In Mexican Prisons

A pencil sketch of Harkort in 1833 done by Johann Moritz Rugendas
(*Courtesy Staatliche Graphische Sammlung, Munich*).

IN MEXICAN PRISONS

The Journal of Eduard Harkort,

1832–1834

Translated and edited by

LOUIS E. BRISTER

Texas A&M University Press

College Station

Library of Congress Cataloging-in-Publication Data
Harkort, Eduard, 1797–1836.
In Mexican prisons: the journal of Eduard Harkort, 1832–1834.

Translation of: Aus mejicanischen Gefängnissen.
Bibliography: p.
Includes index.
1. Harkort, Eduard, 1797–1836. 2. Mexico—History—1821–1861. 3. Santa
Anna, Antonio López de, 1794?–1876. 4. Soldiers—Mexico—Biography.
I. Brister, Louis E. (Louis Edwin), 1938–   II. Title.
F1232.H2813 1986   972'.04'0924   86-6014
ISBN 0-89096-259-6

Manufactured in the United States of America
FIRST EDITION

To
Marilyn,
Evelyn, Edwin, and Susan

Contents

Contents

Acknowledgments

By a fortunate coincidence I discovered Eduard Harkort in 1978, while preparing a translation of William von Rosenberg's *Kritik,* the earliest documented history of German immigration to Texas. Among the names of about one hundred German immigrants in Texas who had supported the Anglo colonists' struggle for independence from Mexico, von Rosenberg gave special mention to Harkort as chief of engineers in Gen. Sam Houston's army. Von Rosenberg's remarks piqued my curiosity. A preliminary search for historical and biographical information about Eduard Harkort in the Texas State Library yielded a book with the cryptic title, *Aus Mejicanischen Gefängnissen* (From Mexican Prisons). This discovery of Harkort's personal account of his travels in Mexico, of his months in prison, and of his many military engagements under Gen. Santa Anna's command prompted further research. As Harkort's story began to unfold, the desire to prepare a critical translation of the journal of his fascinating career in Mexico and Texas naturally followed.

Eduard Harkort was probably the only European immigrant fighting *against* Santa Anna in the Texas Revolution who just a few months before had served as a unit commander in the army of the *Benemérito de la patria.* He was certainly the only German in Santa Anna's army whose record of his experiences was published. It is regrettable that Harkort died before he was able to carry out his plan to expand and to rewrite his notes, many of which are mere telegraphic fragments, hastily jotted down at the end of a day in battle. Through the courtesy of the Texas State Library, which supplied me with a photocopy of the German edition, this interesting narrative is now made available for the first time in English translation to students of Texas and Mexican history.

I wish to express my sincere gratitude to Southwest Texas State University for a faculty development leave, which made it possible to devote a full semester of research and writing to the preparation of the manuscript, and for an organized research grant, which enabled me to spend time in Mexico researching historical and geographical details of Harkort's experiences in that country. I am indebted also to the Staatliche Graphische Sammlung in Munich for permission to reproduce Johann Moritz Rugendas's sketch of Eduard Harkort, and to the following persons, who gave of their time and their assistance on various details in the preparation of this book: Eduard Harkort's great-granddaughter, Frau Gertrud Herrmann-Kühne (deceased 1983) of East Berlin, Germany; another descendant, Thomas Haarmann of Osnabrück, Germany; Diplom-Ingenieur Hofmann, director, Freiberg Mining Academy Archives; Helmut Rischert, archivist, Stadtarchiv Augsburg; the great-grandson of Adolf Hegewisch, A. E. Hegewisch, of Mexico City; the entire reference staff of the Southwest Texas State University Library; Robbie Coker, clerk, Brazoria County Clerk's Office; Historiador Miguel Civeira Taboada, chief of public relations, Archivo General de la Nación, Mexico City; Robert Stevens, assistant archivist, Rosenberg Library, Galveston; Dr. C. H. Muller, professor emeritus of botany, University of California, Santa Barbara; and Dr. Charles Richard Carlisle, professor of Spanish, Southwest Texas State University.

Special thanks go as well to Kayla J. Smith, my student assistant, who typed the first draft of the translation; and to Oralia Flores, our eminently patient departmental secretary, who typed the final draft of the journal.

I utilized the resources of numerous libraries in the United States and Germany. Two to which I am especially indebted are the Nettie Lee Benson Latin American Collection at the University of Texas at Austin, and the Texas State Library.

PART 1
Introduction

Introduction

The Narrative

Eduard Harkort's journal, *Aus Mejicanischen Gefängnissen*, is more than a mere description of life in prison during the Federalist rebellion in Mexico in 1832. It records Harkort's life as a civilian and as a soldier in that young republic, beginning with his last months as director of mines and reduction works for a British mining enterprise, the Mexican Company. Most of the journal is devoted, of course, to a description of the hardships of prison life in Perote fortress and at Puebla endured by Harkort and his comrades, the Mexican officers in Santa Anna's army captured by government forces on March 3, 1832. Harkort continued his journal, however, even after he had escaped from prison in Puebla in August, 1832. He recorded, week by week, the progress of the revolution and his own movements as a lieutenant colonel of engineers and artillery in Santa Anna's rebel army. The journal ends finally with the formal recognition of Manuel Gómez Pedraza as interim president of the republic, and with Harkort looking forward to entering Mexico City victorious with Santa Anna on January 3, 1833, the first anniversary of the Federalists' *pronunciamiento* (pronouncement) in the city of Veracruz.

Harkort's prison journal offers glimpses of life in Mexico far different from those presented by most books about that country published in English or in German during the early nineteenth century. Some, such as the famous letters of Fanny Calderón de la Barca, published in 1843 as *Life in Mexico*, offer a personal and highly informative view of the Mexican people and their customs. Many accounts of this type were written in diary form, such as George F. Lyon's *Journal of a Residence and Tour in the Republic of Mexico in the Year 1826* (1828). Others, such as Henry G. Ward's *Mexico in 1827* (1828) and Carl W. Koppe's *Mexikanische Zustände aus den Jahren 1830 bis 1832* (1837) (Conditions in Mexico in the Years 1830 to 1832), attempted to emulate Alexander von Humboldt's detailed treatise, *Political Essay on the*

Kingdom of New Spain (1811).[1] The authors made careful observations during their travels in Mexico, and they recorded, more or less objectively, information about the geography, population, economy, and the political and social institutions of the country. Harkort's journal was not written, however, with the scientific detachment of a Humboldt or even with the reserve of Fanny Calderón de la Barca. He recorded his experiences and observations in prison and in battle with the immediacy of a participant.

The pages of Harkort's journal offer stimulating insights into the turbulent history of Mexico during the early years of its struggle for economic and political stability. His narrative is permeated by an enthusiastic energy and romantic optimism typical of much German literature of the time. Even while imprisoned in a cold, dark cell in Perote fortress, he looks to the future as he begins to record for others' edification the reality of his experience. Eduard Harkort was both inspired and fascinated by his own role in the colorful drama of war and revolution in Mexico. Writing as an heir to Humboldt's heritage, he gives highly personal expression to the European experience of Mexican history in the nineteenth century. Unfortunately, his prison journal remains as fragmentary as many of the novels and essays of his romantic contemporaries.

The editor of the original German edition of Harkort's journal was his son-in-law, Ferdinand Gustav Kühne (1806–1888). An accomplished essayist and the author of several novels and novellas, Kühne had a considerable following among the adherents of the German literary movement Junges Deutschland (Young Germany). With Heinrich Heine, Ludwig Börne, Theodor Mundt, Karl Gutzkow, Heinrich Laube, and others, Kühne fostered the liberal trend among young German intellectuals during the repressive regime of Prince Klemens Metternich in the first half of the nineteenth century. From 1836 to 1856, Kühne lived in Leipzig, where he married Eduard Harkort's daughter, Henriette (1822–1894). In 1858, when he was living in Dresden, Kühne edited and published the prison journal of his father-in-law. As he noted in his foreword and postscript to the German edition, there were several notebooks, sketches, and mapping surveys among the papers in Eduard Harkort's small estate. Kühne chose the prison journal for publication because it was the most detailed and complete narrative among the notebooks.[2] All of Harkort's papers, the sketches of his comrades in prison, his maps, and his notebooks—even the manuscript of the journal—have apparently been lost. Neither Harkort's great-granddaughter, Gertrud Herrmann-Kühne, who until her death in March, 1983, lived in East Berlin, nor the National Archives of the German Democratic Republic, nor the State Archives in Leipzig had any record of the present location of Harkort's papers. The circumstances suggest, unfortunately, that they were destroyed with other family records in Dresden during the Second World War.[3]

In preparing Harkort's journal for publication, Kühne appears to have deviated little from the handwritten original. He no doubt added the episode headings on each page of the German edition, for a letter from Harkort to Professor Breithaupt in Freiberg published by Kühne with the journal has such headings also. It is, of course, unlikely that Harkort would have composed his personal correspondence with episode titles. Hence, I have omitted all of Kühne's headings for Harkort's letter to Breithaupt and some for parts of the journal narrative in the translation; I retained only those headings describing major divisions within the narrative. Minor incidents and transitional passages have been subsumed within the major episodes.

Evidently, Kühne had only a very perfunctory knowledge of Mexican history, and he probably knew little or no Spanish. In his postscript to the journal, for instance, he notes that Harkort's other papers were too fragmentary for his own editorial skills, adding that only an expert such as Harkort's friend Johann Moritz Rugendas, who had spent three years in Mexico, would have been able to understand and to organize them.[4] Hence, some errors, such as the spelling of a few Spanish words and several place names, occurred in the preparation of the German edition. They may be attributable to Kühne's incorrect reading of Harkort's handwriting, to Harkort's own haste as he recorded his experiences, or to the condition of the manuscript itself—now lost and unavailable for examination. In the translation I have noted and corrected these inaccuracies—either by textual comparison and inference, or by recourse to secondary sources. Further, when Harkort had to resort to a Spanish or Indian word in his narrative for an animal, plant, or other object unfamiliar to his German audience, he generally supplied a parenthetical description or translation in German. Those foreign words that he failed to gloss himself—especially later in his narrative, when he merely jotted down in camp some hasty notes for subsequent reference—have been glossed in brackets the first time they appear in the text.

Most persons in Harkort's journal are referred to by last name only. Wherever possible, I have ascertained the full name from secondary sources and have added the individual's given name(s) in brackets. For the sake of clarity and to improve the stylistic continuity of the narrative, I have also inserted, in brackets, an occasional word or phrase suggested by the German text, but evidently omitted by Harkort in his haste. Further, the spelling of all proper nouns has been revised to current English usage (e.g., Oaxaca for Oajaca, Pedraza for Pedrazza, and Bustamante for Bustamente).

Other minor revisions include (1) the forms of personal address and (2) numerical references. Throughout his narrative Harkort refers to most civilians as Herr or Frau. Only French people are accorded their native appellation of Monsieur or Madame—possibly because Harkort was quite fluent in French, and he appears to have had a great deal of admiration for the French people. Consequently, to underscore the different nationalities of the people Harkort encountered in Mexico, I have substituted, where it was discernible, a person's native form of address for Harkort's Herr or Frau. Furthermore, as any Germanist who might read this translation will note, the masculine German form of address, as in "Herr Stangenberg," is used throughout the text only in the uninflected subject form. In his journal Harkort recorded most numbers as numerals; in the translation these have been written generally as words.

A final stylistic revision concerns the third division of Harkort's journal, the portion covering the period from August 16, 1832, when he escaped from prison, to December 28, 1832, the date of the last entry. During these months, he was almost constantly on the move with a unit of engineers and artillery. Most of the journal entries from this period are mere telegraphic sentence fragments recorded in the historical present. No doubt, these battlefield jottings were written only for Harkort's own reference at a later time, when he would have the leisure to recall and record the complete details of his adventures. To preserve the stylistic continuity of the narrative, I have rendered this portion of the journal into the same past tense as the first two parts of the journal. For the sake of clarity, I have inserted an occasional word or phrase in brackets to replace the ellipses in the German text.

The Author

Eduard Harkort was born July 18, 1797, the eighth of nine children.[5] His parents, Johann Caspar Harkort IV (1753–1818) and Henrietta Catharina Harkort, née Elbers (1761–1837), lived near Hagen in West-phalia, on the family estate, Harkorten. Eduard's father, like his father before him, was a wealthy manufacturer of iron and steel. A survey of industries and factories in the County of Mark for the year 1788 showed that the Harkort family held an interest in four steel and iron foundries and in five factories producing scythes, sickles, wire, and steel. But the elder Harkort was not merely a manufacturer mindful of increasing his wealth; he also seems to have been a respected civic leader. In 1799 he helped to establish in Hagen a first-rate school of commerce. The curriculum included natural history, natural science, mathematics, geography, history, French, German, English, Italian, Latin, religion, business and bookkeeping, music, drawing, dancing, and fencing. Eduard Harkort began attending the new school in Hagen with his older brothers after completing his elementary education at the public school at Quambusch near Harkorten. Each day, in sun and rain, the boys were made to walk about two miles to the school, even though their father could easily have let them ride in the family coach. In school Eduard excelled in foreign languages, mathematics, and the natural sciences.[6]

After graduating with distinction from the school in Hagen, Eduard began an apprenticeship in his father's business. The work did not ap-peal to him, however, and the few months he spent in this job were not happy ones.[7] According to his daughter, Henriette, who many years later recorded her recollections for a projected autobiography, Eduard Harkort set out in 1819 on a trip to England—possibly to find work there. But he had not even reached the Westphalian border when he was suddenly taken ill. Instead of returning home, however, he retired to a nearby inn to recover his health before continuing his journey. The owner of the inn was a widow, Frau Gudula Cormann, née Reuter (1782–1857), who personally cared for her young guest. She min-istered to him so expertly and with such kindness, evidently, that Eduard Harkort made up his mind to marry this angel of mercy. Nei-ther the difference in their ages (he was only twenty; she was already forty), nor the fact that she already had six children seems to have mattered a great deal. Moreover, his feelings of affection and gratitude must have kindled some emotional response in the heart of Gudula Cormann, too, for shortly afterward they were married. The groom's family was bitterly opposed to this union—not just on account of the age difference and the bride's background, but also because of religious differences. The Harkorts were staunch Protestants and Gudula Cormann Harkort was a Catholic. But the two remained married in spite of his family's protestations, and Eduard Harkort moved with his ready-made family to nearby Siegburg, where he supported himself and his family by giving private lessons in geometry and surveying.[8]

Within a year or so after his marriage, Eduard Harkort was summoned to service in the Prussian army. After serving an obligatory year in the artillery, he returned to his wife and children in Hagen, where he found employment as a surveyor for the recently established land registry. The following year, in November, 1822, his daughter, Henriette, was born. Then in 1824, when the land registry offices began to be consolidated, Harkort found himself again out of work. Desperate to obtain some means of support for his wife and seven children, he went to Austria, where a relative had been able to secure for him another position as surveyor. By the fall of 1825, however, he had decided to give up the uncertain occupation of surveyor and to prepare himself for a career in mineralogy and mining at the Royal Mining Academy in Freiberg, Saxony. He returned to Hagen, and in January, 1826, he traveled to Freiberg, where on February 4, he submitted an application for matriculation.[9]

On February 14, 1826, the Board of Mines in Freiberg recommended the matriculation of Eduard Harkort. One week later, on February 22, His Highness Frederick August III, Elector and King of Saxony, authorized the applicant to attend lectures at the mining academy and to receive practical instruction in the local mines and smelters. Permission to enroll at the Royal Mining Academy at Freiberg was formally granted on March 4, 1826, by the Board of Mines.[10]

For almost two years Harkort studied mineralogy, mathematics, geodesy, and mining. He became especially interested in the improved blowpipe technique developed about a decade earlier by the Swedish chemist Jöns Jacob Berzelius for the quantitative analysis of minerals.[11] During his first year at Freiberg, Harkort mastered Berzelius's technique and went on to discover a new blowpipe procedure for analyzing silver ore and other minerals. The main advantages of Harkort's method were the small amount of ore necessary to produce a reasonably accurate analysis and the short time it required to analyze a single dry ore sample.[12] By December of his first year at Freiberg he had perfected the procedure. As news of his innovative technique spread, Harkort was called on to teach his new procedure to several specialists in mining and ore reduction at Freiberg. Among these specialists was Carl Friedrich Plattner, later senior professor of metallurgy and blowpipe analysis at the Freiberg Academy. Plattner is known today for having perfected the quantitative application of the blowpipe, a technique that he learned from Harkort, and for the authoritative treatise he published in 1835 on its use, *Die Probirkunst mit dem Lötrohr.*[13]

In July, 1827, all members of the faculty at the Freiberg academy were required by the Board of Mines to submit reports on the lectures attended by the foreign students at the academy, on their scholastic progress, and on their general conduct. Eduard Harkort was one of the three "foreigners" who had come to Saxony from other German territories to study. His professors in mathematics, mineralogy, and geognosy were unanimous in their praise of his achievements. The attestation submitted by Prof. Johann Friedrich August Breithaupt offers perhaps the most telling appraisal of the young scholar's intellect and personality:

> Herr *Harkort* is a young man of the highest distinction. He came here with a fine background, but within one year he has already made so much progress that many of the more experienced scholars seek his help. In a very short time he has also made extraordinary progress in geognosy, which he is learning in my lectures. From frequent conversations with him, I have had the opportunity to get to know him in all his moods fairly intimately. He seems to possess no great strength of character, but he is certainly very good-natured and amiable.[14]

On July 26, after all his professors had submitted their reports, Eduard Harkort received from the Board of Mines a *testimonium* commending him for having "attended the academic lectures with uncommon diligence and extraordinary achievement, while exhibiting steadfast and moral conduct."[15]

By the time he left Freiberg, sometime in August or September, 1827, Eduard Harkort had gained a reputation among the faculty and students there as something of a *Wunderkind*. He had excelled in all his courses, had developed a new blowpipe technique for the quantitative analysis of dry ore, had instructed others in the method, and at the end of his second year at Freiberg, "at the urging of friends and colleagues," had published a small handbook on the subject. The booklet was to be but the first of several handbooks on the use of the blowpipe in the quantitative analysis of different ores and minerals: *Die Probirkunst mit dem Löthrohre, oder Versuch einer Anweisung, wie man Erze, Mineralien und Hüttenproducte mit Hülfe des Löthrohrs auf verschiedene Metallgehalte mit hinreichender Genauigkeit untersuchen kann. 1. Heft: Die Silberproben.* The list of more than fifty professors and mining specialists at Freiberg named as subscribers to Harkort's book, including Carl Friedrich Plattner, attests to the significance ascribed by them to its publication.[16] On July 27, 1828, the Board of Mines directed a letter also to the king of Saxony, reporting to His Highness Harkort's fine instruction in the use of the blowpipe and his publication on that subject, a copy of which had been presented to the academy library.[17]

After completing his studies at Freiberg, Eduard Harkort traveled to nearby Leipzig to visit his brothers Carl Friedrich and Gustav Harkort, who together operated a large export firm there, Both men were already successful and respected businessmen with international interests. Seven years later, in 1834, Gustav Harkort would gain fame with Friedrich List as cofounder of the second railroad in Germany, the Leipzig-Dresden line.

Eduard Harkort first considered the idea of seeking his fortune in the rich mining regions of Mexico probably while visting his brother Carl Friedrich. The latter's father-in-law, Johann Jacob Aders, was one of the founders and major stockholders of the Rhineland–West Indian Company (Rheinisch-Westindische Compagnie), which, through its subsidiary, the German-American Mining Association (Deutsch-Amerikanischer Bergwerkverein), had received permission in 1823 to operate commercially in Mexico.[18] By this time, several British mining companies were also beginning to establish mining operations in Mexico and South America. From 1820 to 1835, there was a keen interest among many business leaders of England and Germany, especially in the Rhineland area, in developing the vast mineral resources of Mexico. British and German entrepreneurs competed to establish mining rights in the mineral-rich young republic. European investors and mining specialists alike responded eagerly to the promise of quick profits from the gold, silver, and copper mines there.[19]

One of these British joint-stock associations, the Mexican Company, had recruited most of its skilled mining personnel in Germany for working its mines in Mexico. It hired Eduard Harkort as chief director of the reduction works, and in December, 1827, he and a number of other German mining specialists sailed from Hamburg aboard the *Dido* for Veracruz.[20] According to his daughter, Henriette, he left Germany without even a farewell to his wife and children. Whether he went to Mexico because he could not find work in Germany that appealed to him or, as his daughter suggests, because the Harkort family had persuaded him to abandon a wife of whom they disapproved— Eduard Harkort's own reasons will probably never be known.[21] Clearly, he seems to have been emotionally ill-equipped, even by 1827, at thirty, to cope with the responsibilities of a wife and seven children. Perhaps he had even come to regret his marriage to Gudula Cormann, for later, in his prison journal, he notes that he had been wearing a golden locket containing a lock of his daughter's hair, but omits altogether any mention of a wife.[22] In 1829, at seven, and two years after her father's departure for Mexico, Henriette went to live with her uncle Carl Friedrich and his wife, Augusta, in Leipzig. Her mother, who died in 1857, evidently lived out her life rejected and shunned by the Harkort family.[23]

Eduard Harkort, chief director of the Mexican Company's reduction works, and his group of about twenty German mining and reduction specialists arrived on March 30, 1828, in Veracruz. The directors of the company reported in May of that year at the annual meeting of the stockholders, "Mr. Von Harkorten accompanied the Smelters to Mexico as chief of that party. He is a gentleman well known in Saxony, where he has acquired great skill in all the branches of the Art of Smelting."[24] As the new director of the reduction works, Harkort's first and chief task was the construction and operation of the smelting furnace Santa Ana for the reduction of silver ore. It was located in the Yavesía River valley, a few miles north of the city of Oaxaca.[25]

The Mexican Company operated mines in three states: Veracruz, on the Gulf Coast; Oaxaca, on the southern Pacific coast; and Zacatecas, in central Mexico. The copper mines in Veracruz were in 1828 still largely undeveloped. The company's silver mines in Zacatecas were not yet being worked intensively, either, but in Oaxaca, where the company had nearly thirty silver, copper, and lead mines of varying size and yield, Eduard Harkort and Justus Ludwig von Uslar, the chief director of mines, were hard at work by the end of 1828 with about sixty other German mining and reduction specialists, earning large salaries for themselves and quick profits for the Mexican Company's stockholders in England.[26]

Harkort remained in Mexico a little more than seven years, from March, 1828, to October, 1835, when he was deported at Veracruz by order of the president of Mexico, Gen. Antonio López de Santa Anna.[27] During these seven years, he was absent from Mexico only once, for a period of about six months in 1829, to attend a meeting of the Board of Directors of the Mexican Company in London.[28] The story of these years in Mexico is best recounted, of course, by Harkort himself in his journal and in his correspondence with friends in Germany. Unfortunately, his journal is in places very sketchy, and his extant correspondence from Mexico amounts to a mere three letters, two of them written in 1834 and another in 1835. All three of these letters are reproduced in translation at the end of the journal.

It would be presumptuous of me to adumbrate here any part of Harkort's narrative, or to attempt to summarize the chief features of his remarkable adventure. Hence, I shall note only that Harkort became an officer in the Mexican army only after problems with a superior in Mexico had prompted his resignation from the Mexican Company, and the political climate there in 1832 prevented his continued career as an independent surveyor, mineralogist, and cartographer.[29] In the army of General Santa Anna he ascended by 1834 to the rank of colonel. He served his commander with pride and loyalty until Santa Anna himself betrayed the federalistic principles that had initially attracted Harkort to volunteer in 1832 for service in the general's insurgent army at Veracruz.

Of course, once having shed the cloak of federalism in 1834, Santa Anna, the reborn centralist, naturally expected the continued loyalty of those same army officers who just a few months before had hailed him as the champion of federalism and reform in Mexico. Some of these officers, including Eduard Harkort, abandoned their perfidious leader and regrouped as the new opposition to Santa Anna's government. Naturally, as Harkort must have known, it was then merely a matter of time before he would have to meet his former friend and commander in battle. And meet they did in a major engagement near Zacatecas in May, 1835, which ended with defeat for the federalists and Harkort's capture. After being imprisoned for the second time in Perote fortress (the first time had been in 1832, soon after joining Santa Anna's rebel forces), Harkort was placed aboard a ship in Veracruz harbor in October, 1835, and deported as an undesirable alien. From Veracruz he sailed aboard the Mexican schooner *Concepción* for New Orleans, where he entered the United States on November 23, 1835.[30]

Within a few weeks of his arrival in New Orleans, Harkort had found some old friends and other exiles from Mexico who were now living in that port city. Chief among these federalist patriots was Gen. José Antonio Mejía and Santa Anna's own former vice-president, Valentín Gómez Farías. The latter was actively working in New Orleans to overthrow Santa Anna's centralist government. Gómez Farías ardently supported the Texans who desired to preserve the spirit of liberal federalism in the northern provinces of Mexico, but he did not endorse the campaign for independence in Texas led by Lorenzo de Zavala, another federalist exile, and Sam Houston.[31] Harkort had served with Mejía on three occasions in Mexico; the first two times both men had fought for Santa Anna, once in October, 1832, at the siege of Chapultepec, and again in the spring of 1833 in Querétaro. The third time was in 1834, when Harkort served under Mejía as commander of the artillery and engineers in the state militia of Jalisco before that state was forced to recognize Santa Anna's new centralist government.[32] In New Orleans, Mejía probably introduced Harkort to Stephen F. Austin, the leader of the Anglo colonists in Texas.[33] At any rate, within two months of his arrival in New Orleans, Harkort had met Austin and had been persuaded by him to join the Texans in their struggle for independence from Mexico. When he left New Orleans for Texas sometime before mid-February, 1836, *Edward Harcourt,* as he then called himself, had in his possession the following letter of introduction to Gov. Henry Smith:[34]

New Orleans, Jan. 22, 1836

Govr. Henry Smith

This will be handed to you by Col. Edward Harcourt, an experienced and scientific engineer—Such an officer will be very usefull in Texas and I recommend him particularly to the Govt.—He was in the service of the liberal party & was taken prisoner at Zacoticas—he knows Santana and his mode of warfare.

Yours respectfully

S. F. Austin

With other recruits to the Texas cause and a certain [Edmund] Andrews of Brazoria, Colonel Harkort traveled from New Orleans to San Felipe de Austin. He had brought along with him ten other Germans, whom he was recommending for service in the Texas army. They arrived at San Felipe sometime around the middle of February, when Harkort and Captain Andrews reported to Col. Don Carlos Barrett, the judge advocate general. In a letter of February 23, 1836, Barrett wrote to Acting Gov. James W. Robinson and the council of the provisional government, describing his impressions of Harkort, and recommending him for service:

> Col. Hercourt, I have spent some little time with and enclose his papers. I am decidedly of opinion that his services at this time with the army as head engineer would be more valuable than we can even now imagine. I hope he will be provided for at once. He is a gentleman, a schollar and a man of property, & has the reputation of a Soldier! If expedient and possible let his commission and instructions be forwarded by return express.[35]

Barrett had discussed with Harkort the latter's service with the army as chief engineer in considerable detail, for Barrett went on to recommend that Harkort be dispatched immediately with his men to Galveston, where he was to begin the work of fortification. From Galveston, Barrett suggested, Harkort would then proceed with similar orders to Goliad. Barrett concluded these remarks by adding that he was "pleased with the candour of his [Harkort's] statements." In his report Barrett also enclosed a letter from Harkort to the governor and Council, recommending for service in the Texas army the ten Germans who had accompanied him from New Orleans. One of the men was a surgeon who in Barrett's report was described as "well provided with instruments and medicine."[36] Most of the others were apparently volunteers for service in the engineers and artillery under Harkort.

Eduard Harkort remained at San Felipe for several days awaiting the response of the government to Barrett's and his own proposals. In the meantime, the advisory committee to Governor Robinson was drafting its recommendation, but it was a cautious reply and one completely contrary to the best ideas of Colonels Barrett and Harkort. The committee suggested that the latter's offer be gratefully acknowledged by the governor with a note that Harkort "and the other two [sic] gentlemen with him, should go on to the west, and join the army, as we now think their services are more needed there than any where else."[37]

The conflicting recommendations of Colonel Barrett and of the governor's advisory committee seem to have only delayed a response from Governor Robinson and the Council. Harkort probably grew tired of waiting for some definite reply to his proposals and went personally to the provisional capital at Washington-on-the-Brazos. There, on March 14, he drafted for the convention, which was meeting to form a temporary government for the new Republic of Texas, a representation probably very similar in content to the letter that had been forwarded by Colonel Barrett to the governor. In this *pro memoria* Harkort offered essentially two suggestions. First, he proposed the *"erection of a flying hospital* for the army." His friend, Dr. C. Hermann Jaeger, and apparently the same surgeon who had come with him from New Orleans, should be placed in charge of this mobile hospital. At that very moment, Harkort noted, Dr. Jaeger was "occupied in Brassoria with collecting and preparing bandages and lint, and possesses himself a selected stock of medicines, which he puts voluntarily at the disposal of the government under the present circumstances." Second, Harkort proposed the *"creation of a section of military* Ingeneers," with the function of making military maps and constructing fortifications as required and ordered by the commander in chief of the army. This unit of engineers, he added, "will be found very usefull in the construction of ammunition, even in casting cannon balls when it should be required, and in the direction of the artillery pieces, when in batteries or in field." He concluded his representation with a request that he and his companions, evidently those who had accompanied him to Texas from New Orleans, be issued orders organizing them into an engineering unit and attaching them to the army. On March 15 Harkort's petition was read to the convention, and then without any further action being taken on his proposals, it was referred to the Committee on Military Affairs.[38]

While he was in Washington-on-the-Brazos presenting his petition to the convention, Eduard Harkort paid a call on another exile and for-

mer friend of Santa Anna, Lorenzo de Zavala. Once the ally and supporter of Santa Anna in his struggle to overthrow in 1832 the centralist
government of Anastasio Bustamante, Zavala had been named Mexico's
minister to France in 1833, after Santa Anna's election to the presidency. But in 1834, when Santa Anna repudiated the liberal goals of his
own party, dissolved the congress, drove his own vice-president into
exile, and placed himself at the head of a new centralist government,
Zavala had resigned his diplomatic post and had taken refuge in the
territory of Texas, where he owned an estate on the San Jacinto River.
Like Austin, Zavala held an *empresario* contract granted some years
earlier for the colonization of Texas. Soon after arriving in Texas, Zavala
had allied himself with Sam Houston and other Anglo colonists to seek
the independence of that province from Mexico.[39] On March 14, 1836,
in Washington-on-the-Brazos, Lorenzo de Zavala wrote for Colonel
Harkort the following letter of introduction to Gen. Sam Houston:[40]

> My dear Sir,
> I take the liberty of recommending to a patriot as yourself the bearer of
> this letter. Harcourt, having given his service in Mexico under the flags of
> liberty, later suffered the misfortune of being taken prisoner at Zacatecas,
> and of being expelled from Mexico.
> According to the information I have, his services were very valuable
> [to the Zacatecans], and I have no doubt that under your command, his
> services will be equally valuable to Texas. He is trained in artillery and is
> an engineer.
>
> > Your affectionate servant,
> > Lorenzo de Zavala

From Washington-on-the-Brazos Harkort must have returned to
San Felipe to await his orders from the government. A few days later,
on March 28, General Houston himself arrived in San Felipe with his
army on a retreating march from Gonzales. The same day, apparently,
Harkort went to General Houston with Zavala's letter and with his proposal to organize an army unit of engineers. Harkort's suggestion was
finally heard, for that same day Houston appointed him "principal engineer of the army" and ordered him "to proceed to Velasco or some
eligible position on the coast or below Columbia, and [to] fortify it."[41]
In the meantime, the Military Committee had also decided to accept
Harkort's suggestion, for on March 31, Robert Potter, secretary of the
navy, wrote to Capt. Thomas B. Bell at Velasco, "Col. Edwd. Harcourt
an experienced and scientific engineer has been ordered to Velasco and

Galveston to superintend the construction of fortifications at those respective points—in all matters therefore relating to that branch of the public service at Velasco Col. Harcourt will have the command."[42]

From San Felipe Harkort went directly to Velasco. No details of his activities at this time have been recorded, but he must have gained at least a glimpse of the difficulties facing him as captain of the engineers, for in and around Velasco the materials, equipment, and labor needed for the construction of fortifications were in short supply. About a week before his arrival there, Robert Potter had written to Captain Bell, the commanding officer at Velasco, ordering him to collect laborers, teams, and equipment for constructing the needed fortifications. Men who were not willing to aid in the defense of their country, Potter added, were to be compelled to contribute their labor, teams, and other resources as required.[43]

From Velasco Harkort traveled to Galveston Island, where he reported to the commander of the island, Col. James Morgan. In his report of April 8, 1836, to Thomas J. Rusk, secretary of war, Morgan noted that Harkort had arrived a few days earlier, "but without men or aid of any kind." Morgan had been charged with the fortification of Galveston Island, but he had not had much success in obtaining laborers for the project. At this time an invasion of Mexican forces by sea near Galveston was considered imminent, and Morgan still had no satisfactory defenses. In his report to Rusk he pressed these points with a plea for more assistance:

> I am using every effort to get our fortification thrown up here, as we now have the best of evidence of the enemy's intention of possessing himself of this port, if possible. We are in great want of ordinances [sic] for the Fort—I trust the Sec.of the Navy will give orders for one of the vessels of war to remain at this place until we are prepared to receive the enemy.[44]

Harkort's arrival on Galveston Island with little more than his orders from General Houston and from the secretary of the navy to supervise the construction of fortifications on Galveston Island appears to have been the cause for some rivalry between Colonel Morgan, commandant of the island, and Colonel Harkort, commander of the engineers. A letter from President David G. Burnet to Morgan of April 14, 1836, suggests that Morgan was proceeding with his own plans of fortification and treating Harkort as a subordinate:

Do make all possible haste in getting Your island in a defensible State—
it will be necessary to plant some guns at the West and I think two or
three at or opposite the Carandawa—All would be well located—but
these are your matters . . . Col. Harcourt is quite destitute I am told—I
believe he is a "very" valuable officer[;] he ought to be decently supplied.[45]

A week later, on April 21, Gen. Sam Houston's small army engaged
General Santa Anna's far more numerous forces at San Jacinto. After
a decisive victory by the Texans, losses on the Mexican side numbered more than 800 killed and 730 prisoners.[46] Soon after the battle,
Harkort evidently was sent to army headquarters to escort a number of
Mexican prisoners to Galveston Island for service as laborers on the
construction of fortifications there. On April 23, President Burnet
wrote from Post Galveston to Thomas J. Rusk, who at the time was at
the home of Lorenzo de Zavala near the San Jacinto battleground,
"Should the enemy make a descent upon us, we will do our best; but I
fear the result with our present means. Col. Harcourt should be returned as soon as practicable. This point must be kept."[47] By May 1,
Harkort was back at work on Galveston Island. On much of his correspondence after this date he signed himself Colonel of Engineers and
Commander of Fort Travis, signifying probably that Colonel Morgan
had finally relinquished his personal supervision of the fortification
projects on the island. The fort on which Harkort was now working had
been begun by Morgan in early April, 1836, as the first coastal fortification near Galveston. In mid-April, when President Burnet and other
members of the ad interim government had taken refuge on Galveston
Island, the fort was officially named Fort Travis and the camp, located a
short distance away, was called Camp Travis.[48] Fort Travis, which at this
time was still in an early stage of construction, was nevertheless crude
by any standard—nothing like the massive stone fortresses built by the
Spanish in Mexico or by the feudal lords of Germany along the Rhine
River. But the only materials and equipment available on Galveston Island were sand, a few large timbers, axes, and shovels. The laborers on
the fort were mostly unskilled Mexican captives. The fort's first battery
was furnished with guns from the steamer *Cayuga*.[49] A native of Galveston later described the fort soon after the battle at San Jacinto as
follows: "The fort consisted of an octagon-shaped earthwork (or sand
work); a huge ditch was dug and sand piled in the inner margin; a num-

ber of huts for the troops were within the embankment."[50] Both Fort
Travis and Camp Travis were located on a narrow spit of land about 150
yards wide, not far from the northernmost point of the island at the
entrance to Galveston Bay from the Gulf of Mexico. Camp Travis was a
collection of drafty tents housing troops, supplies, and a field hospital
where Colonel Harkort's German friend, Dr. C. Hermann Jaeger, was
occupied treating the sick and wounded prisoners.[51]

During May, June, and July, 1836, Col. Eduard Harkort's energies
were severely taxed. He had to supervise the construction of defensive
fortifications against an assault by sea that was expected from Mexico
virtually any day.[52] His job was made even more difficult by the scarcity
of materials, tools, and skilled labor on Galveston Island, and by the
daily responsibility for the welfare and work of more than three hundred Mexican prisoners.[53] Two letters to Colonel Morgan written during the first week of May express Harkort's frustration over the scarcity
of supplies in the fort: in the first he reports the lack of irons to restrain
one prisoner; in the second, that other prisoners, for want of shelter,
"are situated under the battery."[54] The harsh living conditions in the
camp and in the fort at the time led one prisoner later to refer to Galveston Island as "the hell island." Among the discomforts suffered by
the prisoners and their Texan captors alike were heat, flies, mos-
quitoes, poor food, and brackish drinking water.[55] Yet, Harkort appears
to have taken a personal interest in the humane treatment of the captives. On May 1, he wrote to Morgan on behalf of the prisoners taken
from the captured brig *Pocket*, asking the commandant's aid in retriev-
ing their mattresses from the vessel.[56]

Most of Harkort's correspondence with Morgan during May con-
sists of intermittent reports on the disposition of prisoners in his charge
and on the progress of construction at Fort Travis. But by the end of
May, Harkort had apparently had his fill of guarding prisoners and had
resolved to attend to his primary duties as chief of engineers in the
Texas army. He wanted to get on with the task of preparing surveys and
plans for fortifications along the Texas coast. By May 30, his successor
as commander of Fort Travis had been appointed, and a certain Mr.
Bromley had been chosen to continue the construction of the fort.
Harkort obviously wished to retain supervisory control of the work,
however, for he asked Morgan to support him by "insisting to these

gentlemen, to execute the works conform to my plans and instructions, which to inspect, I have to come back from time to time."[57] The following day, he addressed to Morgan another letter describing briefly his plans to travel to the west end of the island and then on to Velasco, his orders for the work to be done on the fort in his absence, and his appointments of several subordinate officers who would be responsible for the various tasks during his absence. One of these projects was a survey of Point Bolivar and possibly of Galveston Island itself, which he had assigned to two junior officers in the corps of engineers.[58] One of them, a certain Lt. William S. Stilwell, had apparently refused an order from Colonel Morgan on the grounds that, as an officer in the engineers on a mission for Harkort, the orders of his own commander superseded those of Morgan.[59] At any rate, this incident served only to fuel the fires of rivalry between Morgan and Harkort. Morgan reacted by announcing his intention to bring charges against Stilwell. In his letter to Morgan of May 31, Harkort attempted to defuse Morgan's anger by explaining to him the circumstances of his own orders from the cabinet and of his orders to Stilwell, and by taking the entire blame for Stilwell's error on himself.[60] But Morgan would not be mollified. When Harkort arrived at Velasco a couple of weeks later, he conferred with President David G. Burnet, and possibly with some other members of the government, concerning his surveying and fortification projects along the Texas coast. In the meantime, Morgan had written Burnet also, charging Harkort with insubordination. Lieutenant Stilwell had rushed to the temporary capital at Velasco, too, and had made a very ineloquent plea to Burnet for a hearing on Morgan's charges against him. Unfortunately, Morgan's accusing letter to the president has been lost, but Burnet's reply of June 20 reveals most details of that petty drama in Velasco in early June, 1836:

> Sir
> I have read your late letters with some surprise. . . .
> In regard to Capt. Harcourt I have to say that I know nothing of his particular friends "at Court." When he was here I told him expressly that You commanded the Island and all upon it and that he was subject to your orders in general. If he is insubordinate let him be arrested and tried. As the highest officer in the engineers, he is Chief of that Corps and within the peculiar functions of that department of Service I presume he would be subject alone to the war office, but in general police of the island he is clearly subject to your orders. . . .

Lieut. Stilwell bothered me here for two days. On the first day he was drunk and saucy and I sent him off in short words. The next he was sober and apologised for his rudeness. He wanted a court of inquiry, and I told him I did not doubt you would gratify him. He said he belonged to the engineers corps and asked, if as such he was not under the orders of Col. Harcourt. I told him he was immediately—but that You commanded the Island and that Harcourt was subordinate to You as Commandant of the Post.

Now I dont know how I could have better got along with these little matters. That you have your own troubles I doubt not—that I have mine, you know. I have much to do and a very sick child calling upon me day and night.[61]

By the time Harkort returned to Galveston, Morgan had apparently reconsidered his charges of insubordination against both Harkort and Stilwell, for no formal charges were ever filed. The entire matter must have been resolved amicably between the two senior officers, for on June 27, when Burnet wrote Morgan again, warning him of an imminent invasion by a very large force of fresh troops from Mexico, there is no more mention of Harkort's insubordination: "Husband Your provisions. Be vigilant and urge Capt. Harcourt to forward his defenses. Galveston must be Sustained. It may be attacked at an hour you think not."[62]

After this urgent warning from Burnet, Harkort must have redoubled his efforts to complete and reinforce fortifications on Galveston Island. Under the threat of this new assault, he and Morgan must have put their differences aside to work together more closely on fortifying Galveston, for Harkort's written communications to the commandant of the island practically cease. Only one additional report to Morgan, dated July 27, has been preserved:[63]

Macombs Sawmill
July 27, 1836

Col. James Morgan
Sir.

Col. Macomb will some time ago have you informed that he was going to cut on his sawmill boards for the fort at Galveston and that the gov't gave him an order to get twenty Mexicans from citizens, where ever he might find them. The citizens generally refuse to give them up and this is the reason that the sawmill is not yet agoing.

It being now of great importance to have the lumber and there being no other way to procure it or make the mill cutting, I would beg you to send about ten strong and healthy Mexicans up here by the first chance. . . .

> Your most obedient serv.
> Fr. Willm. Houseman
> per Edwd. Harcourt
> Col. and Chief of Eng. T. A.

Frederick William Houseman, who wrote and signed this letter for Harkort, was the same German volunteer, Friedrich Wilhelm Huesman, who had accompanied Harkort to Texas from New Orleans.[64] This letter, in the context of subsequent events, suggests that Harkort had fallen ill earlier in July and was unable to write this report himself. He died of a fever, probably yellow fever, on August 11, 1836, at the home of David L. Kokernot, a Dutch immigrant who operated a lumber business on nearby San Jacinto Bay.[65] A notice of his death appeared in the *Telegraph and Texas Register* of September 13, 1836: "At Kokerouts [*sic*], San Jacinto Bay, the 11 ult[imo] Col. Edward Harcourt, Texian Army and a native of Germany, who commanded the Artillery of Zacatecas when Santa Anna invaded that state."[66] Harkort probably became ill while negotiating a purchase of lumber from Kokernot for the construction of Fort Travis. The Kokernots, that is the family of David L. Kokernot, took the ailing chief of engineers into their home and cared for him until his death. He was perhaps even attended by his friend, Dr. C. Hermann Jaeger, who later gave testimony to Harkort's death and was named administrator of his friend's estate.[67]

When Harkort died, he left behind few permanent records of his service to Texas as chief of engineers, Texas army. There are only three documents in his army record file in the Texas State Archives: a voucher dated February 19, 1836, for "six days board, boots cleaning, etc."; a military payment certificate for his term of service from March 28 to August 11, 1836; and the auditor's voucher for the amount of military service pay due his estate.[68] Fort Travis, the crude structure of earth, sand, and timbers that he had labored almost four months to erect, was destroyed in a storm over Galveston Island early in October, 1837.[69] Any letters, notes, or other personal records of his service in Texas that came into the hands of his only heir, his daughter Henriette, were later lost or destroyed. Nevertheless, after reading his *pro memoria* written on March 14, 1836, to the convention, and his many official reports written during the succeeding months to Colonel Morgan, one cannot help wondering what private thoughts about the revolution in Texas Harkort might have shared with his friend at Camp Travis, Dr. Jaeger, or with members of his family in Germany.

One product of his efforts as chief engineer did survive him—at least for a while. About a year after Harkort's death, a lithographic chart of the Galveston Bay area was printed in New Orleans bearing his name. The exact nature of Harkort's connection with the map and whether he did, in fact, draw it himself is not known. The editor of the *Telegraph and Texas Register* did not think so, however, and in a brief review dismissed the chart as the work of another. The editor's concluding remarks suggest that he had known Harkort personally, or at least was acquainted with his work: "This gentleman died before he had completed the survey of Galveston Bay. Had he lived, we feel confident his name would never have been attached to a sketch so very rude and inaccurate as the one above mentioned."[70] The chart must have experienced a brief popularity at least locally, however, for the French diarist Eugene Maissin, who visited Texas in 1839, knew the map ascribed to Edward Harcourt and cited it in locating the city of Galveston for his readers.[71] The present location of the map, if it still exists, is unknown. The chart was probably published by one or more of Harkort's subordinates, who used the chief engineer's preliminary draft of a map drawn from surveys conducted in the summer months of 1836. On May 31, Harkort had written to Morgan that Lt. William S. Stilwell was "occupied for a few days with the drawings of his and Mr. [illegible] surveys of Bolivar point."[72] Harkort was probably working these and his own surveys and drawings into a complete chart of the Galveston Bay area when he died.

In May, 1838, almost two years after Harkort's death, Dr. C. Hermann Jaeger testified in Brazoria County Probate Court to the death of his friend and petitioned the court to name him administrator of Harkort's estate on behalf of the heirs. The petition, submitted by Jaeger's attorney on May 14, 1838, was approved two weeks later. For two years, then, Jaeger worked to collect Harkort's military service pay, to obtain the certificates for land to which the heirs of the deceased were entitled, and to have the land located and surveyed. In 1840, when Jaeger submitted an inventory of the estate, it included more than three hundred dollars' military service pay, 1,920 acres bounty land for service during the Texas Revolution, 1,476 acres (one-third league) first-class headrights, and one pair of pistols. The headright land and the bounty land were located in the Bexar District, the latter within the present boundaries of Atascosa County. But Harkort's heirs were either ignorant of Jaeger's efforts on their behalf, or dissatisfied with the results, for on May 4, 1840, John S. Lindner, a New Orleans lawyer, filed a petition in Probate Court of Brazoria County, naming Edmund Andrews of Brazoria as administrator of the estate. When Jaeger was notified of Lindner's petition, he submitted his account and asked to be relieved of his responsibilities as first administrator. Andrews then set about concluding the business begun by Jaeger. In July, 1844, he rendered his final account to the probate judge of Brazoria County, and the estate of Col. Eduard Harkort, after six years of correspondence and one change of administration, was declared by the court to be finally settled.[73]

Thus ended Eduard Harkort's life and his odyssey of almost nine years through Mexico and Texas. In his youth he had shown promise as a scientist, but that promise remained largely unfulfilled while he used his talents to serve the ambitions of other men—first the proprietors of the Mexican Company and then General Santa Anna. Eduard Harkort continued to serve Santa Anna until the latter betrayed his principles, his country, and his friends. Harkort came to Texas then, not in search of material gain—the political climate at the time certainly did not favor entrepreneurial ambitions—but after his capture at Zacatecas probably to meet Santa Anna once more in battle. Harkort wanted to train his cannon again on the man who had made him and other prisoners march from Zacatecas to Mexico City and who had sent him for a second time to Perote prison. Harkort was denied this second confrontation, however. In Texas he never actually engaged the enemy in battle, and in that sense he did not die a hero of the Texas Revolution. Indeed, his publications in mineralogy and geography were scant, and most of the records of his travels in Mexico were lost or destroyed after his death. His single largest legacy was the land and liberty in Texas that he purchased with his life.

PART 2
Puebla Journal

Puebla Journal

1. [San Carlos de] Perote Fortress

June 15, 1832

I have been a prisoner of war in this fortress for more than three months already, i.e. since March 9.[1] Thirty-five comrades share this fate of battle with me. The light of day shines, or rather just shimmers through a grating above the prison door and through a deep firing slit into our arched cell. The cell itself is only twenty-five paces long and just half as wide. The walls of our dungeon are smoke-stained black and brown. The limestone plaster is still visible in only a few places. White saltpeter, which forms everywhere, is the only adornment of our damp abode. Forming along the cracks in the walls and ceiling, it solidifies into formations of various shapes. With a little imagination one can see animals, human profiles, Saturn's rings, the Milky Way, the isthmus of Panama, and other things. Along the side walls of the arched cell are rows of benches constructed of boards on which each of us has prepared for himself—as well as he can—a hard bed. Between these plank beds there is a narrow walkway three paces wide. The floor, half brick and half limestone mortar, is full of holes and not too easy to walk on. The firing slit affords us a very limited view of the outside wall surrounding the moat.[2] In the distance, when the infrequent sunshine disperses the eternal clouds and fog, we can see a portion of the mountain, Cofre [de Perote].[3] Six years ago, when I first approached the shores of this country aboard the ship *Dido* from Hamburg, this mountain inspired entirely different emotions.[4] In one corner next to the firing slit there is a barrel; one can easily guess its purpose even without my describing it. In the opposite corner there is another barrel that contains water, our daily beverage. On wooden pegs, protruding rocks, or on cords we hang our clothes, tools, and other things that our captors did not take, or that we have acquired while in captivity. Boots, shoes, hats, uniforms, pots, plates, cups, spoons, epaulets, sabre sheaths, blankets, saddles, baskets of knickknacks, etc., hang everywhere helter-skelter like the episodes of the *Schildbürger Book*.[5] We store such objects also under the planks that, covered with cotton pads, serve as our beds. Only a couple of us were lucky enough to get mattresses from friends on the march to this place. That completes the picture of our abode. Now one may imagine thirty-two officers and four volunteers locked up here as prisoners of war.[6] Each day we are led outside for one hour into the inner courtyard of the fortress, where four guards permit us to exercise in an area thirty paces long and ten paces wide.[7] However, the cold, damp climate is seldom conducive to this little recreation. During this hour, from eleven to twelve each morning, our cell is cleaned and the barrels cleaned by two chained prisoners. This hour gives us a little relief from the foul gases (as the miners say), which have time to escape out the open door.[8]

Confined to our cell, we have seen no one but each other for more than three months. Neither friend nor enemy may visit us. We see only the officers of the guard when they open the locked door to bring our breakfast and noon meal. But since they are our enemies, our conversation with them, of course, cannot be especially pleasant.

Man is by nature disposed to activity. Even when imprisoned he tries to busy himself—if only to pass the time. So we have devised several ways of amusing ourselves—by playing chess, using chessmen made from bread dough, and by playing dice, lotto, dominoes, cards, etc. A newspaper published by the ministerial party, *El Constitucional* of Jalapa, is sent to us secretly and provides some amusement for several hours each week.[9] We review the articles by writing our annotations in the margins. Two small guitars (*jaranas*), which two of us play quite well, provide the music for daily singing and dancing.[10] My stories and novellas help pass away the somber evening hours. But all of this cannot suffice to fill my time satisfactorily. The revolution in which we participated is taking a turn so that the end now seems no longer in sight. Consequently, to find a more pleasant diversion from this gloomy existence, I intend to devote a few hours daily henceforth to recording my recent adventures—partly for my own recollection perhaps in the future, and partly for my friends on a distant continent. I cannot know what will yet become of me, but let happen what will, I hope that the following lines may be placed into the hands of my good friend Adolf Hegewisch.[11] He will preserve them and send them to my family in Germany if I should be prevented from doing so myself. If I can perhaps complete this account sometime after my liberation, I shall dedicate it to the Freiberg Literary Society in Saxony.[12] Here in this dungeon I think of Freiberg quite frequently and I enjoy the pleasant reminiscences of my two-year sojourn in that mountain city. Many of my friends there would no doubt like some news from me. So, from far away I greet them with the salutation of the German miner: "Glück Auf!"[13]

2. *Mr. Obicini's Insults*

Mr. Ambrosio Obicini, the new commissioner of the Mexican Company, insulted me.[1] So I left the service of this mining company to concentrate exclusively on my scientific and geographical projects, especially on the completion of my general map of the state of Oaxaca.[2] I have been working on this map for three years as often as my duties as director of mining and smelting of said company would allow. On October 30, 1831, I left my "home" for the last four years, the smelting establishment Santa Ana, located in the valley of the Yavonia [Yavesía] River (longitude from London = 96°15¾'; N. = 17°17'20"). The Yavesía River forms the beginning of the Rio Grande [de Quiotepec], which empties into Alvarado Bay.[3] I was not happy to leave the mining area where I had worked so long, but where my only reward, to be sure, had been ingratitude. I left behind me the smeltery Santa Ana (my own creation entirely), the company buildings and stamping mill in Socorro, the mines (that now show some promise), the new roads under construction, the shipping house, the regional mining maps that I had begun, and other treasured objects.[4] I left all this to roam about in the state of Oaxaca with my sextants and theodolites, with my blowpipe apparatus and geognostical equipment, the necessary drawing instruments, and my faithful white horse.

I went to live with my loyal friend, Dr. Adolf Hegewisch, a physician. In his house I had several rooms, including a large room for a laboratory, and my meals—all for a modest recompense. Adolf's friendship (indubitably demonstrated in the course of our four-year acquaintance), the attractive location of his house in one of the main streets, the good food served at the table of my charming host, and my little

menagerie, consisting of my horse, a large black monkey from the
southern coast, a *tejón* [badger], a tame white heron [*garza*], a parrot,
and a dog, all these things together with my scientific projects and several good acquaintances banished any regrets over having resigned the
directorship in the Mexican Company. I experienced an additional in-
sult from Mr. Obicini, who tried to withhold from me my excellent sex-
tant (by Carry) and the chronometer (by Webster).[5] I could legitimately
call these favorite instruments my own, since they were the ones that
Mr. Aristides Mornay had taken with him to Brazil and that he had
given me personally in the name of the Mexican Company on my last
visit (May, 1829). They were never included in the company inventory,
and I considered them a gift like the presentation sword that the directors gave me at a full board meeting in recognition of my devoted service.[6] Anyone engaged in astronomical or geographical studies knows
how important it is to own instruments tested by years of personal use.
I consider these two instruments the best I have ever used. I compared
the chronometer, which I had with me on my last ocean voyage, to a
large ship's chronometer owned by Captain Jones of Falmouth. There
was never any more than a difference of one second between the two
instruments. That chronometer of mine was really reliable. Hence, it
offended me deeply when Mr. Obicini demanded the return of the sex-
tant and the chronometer after my resignation, claiming them as the
property of the Mexican Company and saying that I could use them in
the meantime only on the condition that they be returned. This man
made problems for me, too, when I settled my accounts with the company and behaved on the whole so unfairly and unreasonably toward
me that I cannot resist erecting here a small public memorial to his
friendship. My predecessors had had a salary, respectively, of fourteen
hundred and eight hundred pounds sterling. When Herr von Uslar was
dismissed from the company, he was paid an additional six thousand
pesos compensation and he was not even required to submit an inventory.[7] I, on the other hand, received only five hundred pounds and I
had to submit such a detailed inventory that, ridiculously enough, I was
almost held responsible for transactions from Herr Uslar's administration. This was their gratitude to me, even though for three years I did
the work of two directors who, as I said, had cost the company twenty-
two hundred pounds sterling.[8] I had never asked for the job and did not
even want it. But I put all this business aside. Irritated by Mr. Obicini's

"ungentlemanly proceedings," I literally "shook the dust of that place from my feet" and left, determined to forget the Mexican Company. But it still upsets me even now to know that I sacrificed almost four valuable years of hard work, deprivation, and great responsibility to a mining enterprise that will now probably go to ruin in the hands of a mercenary devoid of the miner's mental attitude and enterprising spirit, if God does not work a miracle. I plan one day to write a history of the Mexican Company and to publish it, supported by pertinent documents and records.[9] I expect that such a historical contribution would not be unwelcome to specialists in mining and smelting, and to those who wish to probe more deeply into the operations of the British mining companies. But back to my story—

3. Ascent on Cempoaltepec

I busied myself as follows: I made the calculations for my geographical observations and compiled the data for the map [of Oaxaca]. For the Institute of Arts and Sciences I organized a mineral collection according to the Breithaupt system.[1] I gave lectures on mineralogy and from time to time made field trips and longer journeys throughout the state for my topographical and geological studies. Of all these excursions I shall always cherish especially my trip through Zaachila [Kühne: Sochila] with the governor of that district, Don José Pando. This trip, which for the governor was his annual inspection tour ordered by the General Assembly, resembled a continuous triumphal parade.[2] Everywhere we were greeted in the villages with music, the pealing of bells, and the thunder of small cannon and muskets. On the outskirts, where triumphal arches had been erected, the people presented us with bouquets of flowers bound together Indian fashion in arrangements that were different in each village. There was an abundance of food at breakfast and at noon. In order not to offend the Indian authorities, we often had to eat breakfast three times and the noon meal two times in a single day. This inspection tour extended from Cerro de Cempoaltepec [Kühne: Cempoaltepic] to [San Pedro] Yólox [Kühne: Yolos] and was in every respect educational and profitable for me.[3] I made geographic measurements, increased my geognostical collections and notations on mining, and studied the antiquities and customs. From Cempoaltepec I had the pleasure of seeing both the

Gulf of Mexico and the Pacific Ocean. Mr. [William] Glennie [Kühne: Glenny], who was here before me, missed this view, although he waited three days for the weather to clear. From an altitude of twelve thousand feet I was able to survey the entire state of Oaxaca. I saw the volcano [Pico de] Orizaba, the volcano [San Martín] Tuxtla [Kühne: Turtla], Cofre de Perote, and a white peak that, according to its position, I took for the volcano of Mexico (Popocatépetl).[4] I saw the fresh sacrifice of the Indians on the highest craggy peak, corn cakes *(tamales)* on stones arranged in a circle, decorated with turkey feathers and sprinkled with blood.[5] It took me back in my mind to a time when on this spot, to satisfy a pious delusion or a bloodthirsty fanaticism that everywhere required the same horrible sacrifices, human beings were savagely murdered and warm human hearts offered to appease the gods. Much more appealing to me than this reverie was a delightful blue flower with a stellate cluster of petals—the only flower that I have found at this harsh altitude among the sparse growth of gnarled spruce trees. I think it is a new species and I have named it for the time being *Cempoaltepecana,* until I can describe it more fully. It is found in no other part of [the state of] Oaxaca.[6]

Also on this trip, thanks to the untiring efforts of Señor Pando, we came across some interesting Indian maps painted on linen, or really on cotton cloth. I copied them and will eventually publish them. They are drawn somewhat in the style of Mexican historical paintings such as one finds in the museum in Mexico City.[7]

4. Excursion into the Mountains

Time passed much too quickly during these pursuits. My recreation consisted of horseback rides in the morning with [Adolf] Hegewisch, trips into the beautiful valleys of Oaxaca, and of musical performances in the evening, especially duets on flute and guitar. Adolf owns several splendid duos, which I shall never forget. One that became well known and popular was a polonaise in A-major. Adolf and I played it occasionally as a serenade in the paradisaical night air and starlight, under the windows of beautiful ladies. Everyone on the street used to listen to the melody of my *flûte d'amour,* which Signor Victor Ferero had given to me. He was one of the principal leaders of the Piedmontese Revolution; his effigy was burned in public beside the gallows by the executioner in Naples.[1] He also worked for the Mexican Company as the payroll officer and shipping commissioner. To commemorate his reward in his homeland, he had all the horses and mules of the Mexican Company branded with a small gallows ladder.

Of my longer expeditions into the nearby countryside I will just tell about one of the most interesting: two neighboring villages had been involved in a lawsuit for more than fifty years over a strip of forest and had already wasted more than forty thousand pesos in the courts.[2] Several investigations had already been undertaken, but to make a final determination in the matter, an accurate map was needed, because the wretched freehand sketches available could hardly furnish even approximate information about the site of the contested land. I was commissioned by the Chamber of Justice to prepare an accurate map. Simultaneously, two surveyors were assigned to the project and a committee was appointed, consisting of the district judge, his secretary, who in turn had an undersecretary (because the secretaries only dictate in such matters), two lawyers with their clerks and copyists, the alcaldes of the two villages with their *topiles* (bailiffs), a number of witnesses, etc.[3] We had been advised to take along a military escort this time to prevent outbreaks of hostility among the Indians such as had occurred previously. But the judge decided against such a show of force because he wanted to resolve the dispute amicably. On the appointed day we rode out to the villages San Andrés Zautla [Kühne: San Andreas Sautla] and Santo Tomás Mazaltepec [Kühne: Mesaltepec].[4] The following day we set out to inspect the disputed tract, accompanied that morning by the inhabitants of the two inimical villages. The women and children had to be restrained by force from going along with us.

The disputed land encompassed several leagues of granite terrain so steep that our animals could hardly carry us up the slopes. But our procession made an interesting picture. We were an extremely colorful group: about thirty people on horseback (the aforesaid committee) and a multitude of Indians, some of them carrying food supplies, beds, mattresses, mats, my instruments, etc. A fight almost broke out once during our inspection, for the Indians already distrusted us, and when we wanted to examine a certain spot, they thought that the act of crossing the territory of one village foretold the loss of that property. The judge was able to restore order only with great difficulty.

Because the area was so remote from any settlement, we spent several nights there in the mountains. We made our camp in a wooded ravine that offered some protection against the cold night wind, and in less than two hours the Indians had with great skill constructed several huts of poles, branches, and foliage in which we set up our quarters. The two villages established their separate camps with watch fires and palisades of bamboo [Kühne: *Bohranstalten*] like two enemy armies.[5] They had brought along food in abundance. More than fifty campfires dotted the dark landscape. The green canopy of the forest over us, the activity of the Indians around us, their songs, and the howl of the wind through the branches of ancient oaks created a romantic atmosphere and a mood that I shall always recall with great fondness. The expedition lasted six days and I earned 250 pesos cash for my part in it. Soon after my return there was a festival lasting several days, which Hegewisch and I spent hunting ducks and white herons on some nearby lagoons.

5. Nocturnal Indian Ceremonies

One evening (I believe it was February 4), I was astonished by a brilliant spectacle.[1] About eight o'clock I had climbed up the tower of Santo Tomás [Mazaltepec?] to enjoy the view of the clear, star-studded heavens and to set my box compass on the North Star. Suddenly, I saw the surrounding villages become illuminated by innumerable piles of burning straw, which had all been set afire simultaneously as if by a stroke of magic. In Santo Tomás I could see that the fires were arranged in a circle on the main plaza while the Indians, young and old, amused themselves dancing around the fires and leaping through the flames. The Indians leaped about, half-naked, with coats or blankets slung around their bodies, disappearing suddenly into the dark smoke and, just as suddenly, reappearing again on the other side, illuminated by the flames. Whoever can imagine this scene will believe that I thought I was witnessing a dance of witches in this eerie festival, which, as I am told, takes place every year in these villages. This bizarre celebration lasted more than an hour.

6. Outbreak of the Revolution

I note that I am digressing in my account. For some time I had been negotiating with the government of Oaxaca about completing my general map of the state. I had been working on it for three years and had incurred considerable expense in its preparation. Everything was ready for a three- or four-month trip down to the southern coast, which I wanted to chart. I wanted also to determine the precise location of [the Gulf of] Tehuantepec and of the Bay of Acapulco.[1] Their position is still quite uncertain, especially the position of the latter—so uncertain, in fact, that the previous summer the captain of a British ship had difficulty finding it. I was extremely interested, too, in the marine salt refineries, the pearl fisheries, the vegetation (described to me as especially luxuriant) on the southern coast, and in the biological specimens that I could collect and then sell. The course of various important rivers in the area also interested me. I intended to survey the Tehuantepec River and the Coatzacoalcos [Kühne: Guasamalco] River to investigate the popular notion of a possible connection between the two.[2] Furthermore, I had been assigned to accompany an investigative government commission charged with monitoring the boundary between the states of Oaxaca and Veracruz. On this expedition I would have gone into areas rich in natural history and until now unexplored by any Europeans. Finally, I had also been commissioned by the government to explore the feasibility of constructing a passable road between Oaxaca [City] and Tehuacán.[3] I was just about to set out on this interesting horseback expedition, when fate, coldly and cruelly, tore me completely from the realm of my scientific work and thrust me into the business of armaments and warfare. The sudden political event that precipitated this reversal seemed insignificant at the time.

On January 2 [1832], the general of division, Antonio López de Santa Anna (generally called Santa Anna), together with the garrison at Veracruz, pronounced against the administration of Vice-President [Anastasio] Bustamante.[4] Santa Anna demanded the removal of the ministers [Lucas] Alamán, [José Antonio] Facio, and [Rafael] Mangino [y Mendívil], who were suspected of being partial to Spaniards and of wanting to introduce centralism to prepare the way for a Spanish prince to sit again on the throne of Mexico. The ministers were said to be guilty also of several other violations of the constitution.[5] Santa Anna's declaration was the signal for a new revolution, for if the vice-president did not comply with these demands, as one could expect he would not, then war was inevitable.[6] Santa Anna was also prepared for that possibility, and better prepared than the enemy since he occupied Veracruz and the almost impregnable fortress San Juan de Ulúa, from which he could cut off the government's best sources of support.[7] In 1830 and 1831 the southern coast of the state of Oaxaca had been the scene of former president [Vicente] Guerrero's war against the present government.[8] It was the scene of atrocities that ended finally with the execution of General Guerrero, who was captured through the infamous treachery of the Genoese, [Francisco] Picaluga. Guerrero was publicly shot to death on February 14, 1831, in Cuilapa, a town about three leagues [west] of Oaxaca. Since that time Picaluga's deed has been immortalized, and even the man himself has been stigmatized by the addition of the word *picalugada* to the Spanish vocabulary, as the term for any cunning, treacherous act.[9] People still use the word in that sense and will probably continue to do so.

Santa Anna had fought loyally for Guerrero in 1828.[10] It was to be expected, therefore, that his friends, Guerrero's friends, and the enemies of the government would soon have the entire state [of Oaxaca] in turmoil. Consequently, my friends advised me to put off for the time being my planned expedition to the southern coast. The government put off signing the contract with me, which had already been drawn up. Of course, I had no desire to risk losing my instruments and my unfinished maps by letting them fall prey to a band of partisans. So, for several weeks I was idle. In the meantime, everyone watched with some surprise and suspense the development of what had to come. The government prepared for war and began to send troops to Jalapa.[11] One after the other, several towns on the northern coast declared their support of Santa Anna. The battalion at Alvarado, for example, placed itself under General Santa Anna's command. In the city of Oaxaca he had strong support. On the southern coast there appeared also a proclamation by Col. [Juan] Alvarez in favor of revolution.[12] There was unrest in the Mixteca [Kühne: Mesteca] region.[13] In short, a general stirring of the population was evident. The government of Oaxaca became very vigilant and in a short while the freedom of the press [there] had completely disappeared. Santa Anna's friends then gathered secretly to share with each other the news they had gathered individually.

7. Harkort Meets Santa Anna

Early in 1829 I was traveling through the state of Oaxaca, which had been the scene of Santa Anna's martial feats during the Revolution of 1828.[1] I was going to Veracruz to embark for England on company business when I had the pleasure of accompanying Santa Anna as far as San Andrés Chalchicomula [Kühne: San Andreas Chachicomula].[2] He was leaving the convent of Santo Domingo in triumph after having brought about the fall of President [Gómez] Pedraza, who had only recently been elected. With only a few hundred men in the convent, he had held off Gen. [José María] Calderón's division of almost three thousand men for several months. From his stronghold he had executed many a strategic strike against Calderón, but to repeat his fascinating feats here would be too great a digression.[3] The General's march (in conversation "the General" always means Santa Anna) from Perote to Oaxaca was also most remarkable. Like a certain Duke of Braunschweig-Oels, he led his small but courageous band, with Calderón's division still in hot pursuit, through the Río Salado (salty river) and the rocky Río de [las] Vueltas as far as Etla [Kühne: Ethela]. There, with the cannon he had brought with him, he ambushed the enemy and got the best of him.[4] With this courageous stratagem Santa Anna won me over, just as I had been inspired in my youth by the deeds of [Field Marshal Gebhard Leberecht] Blücher, [Ferdinand von] Schill, and the brave Prussian hussars in their red uniforms.[5] In his presence my admiration for him only increased. He showed a special regard for me, also, and I soon made friends with his officers, with whom I did some fencing and target shooting (especially with Arista).[6] When I returned from England in June, 1829, I met the General again between Jalapa and Encero, as he was preparing to go against the Spaniards who, under [Gen. Isidro] Barradas, were threatening with an invasion; they subsequently did land in Tampico.[7] In our brief conversation he said to me, "I'll give them a fight like they have never had before!" And really, in Veracruz he embarked with five hundred men in barks and skiffs, sailed without incident up to Tampico, landed right in front of the Spaniards, and forced Barradas to an unconditional surrender. The former oppressors had again been driven from Mexican shores![8]

I was very attracted by Santa Anna's youthful, enterprising spirit, his charming personality, and his generous, liberal character. I had already been partial to him for a long time when his proclamation appeared in Veracruz. My friend Adolf [Hegewisch] had fought for the General at the convent of Santo Domingo in 1828 and was now his ardent supporter. At the time I was a family friend of Don Vicente. He had previously held an important government post, but the Plan of Jalapa, which had elevated Gen. [Anastasio] Bustamante to the position of vice-president, also caused Don Vicente to be reduced to his present position as director of the aforesaid Institute [of Arts and Sciences in Oaxaca].[9] As an eager adherent of Santa Anna's, he had no small part in stirring my enthusiasm [for the General's cause]. Don Vicente's family, Lieutenant Colonel Ortiz, and other friends were very persuasive, also.[10] It is no wonder then that I decided to offer General Santa Anna my services. The current political conditions made the continuation of my geographical projects impossible anyway, and I had already received word by secret correspondence from Veracruz that I would be welcome there. So, I began to prepare for the trip.

8. Departure for Veracruz

Since it would have been difficult to take a direct route to Veracruz without arousing suspicion, I conceived the plan to simulate a geographical expedition, to travel first to [San Pedro] Yólox, and then to [San Juan Bautista] Tuxtepec, where I could travel by ordinary skiff down the Río Grande [de Quiotepec] to Alvarado.[1] From Alvarado I could get to Veracruz with no trouble. This route would have been somewhat cumbersome, but new for me and interesting. Lieutenant Colonel Ortiz had decided to rejoin his old commander also and was going to accompany me, but on the day set for our departure he announced that he was not yet ready to go. I did not want to delay any longer, for I wanted to be in Veracruz before the outbreak of hostilities, which we expected any day. Consequently, that same day I changed my route. I decided to take the most convenient route to Veracruz, the public highway via Tehuacán. My horses and mules were ready, and my equipment was packed for a field trip. Dr. Hegewisch, [Lieutenant

Colonel] Ortiz, Alvarez (a blind but nevertheless eager patriot), and I had a "revolutionary" dinner together at noon. The four of us emptied several bottles of champagne toasting the successful outcome of my enterprise. That afternoon I paid a call on the wife of Commanding Gen. [Valentín] Canalizo to mention casually the pretext of my journey, thus ensuring that my sudden absence would arouse no suspicion.[2] Late that evening I stole away to the house of Don Vicente to take leave of his family—perhaps forever, if that should be my fate. The members of Don Vicente's family were the only persons privy to my decision besides those friends already mentioned. Each of the lovely ladies bade me farewell with an embrace and permitted me to kiss her hand. Wrapped in my cloak, I carried away with me a costly small casket made by the ladies as a present for the General. The casket was a marvel of original floral work. It was covered with flowers, leaves, and animals carved from the pith of the flowering rush *(cacalotes)*.[3] The little carved flowers were shaped and dyed to resemble real flowers, with shell-like petals, spiraling tendrils, and serrated leaves. All of the shapes, flowers, and animals were fastened in place with gum arabic. This casket, richly inlaid with gold and silver, glittered splendidly; it held fifty packets of fine chocolate, each of which was also richly decorated. Such artistry is, I believe, peculiar to the state of Oaxaca, for I have seen nothing like it anywhere else.

On the morning of February 13, I took leave of my friend Hegewisch and asked him, if I were to die on a Mexican battlefield, to publish a small memorial to me in a newspaper in Germany. Accompanied by my servant Félix and several mules, I rode through the city on my white horse in broad daylight. The inhabitants were already accustomed to seeing me leave the city with my instruments. The pricking of my conscience, however, caused my heart to pound as I rode through the streets greeting numerous acquaintances, afraid that one of them might suspect my intentions and send someone after me. I breathed much more freely as soon as we reached the open countryside. The morning was splendid. I rode across the open plains as far as Etla, where three years earlier Santa Anna had attacked and defeated Gen. [José María] Calderón.[4] In the same place one and a half years ago I had almost been thrown from a nearby tower by ignorant Indians as I was measuring angular distance with a theodolite for my triangulations of the valleys of Oaxaca. Quite vividly I remember how they had taken me for a wizard of some sort, and how at their alarm the entire village of Santo Domingo [Nuxaá], including women and children, had rallied with their different weapons. They reminded me of the farmers of Ohnewitz [Witlessville], when they ran off the schoolmaster. After the Indians (by some miracle) had brought me down alive from the tower, they made me their prisoner and took me to Etla, where I was bound in irons.[5] The next day they were going to hang me. Fortunately, a friend of mine, Canonicus Castillo, liberated me from those cannibals.

9. Lerche's Troubles

In the area of Etla, near San Agustín [Kühne: San Augustin] [Etla], there are several aluminous saline springs, several insignificant veins of silver, and several sulfate pits. At these pits there was a Silesian, Karl Lerche, who had been earlier employed by the Mexican Company as foreman of the lead and sulfate mine, Plomosa.[1] This German had then been hired by the Tlalpujahua [Kühne: Tlalpuchahua] Company under Mr. [Vicente] Rivafinoli.[2] Soon afterwards, when this unfortunate company had collapsed, Lerche set out for Mexico City with a travel allowance and his separation pay in his purse. There he lost all his money and was recruited by Gen. [Manuel] Rincón for the cavalry. In 1828 he rode with Rincón against Santa Anna and he fought in the battles at Jalapa and Perote. Lerche joined, too, in the pursuit, as Santa Anna fled to Oaxaca, but only as far as Etla, where he was captured by Santa Anna's forces and taken to the convent of Santo Domingo.[3] Then, according to the popular custom in this country, he went over to Santa Anna's side, that is to say, he served in his army. Lerche participated in the General's triumphant march to Jalapa, where he requested his discharge, which was denied, however.[4] He subsequently deserted and after several adventures (and misadventures), he returned to the mining area in the state of Oaxaca, where I hired him. Mr. Obicini, who probably does not like Germans, then reduced Lerche's wages so much that he soon afterward left the Mexican Company and was tending the aforementioned sulfate mine near Etla for Herr von Uslar, my predecessor.[5] Luckily, Lerche came into town the day that I was there and, since he was happy with his current situation, I agreed to let him, his horse, and his dog Wiedu accompany me.[6]

10. Churches of the Indians

In Etla I still had some business to settle with the Indians of [San Juan] Zautla [Kühne: Santla], who owed me some money, but which I did not get, although I spent the whole day trying to. The next day, therefore, I was able to ride only as far as San Juan del Estado, where I amused myself a while playing the organ.[1] The church was under repair and the open doors were an invitation I could not resist. On my wanderings I always had a penchant for trying out the church organs in the villages I passed through. Often I was delighted to find in even the smallest villages large organs with ten or twelve registers, and finely tuned, as the Indian musicians often have a remarkably keen ear for tonal quality. One can observe this sense in their talent for tuning guitars.[2] The Indians here spend great sums of money on their churches, even in the poorest villages. A community, be it ever so small, considers it a disgrace not to have a church, and the people do not rest until they have built by communal effort a church with the necessary gilded and silver-plated saints, an organ, etc. Actually, it has always irritated me to see the Indians labor and rob one another for a worship service that is conducted so mechanically here. Only the overt ritual is different from their former religious practices, and nothing is done for their education.[3] Does it matter much whether the Indian sacrifices a turkey to his former idols or whether he sells a portion of the corn from his little plot to buy a few pounds of wax and burns this before the painted image of a saint? The wretched, often ridiculous statues and paintings of Jesus Christ, of the Holy Virgin, and of the saints that one finds here—are they not basically the same thing to the Indian as his former graven images?[4] One cannot defend, of course, their horrible human sacrifices, but they were not common in this country. The total of people sacrificed by ignorant and barbaric races is probably no greater than the number of poor heretics, witches, and unbelievers who in religious wars became the victims of blind Christian fanaticism or who were burned to death by the Inquisition. When a widow in Bengal voluntarily burns herself to death with her deceased husband, that in my opinion is not worse than the loss to society of human lives when Christian youths and girls are forced to shut themselves away in monasteries and convents. Going against nature, they deny themselves the normal pleasures and joys of life, only to offer themselves in daily sacrifice and to suffer more in this withering condition than the Bengal women who die in a few moments on a funeral pyre.[5] If the hypocrisy and fraud that one sees practiced here is true Christianity, then I would rather join the Persians who worship the eternal flame or the savages who worship the sun. Are not these things—fire, the sun, and the moon—infinitely more sublime, more beneficial, and more divine to ignorant savages than the printed, painted, and carved images of saints? Is the notion of reincarnation not simpler and more comprehensible to him than the doctrine that three different things are one? Is he not deterred from sin more by the conviction that after a life of evil his soul will return in the body of a vile, ugly animal, than by the threat of purgatory and hell, which he has never seen and which his experience cannot comprehend? I thank God that Christian morality has begun to replace Christian ritual. This morality will one day be practiced, too, among these poor Indians, who at present do not feel comforted by the example of their priests, and who are still offering sacrifices in some places to their old gods. They attend Mass so faithfully only because the ceremonies in the church bear some similarity to their former rituals. In the Sierra de Yólox I was in several churches where stones containing carved figures and hieroglyphs had been fixed with mortar in the threshold and in other parts of the building. Today no one knows what these markings mean. Who knows whether these ancient relics are not the real objects of the Indians' veneration! Perhaps it is no accident at all that they [these relics] are in the churches![6]

11. Corruption among the Clergy

These and other observations intrude constantly upon my thoughts (even here in prison), when in the rural districts I see the mindless religious fervor of the Indians, the useless waste of their bitter labor, and, on the other hand, the way the clergy lives. Almost every priest (with some notable exceptions) has at least one cook, and some nieces and nephews living in his house with him or in the same village. I have seen shocking proof (which I do not like to recite) of the corruption among the majority of the clergy here.[1] I have been in villages such as [San Martín] Peras [Kühne: Las Peras], [Santa María] Ozolotepec [Kühne: Oajolotepec], [Santa María] Peñoles [Kühne: Penoles], and others where, for his own convenience, the priest appears only once or at the most two times [a year]. Then for fourteen days straight he reads masses for all the saints on the calendar. During this time he leads a rich and comfortable life, or, as they say, "like the Lord God in France." He drinks his fill of wine, collects his fees for all the masses he reads, and leaves the village on his mules, which have also eaten pretty well, taking with him all the eggs, cheese, chickens, turkeys, and other things the Indians deny themselves.[2] For the rest of the year, then, the Indian is on his own. He christens his children himself and buries his dead. All alone he goes to the caves and mountain peaks, where he still has a hidden altar to his former gods and where he still offers sacrifices among the broken idols of his ancestors. He sprinkles his fields with the blood of parrots or turkeys and with their blood he marks, too, the door of his house, as the children of Israel did with the blood of a lamb.[3] Before his death he buries his money in places that to him are still sacred. What confusion! But we must be patient. Even here enlightenment shall one day overcome ignorance and superstition. Already people are beginning to talk about tolerance. (May God give Señor [Vicente] Rocafuerte [Kühne: Rocafueste], the apostle of liberalism in religious affairs, a long life!)[4] The Protestant church will also penetrate here one day and bring with it real education for the Indians. Such stories as that of the priest who fathered a child with his cook and then dismissed the mother and hired his own daughter are becoming less frequent.

But enough of such thoughts. A prisoner of war can become quite liberal in his cell!

Back to my journey: as Eos (in Homer's words) ascended with lovely rosy fingers, I arose from my mat just as my companions, [Lerche and his dog], were also awakening. In the refreshing coolness of the morning I climbed up to the calcareous mountain ridge of San Juan del Estado; from there, 6,358 Spanish feet above sea level, one has an excellent view down into the valley of Etla and Oaxaca.[5] Fourteen months previously I had spent most of one cold night at this high altitude.

12. A Previous Trip to Oaxaca

In February, 1831, I had traveled to Veracruz and to the gold mines of Zomelahuacán [Kühne: Somelohuacan], where I stayed for a while.[1] Then I had traveled on to Mexico City. The British packet, by which I customarily sent back my reports, was due in port within the week. Consequently, I had no time to lose if I was to get back to the mining area in time to meet it. I decided, therefore, to leave my horses and baggage in the care of my servant, Félix, and to ride back to Oaxaca as fast as possible on rented post horses. However, from Mexico City to Puebla I was able to get passage on an express stagecoach run by a North American company. We left the next morning at six. Until then I had thought a French coach bouncing over the cobblestones from Paris to Rouen was rough, or even a coach in Hungary with a team of Slovakian horses, but those trips were nothing compared with this race to Puebla. At full gallop the driver negotiated the many sharp turns in the road through the forest of the Río Frío.[2] He did not even slow down for the saplings that are laid across the road to divert the rainwater to each side. At each of these trees the coach flew about two feet in the air, and we (the passengers) held on to our seats just to keep from breaking a rib or cracking our skulls. We arrived in Puebla that afternoon by four o'clock. Discounting an hour for breakfast and lunch, we covered thirty leagues in only ten hours.[3] At five o'clock two post horses and a postilion were ready for me to continue my journey. As soon as I mounted, we were away at a gallop, covering by two o'clock the next morning twenty-seven leagues (five relay stations) all the way to Tehuacán.[4] En route, my postilion made a funny scene when he fell from his horse. It was cold that night and he had buckled on his *armas de agua*, a blanket made from large goatskins that one hangs across the horse in front of the saddle. They provide excellent protection against the cold and rain.[5] My postilion's horse fell suddenly in mid-gallop, causing his rider to fly over his head and slide at least ten feet down the road. He was not hurt, thanks to the pelts he was wearing. We both laughed hard about his fall. Then he mounted again and off we went at full gallop, with the horses and their riders puffing, with the rocks and sparks flying under the horses' hooves.

At the way station [Kühne: *venta*] I had an adventure too—in the manner of Don Quixote.[6] I was supposed to get fresh horses there, but since I arrived in the middle of the night, I had some trouble rousing the stationmaster from his bed. He then had to ride out in the pasture to catch the nags I needed. This business was taking a long time, so I wrapped my tired body in a blanket and lay down to sleep—for lack of a better place—in the middle of the gateway. Immediately I fell asleep. In the meantime the good old goatherd had awakened and decided that it was time to let the livestock out of the pens. One can imagine my consternation when I was awakened by the trampling of sheep, goats, donkeys, and cattle all about me. They crowded one another so closely that I could not even stand up. This stampede lasted at least a quarter hour, and although I drew up under my blanket like a turtle in its shell, I still did not escape without a few bruises.

13. A Marathon on Horseback

In Tehuacán I found that my thighs and hips had been rubbed raw by the ill-fitting saddles. Resting in the cold night air from my ride only made these areas more painful. So I bathed my legs and backside with my usual skin treatment: salt dissolved in brandy. This remedy was very effective, too, for after a couple of hours the pain disappeared and over the area a hard scab had formed that resisted the chafing and rubbing of the rest of the trip.

It was still dark when I rode out of Tehuacán. The road there goes alternately over sandy and rocky soil; sometimes it is only a forest path with low-hanging brush and branches. My postilion, a small, lively fellow, rode ahead of me like a man possessed. In a mad gallop his horse fairly flew over the sand and through the woods. Often in the darkness I could barely see him ahead of me. It was all I could do just to keep up with him. In order not to injure my head on the low-hanging branches and limbs, I rode with my head down on my horse's neck. My heavy Mexican hat could not have protected me anyway against any larger obstacles in the path. So, commending my soul to God, I raced along behind my postilion, for I had to keep him in view in order not to direct my horse into one of the deep ditches on either side of the road. We rode at this pace for several hours until dawn, when we finally reached San Sebastián [Nicananduta].[1] We stopped for a while there among the local Indians (clad in blue frock coats) to change horses and to eat breakfast. My reluctance to recognize my postilion's superior riding skill had already earned me several bumps on the head. Until now I had usually had pretty good horses, even a couple of excellent ones, but this time I was offered two nags that at first I even refused to take. They were small, thin, and generally pretty bad-looking beasts. But my new postilion assured me that they were nevertheless quite strong.

So I let him persuade me to take them—a mistake that I later bitterly regretted. After we had ridden a few hours they were so exhausted that they could hardly go a step farther. Finally, even the postilion's harsh whippings could not budge them any more. I felt sorry for the poor animals, which probably were not to blame for their bad condition. In Venta Salada I left them behind. I turned my saddle and little bit of baggage over to the postilion, who grumbled about the extra weight, and I set out for the next station on foot. From this station on, all my mounts were poor. I missed a good horse even more because the wide riverbed of the Río de las Vueltas is so rocky and the crossing so cumbersome. In a stretch about fifteen leagues long, I had to ride across the river more than ninety times. Near [the village] Don Dominguillo, one of my horses collapsed, and I would have been on foot again if an Indian had not happened along and rented me one of his horses for the short distance to the next station.[2] The next day, in the afternoon, I stopped at [the] *venta* of Aragón [Kühne: Venta de Aragon], where I rested several hours before riding on that evening by moonlight up into the San Juan mountains.[3] I reached the peak exactly at midnight, just as the full moon was going down. The horses were too tired to go on; the woods seemed endless, and now in the increasing darkness, I was having a lot of trouble finding the road among the trees. So, with Oaxaca already so near, I decided not to continue on under such adverse circumstances. I wrapped myself in my blanket and lay down to sleep under a tree. When I finally awakened, the sun was already high in the sky.

Now [February 15, 1832], I found myself standing on that same spot again [on the mountain ridge of San Juan del Estado], as I relived in my memory that hard ride fourteen months earlier: I arrived in Oaxaca that day at eleven o'clock in the morning, and after drinking a bottle of champagne with [Adolf] Hegewisch to refresh myself, I set out again for the mining area that same night, riding in the moonlight. In seventy-two hours I had covered 127 leagues [300.8 miles] with only thirteen hours of sleep.[4] I learned on that trip that my body can endure such hardship with no ill effects, for I was not exhausted when I arrived. But I still would not want to repeat such a ride without some compelling reason.

14. The Torrid Region

From this calcareous summit of the so-called Cuesta de San Juan (6,358 Spanish feet altitude), one descends 1,460 feet by a winding northerly route into the valley of the aforementioned Río de las Vueltas.[1] There one soon comes to the village of Aragón. It is a very small settlement with an inn and general store where hot meals are served to travelers. A few hundred feet away there is a sugar mill, and off to one side there are several large fields of sugarcane. Aragón, which lies only 3,862 feet above sea level, is located in the torrid region. The nights here seem almost heavenly to the traveler at the end of a long day's ride in the hot, oppressive sun.[2] From here almost all the way to Tehuacán the nocturnal air is filled with the delicious scent of flowers. The road from Aragón to Tehuacán winds through the narrow valleys of the Río de las Vueltas, Río Grande [de Quiotepec], and the Río Salado (Saline River).[3] Travelers shun this stretch of road because of the heat. It has always appealed to me, however, because it is so beautiful in the evening and at night. The magnificent tropical vegetation of the valley—sometimes sparsely, but often densely interlarded with the *Cactus polygenetus*—interrupts the monotony of the stark conglomeratic mountains on either side.[4] The dark green color of the cactus contrasts nicely with the green of the luxuriant flora. Yellow and red vines hang down into the riverbed from the treetops, coiled and dangling like the curly strands of a wig. They sway constantly, gently stirred by the river currents and the wind. Podlike fruits of every shape and color hang down over the road, and in the distance the sun glistens on the backs of white cranes. The huts of Indians and Negroes (former Spanish slaves and their descendants) lie hidden romantically under palms and banana trees or among the rows of sugarcane. These huts, scattered over the flat basin of each valley, also afford the traveler an opportunity for some refreshment. He can slake his thirst with watermelon or *tepache*. He should not show his disgust, however, when his dark hostess places an unwashed finger or two into the glass as she hands it to him. (*Tepache* is a fermented drink made from pineapple, water, and raw sugar—found usually where there is no pulque.)[5] Along this route there is a remarkable alternation of landscapes, from the charming little [woodland] scenes to the oppressive, barren, dry, and rocky areas. The dry beds of steep mountain streams, which during the rainy season release great tumbling rock slides, join the main river almost at a right angle. This feature of the landscape should give the topographer a good idea of the steepness of these mountains. Indeed, the tiring ride over boulders, gravel, and other rock debris (limestone, porphyry, and gneiss) would be unbearable for the horse if it were not relieved by intermittent shade and an occasional stretch of dirt road.

The second night (February 16) I spent in the cottage of a plantation worker; it was located off the road about an hour's ride north of [San Juan Bautista] Atlatlahuaca [Kühne: Alatlanta].[6] There, gently swaying outside in my hammock, I abandoned myself completely to the happy feelings evoked by the warm, gentle night. This peaceful rustic scene was a world apart from the dangerous life I was facing. I fell asleep rather late to the rustling of the plantain trees. While staring at the stars above me as they traced their slow arc in the heavens, I became lost in reveries on the events of war awaiting me until Morpheus closed my eyes with sleep. I must have been thinking that I would like to exchange places with the Indian under whose bamboo roof I could sleep so peacefully. Indifferent to the business and revolutions of the republic, he goes about irrigating his small cornfield and planting his *frijoles* (small black beans) and *chiles*—everything he needs. At this very moment he is still going about his rustic chores just as he has always done, while I, suffering from the lingering pain of my wounds, sit in prison passing the time with my writing, to suppress the feelings of pain and chagrin.

The little village of Don Dominguillo, located in a broad expanse of the valley, was my third night stop. As I was crossing the Río Grande [de Quiotepec], which, even during the dry season, is full of water and navigable by canoe, I came near to drowning.[7] A large piece of wood in the river had become lodged behind my horse's hind legs and he was trying to throw me off with his bucking and jumping. I realize now that I was in great danger [at the time] because I had taken my feet from the stirrups and had drawn them up under me. The heavy saber I was wearing and the large Mexican spurs would have made swimming difficult had I been thrown off. I took this incident for a bad omen.

The banks of the Río Grande [de Quiotepec] are only 1,255 feet above sea level and the heat there is quite oppressive. I traveled rather slowly, therefore, and I stopped frequently to make measurements and note my observations—partly to verify previously recorded geographic data and partly to avoid arousing suspicion. On the nineteenth [of February] I arrived in Tehuacán, where I learned that [some of] Santa Anna's troops were already moving nearby and that they were expected there any day. So I packed up all my instruments and papers very carefully, gave them to a Mexican friend for safekeeping, and hurried off to reach Veracruz. On previous trips to Veracruz I had always taken the road through San Andrés [Chalchicomula], Perote, and Jalapa. I could not travel by the same road this time if I did not want to be detained by the division of government soldiers stationed in Jalapa. I left the road, therefore, at Puente Colorado (Red Bridge) and rode through territory new to me to Orizaba, Córdoba, etc.[8] In 1829 I had attended a splendid [state] breakfast in Puente Colorado that the authorities of Orizaba had given to honor General Santa Anna as he was on his way from Oaxaca to Jalapa.[9] Afterward, I accompanied him as far as San Andrés Chalchicomula.

From Tehuacán to San Andrés [Chalchicomula] the road follows the sandy plain between gently sloping limestone elevations and offers little of real interest. The gorge at Puente Colorado is located at the edge of the cordillera, near the snow-covered volcano [Mount Orizaba]. The gorge at that point is constantly filled with a cold fog, driven down the slope by the north wind.[10] Again this day, as I neared the gorge, it was raining and very foggy. The dampness made me even more sensitive to the cold and, after riding several miles, I was happy to find a cantina where I could dry off and eat a warm breakfast.

From this point on, the wide road is paved and enclosed on either side by high protecting walls. It descends a couple of thousand feet, winding down in frequent narrow turns, reaching finally the beautiful valley of Orizaba. This valley, forming a broad plain between two mountain ranges, is 4 leagues [10.5 miles] in length, dotted by a number of haciendas and small villages. The vegetation in this valley is quite luxuriant; hence, one finds large fields of tobacco and coffee in cultivation here.[11] The area around Orizaba is quite interesting, and sometime in the future, when I can, I would like to spend a couple of months here preparing a special map of the region. I would include the volcano with the mountains surrounding it and this remarkable manmade road with the adjacent villages. It would probably arouse considerable interest. Orizaba is one of the three *villas* (market towns) of the region; the other two are Córdoba and San Andrés [Chalchicomula].

Tobacco is almost the sole commerce of Orizaba, but the price of this product is right now very depressed. Consequently, the village is not very prosperous. Córdoba seems to do much better with its coffee trade.[12]

15. Traveling Companions in Orizaba

In Orizaba I met a French physician, Monsieur Martin, who had lived several years in Oaxaca and who was now on his way back to France with his family. Since I did not know to which faction a series of out-posts between Orizaba and Veracruz belonged, I spent a day in Orizaba making arrangements to join Monsieur Martin's small caravan. He had eight pack mules. With the *arriero* [muleteer] and his people, Mon-sieur Martin's family, and myself, we had eleven people and seventeen animals in our party. Traveling only by day made our progress toward Veracruz slow. Until now we had been hearing reports from other trav-elers that hostilities had not yet broken out. But one night as I was lying in my hammock in camp, we were suddenly startled by the first thunder of cannon fire. The shots fell with such regular intermittent pauses that I could not possibly tell whether they were fired in a [field] engagement or in an assault. We were advised to veer off to the right toward Medellín, but I chose to follow the road straight ahead.[1] It took us over broken, hilly terrain and then over a plain covered with brush and small trees. Colorful birds of all sorts swarmed about us; among them I was able to distinguish the *pitorreal* [Kühne: *pittoreal*] (pepper eater?) by his beautiful plumage, his large yellow beak, and his rather odd-shaped body.[2] This bird can become very tame and is skilled at catching pieces of bread or fruit thrown to him from some distance.

16. The Outpost

Because the sound of the cannon had frightened the lady in our group [Madame Martin], I offered to ride ahead, and if I encountered some obstacle or danger I would ride back and lead them on by another route. Otherwise, I would await them at the gate to Veracruz, after giv-ing the outposts along the way (provided that they were Santa Anna's outposts) instructions to let my friends pass after me. The French lady was reassured by this plan, so [Karl] Lerche and I rode on ahead. To my amazement, however, we traveled without any difficulty as far as Pocitos [Kühne: Positos] [a village], just outside Veracruz, where I was startled by a sudden and loud "Alto!" (Halt!) on my right.[1] Several armed men approached me slowly with rifles lowered. While they were looking me over quickly, I explained that I had business in Veracruz. Immediately I was taken to their commanding officer, whom I found standing in front of a bamboo hut, surrounded by about fifty of his men. I learned from this officer that this outpost was, in fact, one of Santa Anna's own; thereupon, I told the officer of my wish to see the General. At this news, the previous formalities were dropped immediately and I was assured that the French family following me would be allowed to pass with no trouble. Right now I wish that I could write like [Sir] Walter Scott so that I could compose a worthy companion piece to his Scottish Highland outpost.[2]

The outpost that had halted me, about ten men in strength, had positioned itself on a slightly elevated point of a wooded brake. From a clearing only a few paces wide, which they had made in the thicket, they could survey the road fifty paces in each direction without being seen themselves and they could also retreat safely into the woods nearby. Whoever knows the wooded territory around Veracruz, the impenetrable brush intermingled with prickly cactus and all types of vines and thorns, he knows, too, that only a native of the area is able to locate and follow one of the obscure paths through that wilderness.

The camp to which I had been conducted numbered about eighty men. It was a highly colorful and strange mixture of Negroes, mulattoes, and brown Indians. It is almost impossible to describe the great variety of their dress. Many were wearing simple shirts and short white pants slit up each side. The shirts had no collar and the sleeves were rolled up. On their feet they were wearing sandals. Others wore light *litewkas* or blue blouses of simple cloth. Yet others wore jackets with red collars—probably the tunics from discarded military uniforms. I even saw a couple of men in black dress coats. Several men, whom I took to be noncommissioned officers and corporals, were wearing worn-out riding breeches decorated with many buttons in the Mexican style and open below the knee to show the white long underpants. Large hats of every shape shaded their wild, mustachioed faces. They wore around the waist a sash or belt, from which a bare machete, often decorated with a silver knob on the hilt, dangled by a leather thong. Each man had also the ubiquitous large knife *(cuchilla)* stuck under his belt and several even had hussar pistols.[3] Finally, each man in this colorful group also carried a musket with a bayonet—the only weapon that gave this unit the slightest military character. Without this one weapon they would have looked like a band of robbers. They wore the cartridge pouch in every place possible: on their backs, over their stomachs, over either shoulder—just wherever chance happened to place it. The commanding officer was distinguishable only by his red sash, his boots, and his saber. Thus was the appearance of this outpost.

The men who were not on sentry duty lay or squatted on the ground in small groups in front of the bamboo hut. At little campfires they cooked their *frijoles*, warmed their *tortillas*, smoked cigars, and played cards. Several old women and their daughters, naked from the waist up, worked busily grinding corn on crude millstones or dispensing to the men their favorite beverages.

17. Reporting to the General

After I had observed this group for a while, I rode on. I rode out of the brushy woodlands and soon caught sight of Veracruz on a hilly stretch of sand before me. Since no one else stopped me, I reached the city very quickly. The gate called La Merced stood wide open, and farmers were going in and out with their burdens, just as in the calmest peacetime.[1] The officer on watch welcomed me cordially, and I encountered no further difficulties at all. I was neither questioned nor searched. I left Lerche at the gate and went into the *posada nacional*, where I was quickly refreshed by a good dinner and a bottle of Bordeaux.[2] The French physician, Monsieur Martin, did not arrive until three hours later. [I learned that] his wife had received a good scare when she saw the colorful group at the aforementioned outpost.

As soon as my equipment arrived, I reported to the General, who also received me most warmly. I presented him the casket of chocolates with the letter of recommendation from his friends in Oaxaca. The casket was, of course, quite admired by everyone, for I had been very careful to let no harm come to it in the course of my journey.

So, now I was in Veracruz, ready to fight for the General and, if necessary, ready to spill my blood for him. The next few days were spent resting, looking around, and equipping myself better for the campaign. I learned at the time that a division of government troops under the command of Gen. [José María] Calderón was still encamped at Santa Fe, three leagues [eight miles] from Veracruz, but that an assault on Veracruz was expected any day.[3] I learned, too, that Santa Anna had initiated the hostilities several days earlier; he had gone around behind Calderón's division and robbed a *conducta* [government convoy] of thirty thousand pesos and other valuables, taking in the process 250 prisoners. He had just returned the day before with the loot. His return to Veracruz amidst the volleys and shouts of joy had been like a triumphal entry into the city. These shots were the cannon fire that we had heard the day before.[4] Everyone now expected Calderón to seek his revenge very soon.

18. A False Alarm

The next afternoon, just as I had lain down on my bed to take my siesta, I suddenly heard in the street outside the roll of drums and the blaring of bugles signaling the call to arms. I threw on my uniform and saber, but looked in vain for my aide to have him saddle my horse, which was stabled nearby in another building, but I did not know where. Finally, I joined on foot the crowd outside of soldiers, riders, and civilians. With all of them I hurried toward the gate La Merced, where I found the General with his officers outside [the gate], assembling and calling the troops to order as they came hurrying along. I must admit that in a little while we were all assembled—even cossacks, that is, the armed and mounted mulattoes and Indians whom I had seen outside of Veracruz; they had been given this name by everyone. I was furnished another horse, since my aide did not show up because he had been quietly getting himself drunk in a saloon. We waited a few hours for the enemy, who was supposed to be approaching. Finally, when there was no sign of him, we marched back into the city in military formation. Each was ready to outdo the other in courage. Because of the victory two days ago, the whole city was filled with an enthusiasm that this alarm had now rekindled.[1] It had probably been an intentional false alarm—instigated by Santa Anna himself.

19. New Entrenchments

I spent a few restful days eating and drinking well, and every morning I strolled out to the docks, where I watched the crowds and visited several ship captains. I looked over the fortifications, rode out to the fortress [San Juan de Ulúa], and prepared to put my maps in order.[1] Santa Anna went quietly about his business, too.

On February 27 I received unexpectedly the order to take command of the series of outposts toward the enemy's camp in Santa Fe. I was to construct concealed entrenchments for five hundred men, from which the General intended to launch an attack. I went immediately to that area and, with the aid of a cossack captain who knew the terrain intimately, I chose a point just in front of the forward outpost—a point quite close to the enemy's camp and near the bridge over the small river there, the Río Medio. Of the hundred men on outpost duty, I took twenty-five to work for me. The first curtains of earth were thrown up in one impenetrable escarpment just opposite the bridge, so that the road and this bridge were completely exposed to our fire. Within these escarpments I had a large area cleared that was to be surrounded by breastworks. The troops would then camp within this cleared and protected area. Inside this clearing I could place a couple of light cannons, too, with which I could rake the bridge and much of the road with grapeshot. In addition, I rendered the bridge itself impassable and I had the river blocked with palisade barriers and beams. The brush there was so thick and thorny that it was impossible for the enemy to penetrate our entrenchments. The only access was by a single camouflaged path. If the enemy were to bring up some heavy artillery against which we could not defend our light redoubt, then we had a safe retreat route open toward Antigua.[2] But from here two light cannons and one hundred infantrymen could hold off a couple of thousand counterattacking enemy troops if our assault were unsuccessful.

We did our work in utmost silence. We whispered among ourselves as we worked, and at the slightest noise, everyone dropped his tool, grabbed his rifle, and threw himself on the ground behind the earthen embankment. Since our presence had to remain a secret, we had left our horses behind. My cossack troops were the same as those I described [encountering] just before reaching Veracruz. The only tools we had for constructing these fortifications were machetes, several mattocks, and wooden shovels. The work did not progress as rapidly as I wished, but I was already finished with the embankment on the front perimeter when early on the morning of March 1, I sent a patrol out farther than usual to reconnoiter the enemy camp. In the meantime, I was eating my breakfast. My loyal friend Lerche always brought me the morning and noon meal with a couple of bottles of wine from Veracruz. This wine tasted delicious in the mild night air when I lay on my serape among the green, fragrant foliage of the thicket and listened to the murmuring of the river and the singing of the cicadas. I delighted then in watching the glimmering lights of the fireflies swarming in the darkness as I pondered my present military adventure.

20. Arrival of the General

The patrol I had sent out returned before very long with the report that Calderón had broken camp very early that same day and that there was no sign of the enemy for a league [2.6 miles] beyond Santa Fe.[1] I dispatched Lerche immediately to the General with this interesting news, requesting at the same time from him further orders for this unexpected situation. That night at twelve, just as I was about to go out myself with a larger patrol to reconnoiter [the enemy's position], the General's pack mules arrived unexpectedly with his field equipage. The accompanying officer informed me that Santa Anna himself would arrive in a few hours to execute some ingenious strategy against [General] Calderón. This officer shared with me also a generous slug from his rum flask. I had the camouflaging barriers removed, and in the darkness the mules, laden with munitions, entrenching tools, and the General's gear, came plodding through the entrance and up the sandy path to the camp. [On March 2,] at four o'clock [in the morning], Santa Anna himself arrived with the cavalry, and right behind them came the infantry. He ordered me to send the outposts back and to accompany him for the time being as his adjutant. Immediately, Lerche brought me the General's white horse, his coat, and some fresh clothes. After a rapid march we were soon in Santa Fe, where we had breakfast. We learned there that the enemy had indeed decamped and was in retreat toward Jalapa. After a couple of hours' rest we set out again, and that afternoon we reached a small settlement of a few scattered houses called Manantiales.[2] Our division made regular camp here in the face of the enemy, whom we now saw a short distance away busily placing cannons on a knoll opposite us.[3] After darkness had fallen, the General told us of his plan to skirt the enemy's position and to seize their fortifications at the pass of Puente Nacional.[4] Lt. [Nicolás de la] Portilla [Kühne: Postilla], an officer in the artillery, was sent out ahead of us with the demand for surrender.[5] At eight that evening, to deceive the enemy, our drums and bugles sounded the call to retreat. Instead, we moved out in a very orderly manner and silently to the left flank, following our native guides through bottoms, ravines, and paths in the underbrush for several leagues until we came out in a large, uneven plain where we halted in camp array. This clandestine procession had something romantically sinister about it. No one was permitted to smoke, and we talked to one another only in whispers. From lonely huts scattered in the distance we could hear the barking of a dog or the crowing of a rooster. Now and again we were startled by the cry of a bird awakened from his sleep. The fireflies hanging in the air and the pitch-black darkness of the night (so dark that marching in file one could not see the man before him)—all these things heightened our excitement, and my heart was pounding with anticipation.

It was about midnight when, fatigued from our strenuous march, we lay down to sleep on the hard, rocky ground. We were lying in rank and file, virtually on the spot where we had been standing at the end of the march. Soon everyone was asleep. Only the General, a couple of officers, and myself were still awake, quietly whispering to one another. Finally, Santa Anna himself lay down to sleep. I made a pillow of my rolled-up coat for his head (which he gratefully acknowledged) and, like Jacob, rested my own head on a hard stone as I stretched out on the earth to sleep. The night was clear and rather cool. Soon not a sound was to be heard. It seemed that not even the horses wanted to betray our clandestine march by snorting or neighing. My head was full of thoughts on the adventures of the last few days when I finally fell asleep, but I did not find a ladder to heaven like our aforesaid ancestor.[6]

21. Preparations for Battle

It was about three o'clock in the morning when I was awakened by one of the General's aides and given the order to have the [supply] park readied for travel. I ran through the long rows of sleeping infantrymen looking for the muleteers and their animals in the darkness. I had considerable difficulty locating my muleteers, whom I immediately put to work loading the mules. As I slowly walked back from my errand, carefully walking among the sleeping soldiers of the battalion, I thought about how many would today fall asleep for all eternity.[1] I had vivid thoughts of Edward Waverly as he strode through camp with his friend on the eve of that famous highland battle.[2]

At four o'clock the order came to break camp. The officers were awakened first; they in turn roused their troops. At five o'clock we were all ready to march again. I was summoned to the General to have an early drink with him. Then, just as the first rays of the sun were beginning to disperse the Ossianic apparitions of the nocturnal fog, we continued our silent march over the plain. Santa Anna had promised me the command of the artillery we hoped to capture, for, to my dismay, we had in our unit no cannon, which we could not have brought along on this march anyway.[3] Just before eight o'clock [that morning] we came up behind the village of Tolomé. Consisting only of a few miserable huts, this settlement is in itself unimportant, but on this day it was to become a place of infamy. We positioned ourselves near a bridge, the only crossing [over this stream] on the main highway from Veracruz to Jalapa.[4] We were between the enemy and Puente Nacional, cutting off, therefore, Calderón's retreat to Jalapa.[5] A hiding place was quickly cut out in the thicket near the bridge. Even the General helped by dragging up limbs to help conceal it. Some fusiliers were positioned in this abatis with orders, if we were attacked, first to allow the enemy to cross the bridge and then to open fire on his back. Two infantry companies were positioned behind the huts. Their orders were to attack the enemy with bayonets after he had crossed the bridge. The cavalry and the reserves were positioned behind a hill, on a terracelike slope, and in the shallow ravines nearby. In our respective positions we awaited the events that were to come.

I was sitting with Santa Anna and several of his aides in the breezeway of a bamboo hut. We were talking among ourselves, and the General, who had bought a basket of oranges, was distributing these among us. I was just about to bite deeply into a freshly peeled orange when we were startled by a volley of rifle fire. The enemy troops, who had been suffering badly from thirst, had started coming down from their position on the next rise to fetch some drinking water from the river. The officer in command of our fusiliers had disobeyed the order to hold fire until the enemy had passed the bridge. He had greeted the approaching troops with intensive rifle fire, which was returned immediately and no less intensely, too. The blue smoke rose in thick columns from the verdant thicket. After exchanging fire for about a quarter hour, the government infantry unit withdrew. Slowly the men made their way back up the slope, but we had betrayed our position before the enemy had crossed the bridge. A lot of blood had already been spilled in this prelude to the main assault. The first shot had been fired about nine o'clock, and now, about a half hour later, it was quiet again.[6] "Vamos a ver lo que harán!" (Let's see what they will do!), said the General to me, delighted about this first little lucky success.

22. The Battle near Tolomé

Suddenly we heard the roar of several heavy cannons that the enemy in the meantime had brought up against us. I was with the General at that moment as the first grenades whizzed over our heads and exploded close by. For the next four hours it rained grenades, cannonballs, and grapeshot. We withdrew slowly to the aforesaid terrace, where we prepared to sit out the cannon assault. Since we had no artillery, we could only wait for the enemy to cross the bridge and attack him there. Incidentally, Santa Anna had received word that several enemy battalions wished to desert to our side.[1] Consequently, he probably wanted to maintain a defensive posture as long as possible to await his opportunity and to avoid unnecessary bloodshed. For four hours we did not move from our position, exposed as we were to the enemy artillery fire. With cold-blooded composure, even as we joked and laughed, we saw the grenades land and explode among our troops. Many grenades landed, however, in the thicket. Close by the terrace where we sat, a fat ox was grazing, unconcerned about the struggles of men and their revolutions. It was struck by a twelve-pound ball, and for several hours it wallowed in its own blood. The grapeshot did a lot of damage, especially to the troops stationed near the road behind the bamboo huts—which afforded the men very little protection. The balls rattled right through the bamboo walls. The female companion of one soldier sat with us, calmly eating oranges as fearlessly as we and laughing with us when once in a while grenades went whistling close over our heads into the brush, showering branches and leaves down upon us. We just let the laurel leaves rain down on us and let Calderón shoot up his powder. Then [Lieutenant] Portilla came back with the news that Puente Nacional was ready to capitulate if Santa Anna would bring up his division. But we were already engaged and could not possibly abandon our position.

At that very moment we noticed also a company of enemy troops, cavalry and infantry, that had advanced through the brush and ravines on our flank and now was coming up on our rear. Immediately, Santa Anna dispatched his entire cavalry to rout them. We saw then how our few regular troops went charging bravely against the enemy. Our cossacks, on the other hand, immediately turned tail and drew the others after them. They all charged down the hill in the direction of Antigua and in a few minutes our entire cavalry was completely out of sight.[2] During the cavalry fiasco, one of our assault units stationed below had charged across the bridge with lowered bayonets, trying to overrun the enemy's artillery emplacement there. When they had advanced to within forty paces of the emplacement, a load of grapeshot cut down most of the men in the company and their courageous commander, Maj. [Juan] Andonaegui [Kühne: Andonaegni].[3] The others had to withdraw quickly without their leader under a constant hail of shot. The fusiliers positioned in the abatis had already withdrawn to our terraced hillside during the previous cannon fire. So, our company of grenadiers had had no fire support at the bridge at all. We now noticed on our left an enemy unit that had outflanked us. Soon the assault came from everywhere and there was fighting all around. Even our rear guard came under fire.

23. *Santa Anna's Defeat*

I must admit that our men fought bravely against an enemy who outnumbered us three to one.[1] They had to retreat gradually to the aforesaid terrace; here the last and most violent fighting took place. It determined the final outcome of the engagement and ended with our being surrounded and overwhelmed by the enemy. Our men fell into a terrible disorder and then became completely scattered and dispersed. Those who were not shot down or stabbed to death were defending themselves as well as they could. The terrain did not permit the formation of [defensive] squares against the charging cavalry, and these soldiers had had little or no training in such tactics, anyway.[2]

At this point the hour of my own misfortune began to strike. Until now I had remained on the terrace with General Santa Anna, who had ordered me not to leave his side. Meanwhile, I urged our soldiers on; many, as they fell back, I physically shoved forward again into the line of defense. Of all Santa Anna's European officers, I was the only one who had stuck by him.[3] Lerche had disappeared, too. Holding his head in both hands, Santa Anna ran to his horse. Intent on following him, I ran to my white horse, too, but my mount, tethered to a tree, had either been wounded by a stray bullet or merely frightened by the terrific din. In any case, he had become so skittish and wild that as I approached him, he reared and kicked and did not want to let me mount him. He snapped the reins in two and galloped away like the wind. Reacting automatically, I ran after him, hoping that he would soon entangle himself in the brush. In this endeavor I forgot momentarily the fighting going on around me and the direction I should take to save my own skin. It was my misfortune to rush headlong upon the first rise into a scene of bloody fighting. I met here the aforesaid cavalry unit that had attacked on our rear, and now, having advanced to the top of the hill, it was slashing and stabbing to death the fleeing soldiers, even those who had thrown down their weapons and surrendered. It was here that Col. [Pedro] Landero, weaponless and defenseless, met his death, too.[4] I stood motionless for a few moments, witnessing this gruesome spectacle, and then I drew my saber, my only remaining weapon. I had no intention of allowing myself to be stabbed to death without a fight. My death would at least be a gallant one. Immediately, three dragoons from the Tenth Regiment came galloping up at me.[5] For more than ten minutes I held them off. The fencing skills I had acquired in Freiberg, taught by Sprange of the Royal Saxon Regiment Prinz Maximilian, served me well. One of the dragoons, enraged at having his thrusts and blows constantly parried, finally drew his pistol, which he aimed at my breast to finish me off. Quickly, I tried to knock the weapon from his hand, but in the same moment that he fired, my blade struck his fist, deflecting his aim from my chest, of course, but the bullet hit me in my outstretched right arm. Still holding the saber, my right hand fell paralyzed to my side, and now I stood there defenseless. Even then, I parried several more thrusts of a lance with my left hand, but a saber blow to the neck sent me sprawling to the ground. Then the dragoons and those following them went galloping over me. Several of them shot at me or stabbed at me, but luckily they all missed. Their horses, however, trampled me pretty badly. Fortunately for me, the horses of the cavalry in this country are seldom shod. They left me lying for dead. The last grenade landed only a few feet away from me and exploded. It did not harm me physically, but a fragment falling back to earth landed on my chest and broke open a golden locket containing a lock of hair from my daughter Henriette.[6]

24. Captivity

Although my wounds hurt me terribly and the saber blow had completely stunned my senses, I was still conscious and had enough presence of mind to avoid making the slightest movement. I pretended to be dead in order not to attract the attention of the enemy to myself. I must have lain there a half hour when several soldiers came along plundering the dead. They saw that I was still alive and were about to finish me off when one of them happened to ask me if I had any money on me. I had three doubloons in my vest pocket, which I motioned for them to remove.[1] These noble disciples of Mars were so thrilled at this prize that they decided to spare my life. Of course, they took everything else from me: my dolman, hat, vest, sash, and the sheath for my saber. They led me a short distance away, where they bound me and another captured officer together. Then they dragged us to the large hill where the other captives were being held. Here an officer of the dragoons wanted to run me through—probably because he recognized me as a foreigner from my blue eyes. He showered me with threats and insults, which I had to listen to patiently.

So, there I stood: shot, stabbed, cut, trampled, bound, and almost naked on the same terrace where a few hours ago I had been sitting beside the General. Together we had courageously and cheerfully observed the battle. I looked out over the huts, the road, the bridge, and the green thicket. Everything seemed unfamiliar and alien to me. I could not remember at all what had happened nor how I had come to be in this situation. Then I recognized among the other prisoners several comrades as sad-looking as myself. They gave me a sorrowful nod and directed their eyes to the heavens. This strange reunion, however, seemed to me like a dream. The thunderous roar of the victor's cannon, the rumble of his drums, the fanfare of his trumpets, and his victorious cries are all that I remember of that hour. My pain and the great loss of blood had clouded my mind so much that I am now unable to re- call anything more that happened. Darkness suddenly enveloped my senses.[2]

I finally regained consciousness in the small room of a hut. I lay on the bare, damp earth among other wounded captives, some of whom were already dying. My head rested on a sack of corn, and I was covered with blood.

My memory gradually returned, and I was able to recollect bit by bit the events just past. I recognized the hut we were in as the same in which I had breakfasted that morning with the General. Now it was filled with captives and the wounded. Fortunately, I noticed among the men a young physician, but he was so deaf that he ignored my plea to look at my wounds. With the aid of another prisoner I finally succeeded that evening in getting his attention and communicating my needs to him. Some of the blood was then washed off, revealing that the pistol ball, which had entered my right arm just below the wrist, had trav- eled closely along the bone into my upper arm, stopping finally just above the elbow. At my insistence on an immediate operation, the preparations were made. Several officers held lanterns and others held me still on the ground while the physician, who had lost his kit of sur- gical instruments, made a large transverse cut with a dull knife. The ball was lodged so tightly against the bone that it took a while before the "blue bean" [lead ball] was removed with the aid of a pair of pliers. It amazed my companions that I endured the pain without uttering a single sound. Upon examining my other wounds, they found that the strong silk embroidery on the collar of my British dolman had broken the force of the saber blow. I had sustained only a bad contusion to the neck. My neck had hurt so badly that I had not been able to turn my head, but because I had repeatedly placed my hand there to feel the wound, a lot of blood had rubbed off my fingers. At first, therefore, the other prisoners had thought that I was dangerously wounded. The lance wounds, however, turned out to be only superficial lacerations, for I had parried the lance thrusts quite skillfully. We found, however, that my finger was cut half through. Since my shirt was full of holes from the lance thrusts, anyway, it was cut up to make bandages for my wounds after they had been thoroughly washed with vinegar and water. Then I retired again to my corner, lay down on my corn sack without a blanket or any further medical care, and observed what was happening around me. I listened to the groans of the other wounded and to the plaintive conversations of the other captives. I learned that they thought our General was dead, that some thought they had even seen him lying dead in a ravine. A few moments earlier, someone had even offered his coat and hat and my dolman for sale. Santa Anna's death seemed to me now only too probable. We all wept for the man whom we had seen full of spirit and courage in our midst just a few hours earlier. His fate had caught up with him—"had hurled his cold, dead body under the hooves of horses."[3] Nothing seemed now more certain or more natural than [the belief] that after this victory Calderón would immediately march on Veracruz and would take the city without resistance.[4] In that case, then, the revolution was over, and we were clearly rebels. What would be our fate?

25. Fever and Delirium

We spent the night pondering such thoughts—without food or drink, and without any blankets to protect us against the wind blowing through the flimsy bamboo hut. The whimpering, groaning, and wailing of several badly wounded comrades, the shouts of the guards surrounding our huts, the clatter of the gun carriages and wagons passing by, the pain of my wounds, and anxious thoughts about the future did not let me sleep much, although I examined my situation rationally and philosophically while trying to get some rest. I must have had some fever from my wounds, for whenever I closed my eyelids to attempt sleep, I was haunted by the most bizarre images. I remember especially one peculiar dream. I dreamt that I was in the company of several administrative officials of Wermelskirchen and Hückeswagen (villages in southern Westphalia)—places that I had not thought about since I left Germany.[1] These gentlemen were sitting with me at a table full of old documents and manuscripts from which they were trying to show me the origin and history of both villages. Their boring recitations gave me the most violent headache. I kept wanting to rise to my feet and break off the conversation, but they would not let me. This dream finally became unbearable to me, and I could banish it only by opening my eyes.

But as fatigue closed my eyes once more, there they sat again—the burgomasters and councilmen of Wermelskirchen and Hückeswagen— with their documents and inkwells, and above the door behind them I could see the Prussian eagle.[2] At times, familiar faces would peer through the wall and laugh at me or motion to me to get up and leave the wise magistrate sitting there. I saw Frey, the painter from Danzig; the late Professor Stark from Bremen; Chief Surveyor Eichelberg, who in an unfortunate accident fell and broke his neck; my friend Halle from Hagen, with his violin in his hand; Artillery Captain Streit, who is also an industrious cartographer; and others. To free myself of these images, I forced myself to remain awake, although I wanted very much to sleep. A young captain with curly black hair, whose head rested with mine on the corn sack, died of his wounds during the night. The next day, as the morning sun illuminated this scene of our misfortune, I saw him lying dead and cold at my side.

26. Causes of the Defeat

Before I conclude my description of that eternally memorable day, the third of March, I want to make a few more remarks about the battle. Our defeat could not be blamed on a lack of courage, for even the enemy did us justice on that score in his public account.[1] Only our cossacks would not deserve his praise. Our debacle can be charged to the following causes: In the first place, the enemy outnumbered us three to one. He had twenty-five hundred men, and they were all regular army troops.[2] [Second], the enemy had artillery, and we had none.[3] [Third], our General was going to wait out the enemy's attack instead of launching a counteroffensive. The enemy should not have been given time to outflank us and to intimidate many of our troops with a lengthy cannonade. Fourth, our fusiliers in their hidden position opened fire prematurely. [Fifth], the uniforms of our troops and of the enemy were so similar that we often withheld fire in the mistaken notion that we were firing on our own men. Sixth, we had in our cavalry about three hundred turncoat captives from the capture of the *conducta*, and other deserters who had joined our cause.[4] Seventh, our position was below that of the enemy, who held the hill overlooking us. One could certainly fault Santa Anna for this error, for one should not choose such positions. But it must be noted that he did not intend to engage in serious battle, but merely to give several enemy battalions, whom we believed friendly to our cause, the opportunity to surrender or desert.[5] If [Lieutenant] Portilla had returned a couple of hours earlier, then we probably would have marched on immediately to Puente Nacional, which we could have seized, thereby cutting off the enemy completely from Jalapa and causing him considerable difficulty. There we would have found several cannons. The expedition would have had an entirely different outcome, and we might have entered the capital [Jalapa] as victors.[6] But now, back to my story.

27. A Death Sentence (and a Reprieve)

The day after the battle (if one can call only three thousand men in combat a battle—in Europe it would be scarcely more than an outpost engagement), on the afternoon of March 4, all of the captive officers, thirty-two in number, and four volunteers were led off in ranks of four by a cavalry escort of twenty-five riders up the highway to Jalapa. Several of the badly wounded, myself among them, remained behind. During the night my arm had become so swollen that today one would not have been able to remove the bullet. Since I was almost naked besides, I did not want to expose my wound to the blistering sun. So, when the others were marched away, I thought I was doing the smart thing to remain behind with the others. I thought that we would be taken along to Veracruz, and there I would be well taken care of by my friends.

After the other prisoners had marched away, I lay for about an hour in my corner—rather pleased with myself for my Prussian cleverness. Suddenly, General Calderón came storming into the hut, shouting, "Where is the foreigner we captured?" I raised up and made a motion identifying myself. Without further ceremony he gave the order to have the [foreign] scoundrel *(pícaro estrangero)* immediately shot. In an instant I was actually being taken out of the hut. I could see in the eyes of the soldiers their delight over my execution, which reminded me of Fridolin going to the forge:

> That delights the two brutish men,
> Filled with murderous glee.
> As cold before the iron had been,
> Must the hearts in their breasts be.[1]

I shrugged my shoulders, said nothing, screwed up my courage, and resigned myself to my fate, saying to myself, in Solomon's words, "All is vanity!" There was no indication that I would be able to keep my arm, and what can one do in the world with only one arm? A company had already been assembled. From these men some were going to be chosen who would do me the favor of drilling a few ounces of lead into my body. Then Calderón gave the order to bring me before him again.

He asked me my name and where I came from. I answered him very calmly, and then in a coarse manner he flung these questions at me: "You scoundrel, what are you doing in our country? Why are you meddling in our political affairs?" [And then to an officer he said,] "Take this rascal out and kill him!" Indeed, I was being led out now for the second time, when outside a corporal took me by the arm and told me to run. I asked, "To where?" "You'll see!" was his curt reply, as he propelled me ahead of him in the hot sun. Without a vest, coat, or hat I ran as fast as I could just to get out of the sight of that boor Calderón. I still could not figure out what they had in store for me, but I suspected that my execution was to take place at another location, farther to the rear instead of in the presence of the other wounded. After an hour we caught up with the prisoner detail. I was handed over to the senior officer, and off we went again at a run. After having escaped death several times already, I thought that I had for sure fallen into his grasp this time and would drop dead somewhere on this march. I was weak from the loss of so much blood, and I was suffering from hunger and thirst. Sweat was dripping from my whole body, and the sun was burning down more painfully on my head than it had done to the prophet Jonah.[2] My arm was turning red, blue, and green, but I did not despair, thanks to my natural good spirits. Fortunately, things also began to get better.

The senior officer was a humane man, for as a soldier he knew firsthand the vicissitudes of warfare. Consequently, he did not carry out the orders given him by Calderón to treat us as severely as possible. After a forced march of about two leagues [five miles], he allowed us to stop at a group of several huts and receive some refreshment. He gave us a hundred thalers with which to purchase our food and drink.[3] A friendly Indian gave me an old shabby hat; to me it was a great treasure! My friend Captain Veitia [Kühne: Veitga] tossed me a worn coat that the day before had been stolen from a dead fusilier.[4] So, I was somewhat outfitted again. This *litewka* was now going to be my mattress and my blanket. From here we continued our march at a slower pace and with more comfort. Several burros that we met on the road were hired for the weak and disabled to ride on by turns. That evening we arrived in Puente Nacional—the town that just the day before we had planned to seize.[5] Man proposes and God disposes!

In Puente Nacional we were well received by the owner of the new inn. Soon after I had eaten some supper, I wrapped myself in my *litewka* and slept sweetly beyond all expectations on the hard tile floor of the dining room in which we were all locked up. It is remarkable, by the way, that from this day until we reached Perote fortress, my sleeping hours were filled with the most delightful images. One time I was taking a stroll in a forest grove at Harkorten, the old estate of my family near Hagen. Another time I found myself at a festive ball, and once I was dining on shellfish and potatoes and a couple of glasses of Mosel wine at Lempertz [restaurant] in the Sternengasse in Cologne. Another time I was eating trout with asparagus sauce at the Stadt Gotha [restaurant] in Dresden. Such delicious dreams were, of course, much more pleasant than the lectures of the councilmen in Hückeswagen and Wermelskirchen. They were, in fact, a real source of strength for me. But why was I having such delightful fantasies under such wretched conditions? This question puzzled me as much as the circumstance that had allowed me to escape the execution order of the boorish man with the name of the famous Spanish dramatist.[6] Even if he was taken by a slight attack of generosity, I shall nonetheless never forget his coarse manner. A victor should never mistreat his prisoners; they are already humiliated enough. To curse one's enemy when he is already bloodied makes one only more a barbarian. In this connection Santa Anna's character seems so much more noble! After the capture of the *conducta,* he granted the captured officers as well as the soldiers their complete freedom.[7] It probably never occurred to him to say a harsh word to any of them.

28. The Journey Continues

After breakfast on the morning of March 5, we set out on the day's journey. Twenty-five burros were hired, several mules and horses, too, so that we all were able to ride. So, somewhat comforted now, we set out

rather merrily. We really made a strange procession. There were more
than thirty officers in their uniforms and epaulets, but without sabers
and spurs, riding on burros and packsaddles, laughing and joking, accompanied by twenty-five dragoons all mixed in among us! As comical
as this scene appeared to me, I was still suffering constant pain from
my wounds. I was anticipating, too, the loss of my arm very soon, so
that as I was riding along on my lazy burro, I was thinking up projects
that I could undertake without one arm—if I survived the operation at
all. If I were of the Roman Catholic faith, then as a *manchot* [one-
armed person] I would become a monk, for monks, as far as I know,
need their hands only for eating and drinking. With the left hand one
can make the sign of the cross, bestow blessings, and even receive
tithes, if that is still customary. Finally, I put these thoughts out of my
mind and decided to wait a while to see how I would feel about being
one-armed after it actually happened.

In Paso de Ovejas we rested a couple of hours.[1] We were lying
quietly in huts surrounded by dragoons, enjoying a noonday siesta
when we were suddenly awakened by the loud trampling of horses'
hooves. It was Minister of War [José Antonio] Facio, who had already
been informed of Calderón's victory and who now, with his mounted
guard, was hurrying from Jalapa to Veracruz to be there for the triumphal entry into that city.[2] While all the other prisoners rushed outside to greet the minister and to plead for their lenient treatment, I
remained inside, lying quietly on a bamboo cot, for I did not want to
attract the minister's attention to myself. But one of the minister's aides
came running in, explaining to me that Facio had sent him to learn my
name. I now began to fear the same kind of business with him as I had
had with Calderón. Perhaps Señor Calderón had spared me from the
firing squad just so Señor Facio could have the pleasure of shooting me.
I told the aide my name and thought to myself, "All's bad that ends
badly."[3] But after a short while the minister rode on without insulting
me or even speaking to me. Silently I thanked my creator and Señor
Facio for this beneficence.

29. *Arrival in Jalapa*

We continued on our way, then, riding on each day astride our burros
until March 7, when we reached the romantic city of Jalapa. Our ar-

rival was almost like a triumphal entry, for a majority of the inhabitants of this very attractive and delightful city supported Santa Anna's party.[1] Moreover, some of the prisoners had family and friends living here. Others in the city were simply curious to see the heroes of Veracruz, who, though few in number, had nevertheless dared to rise up against the Mexican government forces and who had fought so bravely before their eventual defeat.

Everybody poured out into the streets to greet us, and then they followed us to the large barracks at Constitution Plaza, where we were quartered in a large hall.[2] Our life here was as happy and as colorful as prisoners anywhere could have. Friends and acquaintances brought in beds, mattresses, chairs, food, drink, clothes, even money to us. It was as if Hieronimus Jobs had just become pastor.[3] Five hundred pesos, the proceeds of an earlier collection, had already been presented to us outside the barracks. We used the money to establish a common fund for our future use. Monsieur Henriet, the French innkeeper whose hospitality I had enjoyed on several previous occasions, brought me a bed, some clothing, food, and other things. In addition, I was given two shirts, a serape, and some money by Herr [Friedrich] Becher of the German West Indian Company, who happened to be present, too.[4] A surgeon was also sent for, and he dressed my wounds properly—for the first time. I really slept well on my mattress that night!

That same day we learned that our General had by some miracle escaped and that he was even then safe in Veracruz. We heard, too, that Calderón, instead of capitalizing immediately on his unexpected victory by attacking the city as quickly as possible, as a clever general should have done, had even retreated to Paso de Ovejas.[5] There he had taken time to clean his cannons and to burn the dead because he feared the outbreak of a pestilence from the corpses.

Consequently, it was to be anticipated that our cause was not yet completely lost, for Santa Anna would resist with every means available. Calderón's division seemed to me much too small, anyway, to take a place like Veracruz, with its many batteries. The news of Santa Anna contributed a great deal toward making our stay in Jalapa a happy one. We even entertained the fond hope of being able to remain in Jalapa. But already the next day we received the order to pack up for the journey to our destination, Perote fortress. This order dampened our spirits considerably.

30. A Scientific Expedition

We mounted our burros sadly and rode slowly along up the highway, among the balsamic and floral fragrances that make this particular road so delightful. In San Miguel del Soldado [Kühne: San Miguel de los Solados] we met a company of travelers who had stopped there for a while because their wagon had broken down. One young man among them recognized me right away as a European. I learned after talking with him that this group was setting out to investigate the famous [ruins of] Palenque in [the state of] Chiapas.[1] This young gentleman, a Frenchman, typified perfectly the humane and amiable character of his nation. He gave me a pair of finely tailored riding breeches and some money. I was treated kindly, too, by Herr Schmitz, who was traveling with the expedition.[2] I never saw the leader of the party, Monsieur [Jean Frédéric] Waldeck. I wished them every success on their scientific journey, which interested me a great deal. If I had met this group earlier in Veracruz or if I had not already been a prisoner, I would have joined them to forget this political business while climbing around on the ruins of that old Phoenician or perhaps Carthaginian city.[3] Nothing in the world can be as instructive as exploring the history of great past civilizations or the ruins of their structures. A nation that has disappeared from this earth is really a death on a grand scale. World history should be written as a chronicle of these civilizations.

Why are there no general maps on which the rise and fall of former civilizations are represented? If I had the mechanical skills, the time, and the necessary tools, I would make a large globe and attach to it some type of device with which I could show how in one area of the earth humanity evolved and then how the different races and nations migrated to the far corners of the globe. I would show how these nations made war on each other, displaced each other, and annihilated each other; how the victors progressed then to their zenith, declined again, and disappeared. I would show how other nations emigrated en masse—from Asia to Europe and America, from Europe to Africa, however history records such migrations, or however myth presents them. These nations would glide over the globe like wispy clouds that pass before the disc of the moon. One would see and comprehend there a magnificent and awesome, but beautiful and sublime, tragedy that could not be presented on any stage. How insignificant would all the panoramas and mechanical-visual representations appear, after once surveying the entire earth and its history! I am convinced, too, that such a drama of the nations can be presented. I will think about this project some more later, but for the time being, I will leave the development of my idea to the history professors living in Germany right now. However, no one can deny that my idea is an original one!

Oh, how chagrined I felt when after such a high flight of imagination I had to return again to our burros, which were trotting along carrying us nearer and nearer to our dungeon cells. Yes, we were trotting. Our drivers (and I can accurately say *our* drivers, for as we sat on the burros we were driven along, too)—our drivers had gradually become drunk and had gotten the idea of earning their contracted fee to Perote in less than the usual time. To accomplish this feat, they were dealing out powerful blows to our long-eared friends. Each of them tried to outdo the other, so that the poor animals, completely terrified by this treatment, were running as fast as they could. The drivers beat them incessantly, shouting, "Onward, boys!"—a very common cry in leading an attack. Amid all this commotion we had some pretty ridiculous scenes. Now and then, one of us would fall from his burro, to the loud and general amusement of the others, who sooner or later suffered the same fate. So, on we trotted, exhausted from the ride and out of breath from all the laughing. We trotted through the rich fir forest growing on the scoriaceous slopes of the Cofre de Perote. We trotted through Las Vigas, through La Cruz Blanca, and on to the plateau, where, not far from [Los] Molinos, we caught a glimpse of the fortress.[4]

31. Perote Fortress

It [the fortress] is situated on a plain, approximately a rifle shot distant from the village of Perote.[1] The plain is full of holes made by marmots and mice, which brought all the previous incidents to a final, comical climax. As we entered this plain, the burros began stepping into the holes and falling, throwing the whole party one after another to the sandy ground. To spare my arm a *salto mortale*, I had dismounted earlier. All the inhabitants [of the fortress] had come over the drawbridge and were gathered outside the palisade to watch the captured officers of Tolomé make their entrance. Perote fortress is square in shape, each side being three hundred paces in length. It is solidly constructed of hewn stones and is surrounded by a broad, dry moat.[2] We entered the fortress just before sunset. A large door opened, not the heavenly gate exactly, but one that led into the cheerless vaulted cell described at the beginning of this journal. Our eyes and our fifth sense [touch] were confronted only by naked, filthy, and cold walls. Behind us the door clanked shut and we were alone in the dismal darkness, all of us numb with despair. Cursing our enemy and our dreadful fate, we lay down on the damp floor. Some lay quietly crying; others raged in anger; but most simply stared at the blackened wall as if in shock. We spent the first night in prison remembering with envy those who had died in the battle and whose ashes now rested peacefully at Tolomé.

The next morning Lieutenant Escanís and I were taken to the fortress hospital.[3] He had received a grazing blow to the back of his head from a piece of grapeshot. It was high time for me to receive some treatment, too, if my arm was going to be saved. The so-called hospital, located on the north side of the fortress, is in the same type of vaulted room as our cell, which I described earlier; only the walls and the floor are somewhat cleaner.[4] The air there, too, is not so stale, because the door remains constantly open. Several board partitions separated the patients, each of whom had a good mattress, linens, and blankets, a table, and a chair that had been modified to accommodate certain natural functions. I rested here quite comfortably and quietly, since there were only two other patients with wounds, and I was glad to be able to enjoy finally the rest that I needed so badly.

32. The Hospital and Its Staff

The routine in this temple of Aesculapius was as follows. Every morning at five our vessels were cleaned and the hospital floor was swept by several convicts. Then the chief surgeon, a large, strong, serious man in a gray coat, appeared for his rounds. His head was bound in a white cloth and on that he wore a hat, as is the Spanish custom. He was accompanied by the physician, a half-crazy, cross-eyed, and funny little man who one day wore a jerkin, another day a dress coat, or a colorful hussar jacket, or some other kind of uniform. Three or four times a day he changed these costumes that one could see had not been tailored originally for him. He was rarely or never clean-shaven. The physician (who, his detractors claimed, was actually only a horse doctor) was followed in turn by two attendants with lamps, for it dawned much later in this vaulted room than in the rest of the world. One of the attendants was a haggard, stooped, but otherwise good-natured little man with a hernia. His clothes were so tattered that the man's skin was visible in several places. He helped the physician in dressing wounds, and those wounds for which a good pair of eyes was needed, he dressed all by himself, for as I said, the physician was cross-eyed. His vision was so bad, in fact, that while cauterizing with lunar caustic he often burned the new and healthy flesh, and placed bandages with poultices on the wrong spot. The other attendant was a runaway servant named Camillo. He had a goiter that he tried to hide by always wearing a large neckerchief. These two attendants were followed in turn by two chained prisoners, one of them carrying a large folio volume, the other an inkwell and quills. They also had their little physical infirmities so that all the members of the staff, with the exception of the chief surgeon, actually embodied the hospital themselves.

With his rich bass voice the chief surgeon wished each patient, one after the other, a good morning. Each one was asked how he had slept and how he felt. Then the surgeon prescribed treatment and medications, which were noted very carefully in the large book. Finally, he supervised the dressing of our wounds. When everything was in order, the team of "experts" withdrew, with the exception of the physician, who usually remained behind on some pretext and cracked jokes with us. Punctually at eight o'clock each of us received a cup of chocolate with toast and water, served by two prisoners whose chains had been removed, since they had been assigned to our service. At twelve o'clock they brought our noon meal, which invariably consisted of a cup of watered-down bouillon, some rice with mutton, and bread. We received either a full or a half portion, according to the orders of the chief surgeon. I did not receive full rations until eight days before my dismissal. At three o'clock we got chocolate again, and at seven o'clock there was some roast mutton for those who were on full rations. This regimen was observed so strictly that I cannot recall a single deviation from the routine.

Immediately after my entrance into the hospital my wound began to fester—so much, in fact, that pus poured out like water when the bandage was removed. The long wound had to be kept open at all costs, which was done with a dry sponge. This operation, which was repeated every two days, caused me the most intense pain. After four weeks of this treatment they drew out with the sponge a piece of my dolman and a piece of my shirt, which had entered my arm with the pistol ball. After that day the festering stopped, and my recovery, to my delight, proceeded very rapidly. It is natural, I suppose, that I became extremely bored during the remainder of my recovery. Several books that had been sent to me, including the story of Napoleon (based on his memoirs), and the diary of Saint Helena by Las Casas, I finished quickly.[1] The rest of the time I had nothing more to do than lie in bed, sleep, and look for faces and shapes among the cracks, spots, and lines in the walls. I even looked for human profiles in tortilla fragments. Once I had the enormous pleasure of finding quite unexpectedly the profiles of the two lawyers, Schluck and Schlauch, from the *Jobsiade*.[2] I laughed so hard about it that the others in the ward did not know what had gotten into me. I passed the time, too, by whistling, singing, and by drawing on the wall with charcoal a map of the world and of the battle of Tolomé. We were all very eager for some news from outside, but we rarely received any. We learned only that [General] Calderón was wasting his time covering the road to Veracruz and that Santa Anna was making frequent assaults on him.[3] One day one of the hospital attendants failed to make his usual appearance. About the same time I noticed some money and clothes missing—possessions that were badly needed at the time.

The hour of my dismissal from the hospital struck finally on May 1, the third day after Easter. My wounds were healed, although my arm was still stiff. I was able to write some, but only with the greatest effort, causing me to fear that my arm might remain lame. At eight that morning the officer of the guard came to take me back to the cell. I was received with loud rejoicing by my old comrades. One after the other they shook my hand or embraced me and congratulated me on my recovery.

PUEBLA

33. *Puebla de los Angeles*

July 3, 1832

Today, exactly four months after the disastrous battle at Tolomé, I take my pen in hand again to record the remarkable change of fortune that unexpectedly occurred eight days ago. Everything has changed: the locale, the prison, and the treatment. Instead of in a dark, vaulted cell, we are confined in the main hall of an airy, spacious, and cheerful barracks with a gallery and a fountain. Instead of the cold, cheerless climate of Perote, we are enjoying the fresh air in the beautiful valley of Puebla.[1] Instead of the stern, rude, and hostile treatment under the commandant of Perote fortress, the attentiveness of the officers in the garrison here is really delightful. Now I shall try to search my memory for details of the last eight days and continue my narrative by relating the pleasant manner in which the Perote episode was suddenly interrupted.

34. *Departure from Perote Fortress*

On June 26, just as I was sitting on my hard bunk, we received the news and the order from the officer of the guard that six of us were being transferred that day to another place. None of us had ever dreamed of a change of prisons. The officers included on the transfer list were Col. [Manuel Fernández] Castrillón, Maj. [Ramón] Hernández, Capt. [Francisco] Macín, Adj. [Nicolás de la] Portilla, and myself.[1] Everyone in our cell became excited over this new order, but we knew no reason for it, nor for the choice of names on the list—even less the reason for keeping our destination a secret. Several days earlier we had heard about the cease-fire agreed to by Generals Santa Anna and Calderón, and about the preparations for peace negotiations.[2] Naturally, we had been praying for the hour of our release, but we expected the doors to freedom to be opened to all of us at the same time. We had no idea that some of us would be separated from the others, nor [any inkling] of our destination.

Our few possessions were packed pretty quickly and then we

waited sadly in silence for the hour of departure. We were all pre-
occupied in speculation on the possible cause of this measure and on
the destiny in store for us. We were all extremely dejected: those on
the list were saddened by the unanticipated separation from comrades
who for four months had shared a common fate with them. Those remaining behind envied us who were about to leave, for they assumed
that our destiny would be a better one than their own. So, for four
uncomfortable hours we waited with our vague, sad feelings until a
rented cart drawn by three mules arrived for us. The door to the cell
was opened and we bade an affectionate farewell to our fellow captives
who remained behind. All of us had tears in our eyes.

We went on foot as far as the village of Perote, where our escort,
twenty-five cavalry troops, turned off to the right with the cart. We
learned then that our destination was [the city of] Puebla.[3] It was already four o'clock in the afternoon, but the weather was so sunny and
clear that we rejoiced in our hearts at the beauty of the green fields, of
the mountainous horizon, and of the blue sky. We were happy, also, to
be able to cast farewell glances at the fortress behind us. I felt like a
man who after suffering with a long painful illness for several months
finally goes out again into the open air. Everything seems new to him,
and more beautiful than before. The most insignificant flower and the
plainest butterfly delight him. He marvels at the fresh sight of cloud
banks illuminated by the late afternoon sun. He marvels at the beautiful sunset and at the golden peaks of distant blue mountains. We
shared such feelings of wonder with each other as we rejoiced in the
new sights. We knew, of course, that in a few days we would disappear
into another prison, but it could not be worse than the one we had just
left. And if it was as bad, then our present journey was at least a pleasant interruption that we intended to enjoy to the fullest. It was a pleasure just to drink in the pure air of this altitude. Happily we rolled
along over the plain in our cart until we reached the hacienda Santa
Gertrudis [Kühne: Santa Gertruda], about four leagues [ten miles]
from Perote, at the foot of Mount Pizarro, which to me was a welcome
sight.[4]

We broke camp the next morning at five o'clock. It was a splendid
morning. The sun's rays were streaming down again between the mountains. On the left the Cofre de Perote and the eternally snow-covered
peak of the volcano of Orizaba towered above us. Before us in the

background was Mount Malinche.[5] In the distance on the right was majestic Popocatépetl, and then right next to us was Pizarro, its impenetrable hills overgrown with thick cactus, the so-called *mal país* (evil or bad lands). With our three mules running at a trot, we quickly reached the village of Tepeyahualco, where we stopped for breakfast.[6] We were visited there by a major who was coming back from Mexico City. One can easily imagine my feelings when I recognized the white horse he was riding as my former mount, complete with saddle and pistols. My heart was breaking at the sight, but I was their prisoner, so I kept my feelings to myself.

35. *The New Rifle Model*

A young Mexican landowner here showed us a rifle of remarkably small caliber. The ball was hardly three lines in diameter.[1] The rifle itself was as light as a pistol. He assured us that this rifle could shoot farther than one of average caliber and much more accurately, too. I was convinced of its accuracy because of the diminished friction of the air on the ball and because of the ratio of the barrel length to the caliber, etc. Professor Benzenberg would definitely find the spread cone of this rifle significantly smaller than that of the weapon with which he was experimenting near Düsseldorf and which nearly cost him his life.[2]

As the young Mexican owner kindly pointed out, however, the actual advantage of this rifle was the small size of the ball. It is more deadly because the opening of the wound is so small that the blood cannot flow out of the wound, so it flows into the interior of the body. Thus, the smallest wound becomes fatal. I would recommend the introduction of these small-caliber rifles to all belligerent nations; they would achieve far greater and more certain results with less expense of powder and lead. The rifle was invented by an eighty-year-old Indian who lived alone in the mountains nearby. Since the Mexican who showed it to us has until now sought no additional advantage from the rifle for himself, I hereby do publicly make claim to the patent rights on this rifle and on all other types of weapons to which this new invention could be applied. If I had not been a prisoner, I definitely would have attempted some experiments on the spot with this new weapon.

36. Arrival in Vireyes

Soon after continuing our march we noticed on the plain to our left a division of cavalry about a thousand men strong. They were riding with an advance and a rear guard. When they spotted us, they immediately deployed into battle position, and reconnaissance groups rode out to approach us on either side. It turned out that this division was coming from Mexico City and was the escort for a *conducta* [bullion shipment] of thirty thousand dollars bound for Jalapa. They were taking the greatest precautions because of the insecurity of this area, which was patrolled by large groups of Santa Anna's partisans. Of course, they had thought we were the advance guard for such a unit. I kept hoping secretly, since our escort was so small, that we would fall into the hands of a group of partisans. But we arrived unmolested at Vireyes [Kühne: Virreges] a hacienda, where we remained for a day.[1]

I should also mention that our poor mules were extremely fatigued by the last four leagues of our journey. The road was covered with deep sand, which tired our animals so much that they could hardly go on, even though we frequently walked long stretches on foot to give them some relief. Imagine a heavy cart with a wooden axle that is never greased and with clumsy wheels, the hubs of which have no box. Imagine the sand and at times deep mud, with six men packed into a cart too small for them, and then one more, the driver, sitting up on his seat. Then one can also easily imagine the misery of those poor mules, which had been so badly beaten and mistreated. The cart had no shafts for the animals on either side and the traces were connected behind the mules directly to the cart in such a way that there was no room between them. The harness ropes, therefore, rubbed them constantly and made raw places on their hides.

Our procession was finally moving so slowly that the dragoons lost their patience. Two of them hitched their powerful horses ahead of the mules and off we went at a trot. The horses were hitched up easily by means of the familiar *lazos* or strong braided ropes that horsemen here always have with them and that they handle with great skill. While riding at full gallop, the Mexican can snare with this lasso anything that tries to escape him. One really needs to see this weapon in action to get an idea of its usefulness. In the first revolutionary war against the Spaniards, a large portion of the Mexican cavalry had no other weapon than this lasso. But the Spaniards had a great fear of these riders. Once a man was snared by the loop of the light rope, he was pulled to the ground and dragged to death. There are even instances of a single strong cavalry soldier snaring a light cannon with his lasso and pulling it away after him. The other end of the lasso is made fast around the strong saddle horn that is shaped for this purpose. So, the horse can even pull from one side or the other without the slightest inconvenience to the rider.[2] I am sure that it was interesting to see our cart with its cover of straw mats, drawn by three mules and the mounts of two dragoons, and followed by our escort trotting along behind us. People must have thought that we were very important government prisoners.

We arrived in Vireyes about two o'clock in the afternoon. We spent the rest of the day talking about our General and his marvelous escape after the battle at Tolomé. Upon giving his word of honor to return, Maj. [Ramón] Hernández had received permission a few days earlier to go to Veracruz to see after some family matters. Now he told us about the great presence of mind of Santa Anna, who had ridden away behind the enemy after the engagement at Tolomé and had taken the road to Paso de Ovejas. There he had stopped at the house of the alcalde, where he even drank some chocolate, while assuring his host that he had defeated the government troops and that his division was following right after him. The alcalde suspected nothing and allowed Santa Anna to continue his journey unhindered to Antigua and thence to Veracruz, where he arrived safely the next morning at six o'clock.[3]

I discovered further that it was Major Hernández who had saved my life in Tolomé. As the enemy was preparing for my execution and I was being led out for the second time, General Calderón had asked the major, who happened to be in the room, what my officer's rank was. He replied that I was probably no officer at all, since he did not know me. The second part of his answer was accurate, for we had never seen each other before. Consequently, I owed my life to the man with whom I was now traveling along to a new prison.

37. The Third Day of Travel

On [June] 28, we did not set out until twelve o'clock noon because we were awaiting reinforcements to our escort—a hundred men under the

command of Colonel Franco.[1] This officer and all his men treated us
with so much attentiveness and courtesy that, after four months of
harsh treatment, we were happy beyond measure at this change. We
got an extra team of three fine mules and off we went at a trot. When
we stopped to eat along the way, the officers treated us to several
bottles of refreshing wine. It was the first wine I had drunk in a long
time. Two leagues [five miles] farther, we turned off to the right from
the road and after traveling for two hours over a good side road and
through cornfields, we reached our third overnight stop, the hacienda
S[an] Antonio de Tamaris.[2] Here we were given a good, clean, white-
washed room with tables, chairs, and the service of the household ser-
vants. A good supper eaten with a fork, spoon, and knife made us almost forget that we were prisoners. All of the officers visited us and we
had ample opportunity to become acquainted with the liberal and
noble character of Colonel Franco. His name certainly is well de-
served. His whole being was frank and open: a large, powerful man
with rather dark skin, small, flashing eyes, handsome white teeth, and
black hair and beard.

The beautiful, large hacienda consisted of several buildings and
lay in a rich plain three leagues [eight miles] from [Mount] Malinche,
which from the hacienda one can see rising nobly nearby. Rain from
several heavy thunderstorms was falling on the slopes of this beautiful
mountain, forming individual columns of clouds, and among these the
frequently occurring dust devils ascended from the green plain into
the atmosphere. These whirlwinds wandered over the plain slowly and
majestically, like Ossian's nebulous spirits of dead heroes, until they finally disappeared in the distance.[3] I observed this delightful spectacle
for a long time. In the meantime, several hundred Indians, tenant
laborers on the plantation, came hurrying along in regular, distinct
groups from the fields toward the hacienda. They were carrying their
tools over their shoulders like weapons, singing, and praying the ro-
sary. The term "tenant laborer" deserves some clarification, for in a
republic it seems inappropriate.[4]

The next morning at four o'clock we were suddenly awakened to
attend mass. Since I am not Catholic, I would have preferred to continue sleeping, but since everyone else was preparing to go to church, I
did so, too, in order not to offend. It was rather cold. We wrapped ourselves in our serapes and cloaks and followed the stream of workers and

soldiers who were hurrying to the small chapel about a hundred paces away. It was clean and airy, but there was no organ. The ringing blare of trumpet was the only church music. The service, incidentally, was a so-called silent mass. The pious padre offered his devout prayers, and then it was all over. After the *Dominus vobiscum* [Kühne: Vobiscum Dominus] we hurried out of the chapel into the dawning morning sun, which at that moment was casting its first beams of light over the firmament. Suddenly, awed by such majesty, I did feel in the mood to say a silent morning prayer.

38. A Hazardous Region

After we had drunk our chocolate, the signal was given to saddle up for departure. Again I had the opportunity to admire the leisureliness of the preparations—a phenomenon that I had frequently observed before. We were not ready until two hours later. How different from the spirited European cavalry! Finally, off we went between the large fields of green corn that cover the rich plains here almost as far as the eye can see. Now we were riding in a new, more spacious cart drawn by six handsome mules, all of which had been supplied by the hacienda. Soon we came to the narrow mountain gorges that interrupt the man-made highway for long stretches between Venta del Piñal, where we stopped to eat, and Acajete.[1] These narrow passes are really highly pernicious for wagoners. The cart tossed about so much that the mules sometimes stumbled and we had trouble just holding on to our seats, which gave the men in our escort much cause for laughter as they gleefully watched our maneuvers.

Venta del Piñal, situated at the foot of the Piñal, is notorious for the dangers awaiting travelers there. Indeed, robberies occur there frequently and the perpetrators flee from their pursuers to safety through the narrow mountain gorges and ravines, and over the brushy hilltops.[2] It is another three leagues [eight miles] from Acajete to Amozoc [Kühne: Amozo], where the terrain begins to change.[3] [In Amozoc] we had some difficulty driving the cart from the highway across the marketplace. A few days earlier the plaza had been enclosed by arcades for the Corpus Christi festival, and the posts and stakes stood so close together that the cart could not pass between them.[4] So, we got out of the cart and went on foot to an uninviting, dirty room reserved for us in the general barracks.

We had arrived early enough to spend some time talking with the officers of our escort at the marketplace where our caravan was camping for the night. They stayed with us the whole evening, and the next morning when we left, our parting was very cordial, for the reinforcements had orders to return. Therefore, we kept only our original escort of twenty-five men. However, it turned out that our wagoner had taken off already with the cart and the mules. It took two hours for a dragoon to go out after him and bring him back. Then, we were finally able to continue our journey through the lovely valley to Puebla, only three leagues [eight miles] away. We passed Las Animas, Chachapa [Kühne: Chalchope], and the *garita* (customs house) more depressed than happy about arriving soon at our destination.[5] Traveling seemed to us much more pleasant than being locked up in a cell. Since my wounds did not hurt any longer, I was in a better mood to observe my surroundings and to endure the exertion. Consequently, I was able to enjoy undiminished the beautiful view of Puebla with the picturesque pyramid of Cholula in the background. Magnificent, snow-covered Popocatépetl seemed to beckon to me.[6]

At the gate of Puebla we stopped to await two coaches that had been ordered for us so that we would not have to ride through the city in our miserable cart. After a quarter hour the coaches arrived; they were beautiful and had large glass windows that allowed the spectators to see their fill of us. The curious, apprised beforehand of our arrival, had already gathered in droves. As we rode through the streets, the people followed us, increasing in numbers, until the whole city seemed to turn out, eager to see the men who everyone said were Santa Anna's general staff. Our entrance was like a triumphal march. No victorious hero could have stirred up more exictement. A surging crowd swarmed about us. Far from feeling any shame, we raised our heads proudly to give a good view to the crowd that rendered us such honor and in whose ranks we knew we had many friends. We rode in this way almost through the whole city until we reached the *Caserna de los Bedemnites,* where we are still imprisoned today.[7] It is comfortable and we are treated well, as I mentioned at the beginning of this section.

I was touched and surprised as I climbed the stairs to my new quarters, for there hung a fresco painting depicting Santa Anna's triumph in Tampico![8] Frequent visitors from the city have shown us every kindness. We live quietly and comfortably and have everything but our freedom. I busy myself a great deal sketching from visual memory a topographical map of our journey so far. I am trying to make it as accurate as possible, based on my observations during the march. In addition, I am working also on a painting of our former cell [at Perote] with all the captured officers from Tolomé in it. Each one is faithfully depicted, one as he busies himself at some project and another as he merely passes the time. The picture will be true to life, portraying the men in varied groups and postures. So far I have not been bored. I miss only my favorite flute a great deal; it is supposed to come by stagecoach soon with my bags, maps, etc., from Veracruz.

39. *An Imminent Parting*

July 7
I had hardly finished writing the above, when we were told that my five comrades would leave next week for Cuautitlán [Kühne: Cuantillan], on the other side of Mexico City, but that I shall remain here.[1] This separation has put us all into a depression. We cannot figure out the government's aim in taking this measure, especially since the [government's] negotiations with General Santa Anna are still in progress, and the revolution, so everyone says, will be settled peacefully.[2] Four weeks ago sixty prisoners of war were transported from here to Mexico City and then on to California. My comrades fear that the same fate awaits them, that they are being sent farther north at intervals in order not to create a stir. We can comprehend even less their plans for me. We surmise, however, that here alone, I will not have a pleasant fate. We have submitted representations to the vice-president, asking that we be allowed to remain here together, if possible. I personally have taken some steps to obtain my freedom.[3] My good friend [Felipe] Alvarez, who had been left among the other prisoners in Perote fortress, arrived here yesterday.[4] But he is being held in another barracks. Several attempts to have him transferred to our group have been fruitless. I hear that he is not doing too well in his narrow confines.

Three days ago I had the pleasure of a visit here by a Russian who could speak German, French, and English. I was able to converse with him for hours in these languages, which I had not heard or spoken in a long time. I had sent for an acquaintance who owns the French restaurant in Puebla to have him get a few things for me. But my messenger made the mistake of going to the express coach dispatcher's office instead and presented my "order" to the Russian who works as the commission agent there. He came to see me, whereupon I apologized for my messenger's error, and soon we got to know one another very well. We learned from him several interesting items of news, and he agreed to have my things sent from Veracruz and to mail our correspondence. Since I am without my own flute, an artillery officer here has promised [to lend] me [one of] his. I am looking forward to the pleasure of a few duets tomorrow.

40. Cooking for Ourselves

For six days we had been receiving our meals sent over from a nearby kitchen. It became so bad, however, that we could not eat the stuff. Each of us was just throwing away four reales a day to have this food prepared.[1] Consequently, our friend [Captain] Macín decided to cook our meals right in our room, which has a spacious alcove.[2] We are managing pretty well by using several earthen pots; and Macín seems to be quite accomplished in Mexican cookery, although his dishes would not be relished by many people in Germany. Everything swims in grease, and every dish has to have chile (Mexican pepper), onions, garlic, and *chilmole* [Kühne: *chieemole*] (tomatoes).[3] Mexicans are no great devotees of bouillon. What they call *sopa* (soup) is a thick mush made from bread, rice, or noodles. Here in Puebla the *aguacates* [avocados], a green fruit with a large seed and pale flesh, are supposed to be excellent. My comrades eat them in great quantities raw and dipped in meat broth, but they have a certain taste that does not appeal to me.

In the two days that our friend has been cooking we have already had a few accidents in the kitchen. Yesterday a pot broke and its entire contents of broth, meat chunks, and vegetables were spilled all over the ground. Today a dog sneaked in and ate up the piece of pork fat we had just bought. We ran after him to punish him good for his thievery, but since our guard stands at the entrance steps we had to cut our pursuit short and the dog got away.

41. *Corporal Punishment*

This afternoon there was a flogging at our barracks. A soldier had beaten a noncommissioned officer, a sergeant, and a corporal. In return, he was to be flogged. All the companies were assembled on the parade ground; then the offender, a good-looking fellow, was led out. He took off his jacket and placed his arms around a tree, where two assistants held him. Two corporals each gave him twenty-five strokes with a strong stick. I took a liking to the fellow because, even though he winced and writhed a great deal, he did not let a single sound escape his lips. After the punishment was over, he calmly walked to the fountain to wash himself. The flogging of soldiers is still customary here, although the country is a republic.[1] Freedom and humane conduct should go hand in hand with one another, but such is not always the case. The government here is a most perfunctory republic, for it lacks any real historical traditions. There have also been republics like the Venetian one, where despotism—terribly entrenched and of course disguised—exercised its power surreptitiously.[2]

42. *News from Veracruz*

The rainy season is in full swing. Every day just before noon heavy clouds gather, accompanied by a strong wind; then it gets still, and amidst thunder and lightning it rains in sheets. Then after a few hours it is quiet again. The mornings are bright, clear, and beautiful. I spend the whole day outside under the colonnade. Day before yesterday we were visited by Gov. [Juan José] Andrade, who is the commanding general here.[1] Two weeks ago he barely escaped an attempt on his life. The assassin mistakenly stabbed a distinguished retired army officer to death. The newspaper that contained an account of the incident reported also the unexpected news of my friend's death in Veracruz: Carl Weber (of the firm Weber & Company) was also murdered by an assassin.[2] Weber, [Adolf] Hegewisch, and I had once lived for several happy months in Oaxaca. One can imagine how deeply I was shaken by the news of his death.

We received the news from our companions-in-misfortune at Perote that they have been receiving soldiers' rations since we left—

probably as a result of several demonstrations and the complaints they had made. The balance of funds owned in common, amounting to three hundred dollars, they divided among themselves.

43. Music in Mexico

July 10

Day before yesterday there was another flogging: a deserter got his fifty strokes. There is quite a bit of leniency here toward deserters. They are shot only for repeated offenses during wartime.

The artillery captain I mentioned above brought me an old mended flute; with the exception of the D sharp, it has no stops. It has not been my experience that a flute gets better the more it is repaired, as do the Cremonese violins.[1] The flute that was brought to me is really bad, but it nevertheless gives me a lot of pleasure, especially when I play on it the concerto by Pleyel that my friend brought along with the flute.[2] My companions in prison want me to play waltzes, dances, etc. Everything else they call *caprichos* [capriccios]. In general, I cannot deny that the Mexicans have a love for music, but they do not have much feeling for it. They much prefer a trifling waltz to the most beautiful improvisation, which they do not understand. At times in Oaxaca when my friend Adolf [Hegewisch] and I played adagios at large parties, it always pained me to see that our music aroused little or no interest. On the contrary, it seemed only to bore everyone. Rondos, on the other hand, and themes with variations were always welcome.

In Oaxaca there are several families in which the young ladies play overtures and sonatas with a great deal of skill, but they are absolutely devoid of taste and feeling.[3] Everything is rattled off in dance rhythm. Until a European music teacher becomes established there, nothing will ever change. The wife of the former state governor [Joaquín] Guerrero is one of the few Mexicans I have ever known who had a real feeling for music.[4] She played the guitar with a surprising amount of tenderness. Unfortunately, I did not hear her play a great deal, but what I did hear was very expressive. Another good musician, I remember, is a small padre who plays overtures on the guitar with a great deal of taste and precision. In Jalapa the harp is very popular, and I have heard of a lady in Orizaba, an excellent harpist, who even plays from notes. Once when I was traveling through that city I had expected to have the pleasure of hearing her play, even of accompanying her on my flute, but I was unable to extend my stay long enough.

44. *Important Dispatches*

July 14

Yesterday we received the news that Gen. [Manuel Mier y] Terán had suddenly died. He had commanded a division of government troops fighting against Gen. [Esteban] Moctezuma [Kühne: Montezuma], who had led the uprising for Santa Anna in Tampico.[1] According to some reports, General [Mier y] Terán committed suicide; others conjectured that he was forcibly launched into eternity.[2] Today we were told that the government's negotiations with Santa Anna in Puente Nacional had been fruitless, and that hostilities had been declared anew.[3] Our General is supposed to have a division of more than three thousand men that he intends to lead to the capital. If he carries out this plan in the near future, then I hope to have my freedom soon, for his route goes right through Puebla.

Yesterday, too, we read the proclamation of general and former president [Manuel Gómez] Pedraza from the United States. Santa Anna has declared his support of this general and has called for his return to Mexico.[4] The fighting will probably become much bloodier now. The state of Tabasco has also declared its support of Santa Anna, and the port of Matamoros has been closed because a fleet of Santa Anna's ships attacked the harbor there and made off with a ship. Now the government no longer controls a single port on the northern coast.[5]

Our daily routine is still unchanged. Besides having a lot of visitors, I spend the whole day sketching and drawing. I have even tried my hand at painting in miniature—which I really like!

45. *An Unexpected Visit*

July 18

Again I am alone in my room in the barracks. I am sitting at a small table, and in the drawer are my writings and my drawing instruments. Taking my pen, I shall record the events of the last four days.

The day before yesterday eighteen of our companions-in-misfortune arrived here unexpectedly from Perote fortress and were quartered in these barracks. (Thirteen still remain behind.) Our usual peaceful routine was interrupted, for everyone was, of course, astir. The guards were doubled, and the number of visitors increased many-fold. Then everyone had to pack his things, for today all the prisoners, myself excepted, were supposed to continue on to Tepotzotlán [Kühne: Tepozutlan], on the other side of Mexico City.[1] Letters were being written; people were haggling with the cobbler and the tailor; and the barbers and cooks were being paid off. There was a hustle and bustle in our rooms, as at a fair.

The hour of departure came finally this morning. In three wagons and riding eight horses (with sufficient escort troops), twenty-three of my companions departed—five who had come with me three weeks ago from Perote, and eighteen who had arrived just two days ago. Our farewell to each other was very emotional. Everyone wanted to recommend me to his local friends. Each of my comrades shared with me some of his money, for since coming to Puebla I had received no payment from the government for my food and other needs. Of course, they did not have much, but the little they gave me was like the widow's mite in the New Testament.[2] It was certainly very painful for me to have to part with my companions. We had shared a common fate for almost five months, and all of them had treated me with an unexpected kindness that money cannot buy. In their company I never wanted for anything.

46. News and Prospects

Now they are gone. Today I sit here with tears in my eyes—it is also my birthday—lonely and uncertain about the fate in store for me. It still seems to me a strange circumstance that it was I who got left behind. Let come what may, I shall meet the worst fate with a philosophical attitude. I am hopeful that they no longer intend to shoot me. I am hopeful, too, that our imprisonment will not last too much longer, for yesterday we heard the news that the states of Zacatecas and Campeche had also declared their support of General Santa Anna, who, by the way, has already taken Puente Nacional.[1] Gen. [Máximo?] Bravo, who everyone said was opposed to Santa Anna, has died, and General Moctezuma has moved into San Luis Potosí.[2] All of this amounts to a real crisis for the government, and if, as a consequence, our General marches on the capital, then the government will undoubtedly collapse very quickly and we shall emerge triumphant from this bold affair. Then I can expect some recompense for my loyalty and my suffering. I am encouraged by this prospect and by the probability that it shall come to pass.

It is a question now of taking me to the city prison, but several officers who have befriended me here are at this moment trying to intercede for me. So I have some hope of remaining in this hospitable barracks. For the time being, I am getting my meals delivered from the *posada francesa* [French inn], which is operated by an English lady. Consequently, I am finally spared from Mexican cooking (with its garlic and such things swimming in grease), which after five months has become loathsome to me. I shall also be able to drink tea again *à l'anglais* [British style]. I believe that the most common farm woman in Germany would throw out such food as our friend [Captain] Macín has been preparing for us.

A few days ago I sent a representation to the governor and commandant, [General Andrade], asking him to allocate an allowance for my maintenance, since in all countries it is the custom not to let prisoners die of hunger. However, he answered me that he was not empowered to do so. If I did not already have some cash (fortunately), things would look pretty bad for me.

They are just now bringing in a prisoner; he will be placed in a tiny cell. He is supposed to have some connection with the aforementioned assassination attempt on the commanding general.[3] Writing is very tiresome today, for I have to use boot blacking instead of ink. Several days ago we were visited by an officer from General Calderón's division who had been present at the battle of Tolomé. From this officer we learned about the critical situation in which Santa Anna had placed his [Calderón's] division at the time because of the particular position we held. This information serves only to justify the actions of our General, who since then has been roundly criticized for his position that day. This [Calderón's] division had worked the whole night before and had been standing ready at arms, expecting an attack all that time. So, exhausted and without food, they had continued their march the next morning, expecting to find water and some respite in Tolomé, but to their surprise they found us there, too. The way to the water was blocked by our ambush positions. It was too dangerous to attempt crossing the bridge. So Calderón's troops found themselves with their backs to the wall. If they could not take this pass, then they would have to surrender. Consequently, they were fighting a battle of desperation—which often makes one fight more fiercely than the greatest amount of mere courage could.

47. Painting Portraits

I was just visited by several officers who, after seeing the very successful portrait I made of our friend [Captain] Macín, want me to paint their portraits in miniature. I do not have the necessary ivory discs, but these gentlemen have found a solution. They are going to steal a billiard ball from the local coffeehouse and are going to have some discs cut from it. The plan is really not such a bad one, especially since all the extra discs will be for me, to provide me with some means of earning a few extra doubloons.[1] Will my share of that billiard ball be placed in the balance on Judgment Day? It is possible and even probable, but I shall point out in my defense that the government paid me nothing to keep body and soul together. I shall see how well I do with this painting venture; there is the possibility that little by little I could paint portraits for the whole city. A lady has already come to me to order a copy of one of my portraits. Well, at least she *asked* whether I would be willing to paint for payment. Why not? If it has to be then, as [Till] Eulenspiegel, I shall paint [portraits], large and small, like the people who go in and out of the [city] gate.[2] The French marquises made salad to feed themselves.[3] With me it will be, "Mr. Artist, will you perhaps paint my portrait?"

48. The Old Musician

July 19

The efforts of my friends to keep me in this barracks have been successful. However, I shall move into another room tomorrow, and I am somewhat depressed about that. Among the friends who visit me, the artillery officer, Cayetano Negrete, stands out as the most devoted.[1] He was formerly with the Spanish regimental band, and [in 1811?] he deserted from Puebla to the [Mexican] insurgents with his entire band in parade uniform, with instruments and music books. He and his band entered Cholula, where Gen. [Nicolás?] Bravo was camped, with drums beating.[2] As a reward [for his defection], he was made an officer [in the Mexican army]. He is now retired, but he rejected the pension of six dollars a month because he supports himself and his family by hiring out to play at different occasions.[3] His hair and beard are already white and, by the way, he is quite well dressed. He is very amiable and talkative, but he has the habit of constantly drawing his conversation partner to himself by the coat buttons—a habit that goes completely against the rules Lord Stanhope gave to his son.[4] In addition, he sprays saliva incessantly through his teeth like King Sputterbeard.[5] It is all I can do to protect my sketches from all that moisture. But I still like him very much for his affability.

Another frequent visitor is a local *bel esprit* (without occupation), who speaks French and some English. He likes to show off his knowledge. His facial features are very Jewish, complemented by the large beard on his chin. He has brought to me a work published in French, namely the *Essai d'une distribution généalogique des sciences et des arts par Diderot et d'Alembert,* condensed into diagram form, by Christian Friedrich Wilhelm Roth, which appeared in Weimar in 1769.[6] He wants to translate the contents of the genealogical tree into Spanish, and I am supposed to help him with it. He always comes visiting early in the morning at an inopportune time, for every night I am engaged in hand-to-hand combat with certain small comical insects that want to share my bed and my blood with me.[7] Consequently, I do not fall asleep until late and, therefore, would like to be able to sleep late the next day.

49. The Storyteller of Perote Fortress

In the evenings I miss having people to tell my stories to, for in the hospital at Perote [fortress] I was the duly appointed teller of fairy tales. In fact, the large painting that I have just completed depicts in this very situation all thirty-six officers from Tolomé who were imprisoned at Perote.[1]

In reading through my manuscript, I note that I have left out a description of our activities in Perote prison. In order not to leave a gap [in my account], I shall supply that information now. I shall go back to the day when I left the hospital. Upon returning to the cell (already

described), I found my comrades' situation somewhat changed—to
their advantage, actually. They had been given the benches I described, on which they could lay themselves—by twos, threes, and
fours. For mattresses they had [straw] mats and sheepskins. In short,
conditions were as I described them in the introduction to my narrative. Don Felipe Alvarez, who had already been very kind to me on
the march from Jalapa to Perote, offered to share his bunk with me. He
had intentionally prepared it large enough. I accepted his offer with
pleasure, because otherwise, as the last one in the cell, I probably
would have gotten the place down by the barrel, where the smell was
almost unbearable. This young man was from Mexico City. Several
weeks before the battle at Tolomé he had been hurrying to Veracruz to
offer his services to Santa Anna, but he had been picked up by [General]
Calderón and sent as a captive to Jalapa, where he remained until we
arrived, when he was incorporated into our group. I want to show my
gratitude for his acts of friendship toward me in Perote [prison], and as
soon as I have the opportunity, I shall richly repay him.

Our life in this prison was every day the same. Every morning
about eight o'clock the door was opened for the first time and we were
brought some coffee or chocolate with bread from the women who
cooked for us. Then the door was closed again. At ten o'clock breakfast
was brought. Again the door was closed. At eleven o'clock the door was
opened again for cleaning the cell, replacing the two barrels, and for
our half hour in the sun. The door was then closed again. At two or
three o'clock it was opened just long enough to give us our dinner.
Then again at five o'clock chocolate was brought and at eight o'clock we
had supper. Each time the door was open only long enough to bring us
our food.

Every day was like that. In groups we all had our different pas-
times: playing cards, dominoes, dice, or chess; writing, reading, singing, playing music on little guitars [jaranas], or dancing (especially
about twilight). When I joined the others in this common cell, I had to
make myself welcome. So, every evening when we had all lain down to
sleep, I told stories for everyone's entertainment. I was even eager
to play storyteller, since it gave me the opportunity to improve my
mastery of the Spanish language. Therefore, I merely served up what
I knew: fairy tales from my youth, anecdotes about Frederick the
Great, the novels of Sir Walter Scott, [the adventures of] Till Eulen-

spiegel, [the story of the outlaw] "Schinderhannes," [Ludwig Tieck's fairy tale] *The Children of Haimon*, [Johann Carl August] Musäus's fairy tales, and [Ernst Theodor Amadeus] Hoffmann's fanciful tales.[2] But these stories were soon exhausted, and I had to resort to narrating the plots of dramas and tragedies such as [Friedrich Schiller's] *Love and Intrigue, The Robbers, The Maid of Orleans, The Conspiracy of Fiesco [at Genoa]*, etc.[3] When these stories started to run out, I had no other choice than to make up narratives from different novels and other stories I knew. Indeed, I really taxed my ingenuity to put together an infinitely long heroic epic, made up partly from the Nibelungen-saga, from [Friedrich de la Motte] Fouqué's [novels], *The Magic Ring* and [*The Travels of*] *Thiodolf, [the Icelander]*, and from [Johann Baptist von] Alxinger's [verse romance] *Bliomberis*, etc.[4] I narrated this epic for the edification of my listeners, who enjoyed it, too, because the events were all so new to them. Since our imprisonment lasted so long, I probably would have been forced to cast in another story some rather diverse characters: [Homer's] Ulysses, [Friedrich Baron von der] Trenck, [Carl Maria Weber's] *The Freeshooter*, [Schiller's] *Maria Stuart*, the crusaders, Emperor Charlemagne, the Baron von Münchhausen, and [Friedrich Wilhelm Baron von] Kyau.[5] Fortunately, it did not come to that.

50. Escape Attempts

Our monotonous life [in Perote prison] was interrupted several times—the first time by an escape attempt. The plan was to break out through a hole in the fortress wall.[1] But a fight between two of our comrades upset the plan and the undertaking was then defeated by the resistance of 5 or 6 men in our group who were afraid to try it. A surprise attack on the guard, indeed on the whole fortress, with the aid of 150 men from the [prison] garrison was frustrated also on the very evening of its execution—we had probably been betrayed.[2] On the night of June 19, the alarm was suddenly sounded in the fortress at the loud screaming of a prisoner. Everyone rushed to arms. The scare had a comical ending, however, when the cause of the excitement was discovered: one of our fellow prisoners had had a nightmare and in his sleep he had uttered the blood-curdling scream.

51. The Prisoners of Perote

Now as I recall that time and relive it in my memory (to capture it on paper and with my paints), the figures of that special group reappear vividly before me. There stands Manuel [Fernández] Castrillón [Kühne: Castillione], a colonel and first adjutant. He was tall and strong and, with his curly hair, he towered over everyone—a true Roman type. He was well bred, educated, and quick. He wore loose-fitting blue trousers. [Inside the prison] he went about only in a shirt, but outside he wore a blue cloak. He was from Havana. His sonorous voice led all conversations and discussions; almost all of his suggestions were well received. As the acknowledged leader, he quietly looked after the affairs of the prisoners. But with all that, he was also domineering. He was at times impetuous and unjust, but otherwise pleasant in social intercourse. The whole group gave him the appropriate respect.[1]

[Lt.] Nicolás [de la] Portilla was an intense young man—not so large, but very strong. He was younger [than Colonel Castrillón], extremely impetuous and temperamental, with a rather fierce-looking and coarse physiognomy. He exaggerated everything, going from one extreme to the other, but free of any arrogance. He was a first lieutenant and adjutant—the one who, before the battle at Tolomé, had called for the surrender of the little garrison at Puente Nacional. He was impatient and easily enraged. He went about lightly clothed. He talked a lot and therefore was constantly plagued by a cough.[2]

Then there was Joaquín Arzamendi, a captain in the fusiliers and the only one who during his captivity was always in uniform with its brass insignia on the visor band. He was large and strong, but quiet and modest. He kept our accounts and was an *hombre de bien* [honest man].[3]

[Francisco] Macín, a captain in the infantry, was small and serious. He was a little cross-eyed and had a bushy beard. A fastidious and vain man, he grasped everything with his fingertips. He combed his beard with great care and brushed his teeth for a half hour. With affected gestures he tried to attract attention to himself. For example, he would arise early every morning and sit on his chair for an hour as though absorbed in serious thought, wearing only his underwear and wrapped in his serape. He liked to play the role of a refined gentleman, and was one to a certain degree, but not always, for he was malicious and engaged in intrigue. But he was knowledgeable and talented.[4]

Lieutenant Escanís [Kühne: Eskains] was from the island of Cuba. He was also a little cross-eyed and had large, black eyebrows. He had what I would call a "camel face." Frequently, he frowned and knitted his brow. He continuously wore a brown jacket, the sleeves of which were worn out at the elbows. He was something of a philosopher (especially on religious issues) and a freethinker. He seemed to come from a humble background. He had received a head wound [at Tolomé].[5]

[Capt.] Juan Arzamendi, the illegitimate brother of Joaquín, was small and agile. By profession he was a printer. He was a real busybody—always moving around, now here, now there. He played the guitar well and he smoked a lot; and with his smoking he was always spitting, which made him somewhat repulsive to me. He wore his serape continuously, but he was a young man of accommodating, complaisant, and good character.[6]

Felipe Alvarez was twenty years old, small and slight of build—almost serpentine. That is, he stood with his legs back, his stomach forward, the shoulders and chest drawn back and his head forward. He seemed to come from a good family and to have had a good upbringing. He became very attached to me, and he played chess very well. A volunteer, he had been captured in Puente Nacional on his way from Mexico City to Veracruz to join Santa Anna's forces. I owe him for a great many of the comforts I had [in Perote fortress]. We shared a bunk.[7]

Capt. [Eusebio] Flores was the brother of [José María] Flores, commander of the fortress, San Juan de Ulúa [Kühne: Olloa]. He had black hair, a black beard, and black eyes with large brows. He was good-natured and quiet, even though he had a catlike face.[8]

Barbagose, a Negro, was a lieutenant and in his fifties. In Jalapa he had liberated a black dress coat in which he paraded around all the time. He was considerate and good-natured.[9]

Daté, small and beardless, seemed to be about fifteen years old. He was already married, however, and had a family. He was very hard of hearing, I am sure, for he had not heard the cannons at Tolomé. He had become extremely depressed when he was captured. He was, by the way, skilled and careful in tending wounds. It was he who had cut out the bullet for me at Tolomé.[10]

Captain Robles was short and fat with straight black hair and beard. He had shifty, mean eyes, and was cowardly, quarrelsome, insulting, and impetuous. He was the only black sheep among us. He spoke very rapidly and took offense at our every word.[11]

The others in our group were a major, of medium height and build, in his thirties, and peaceful and quiet. The other, a volunteer named Montamo, was a mama's boy from Mexico City. He was always in a sweat about his correspondence with mama. He was like a bird that had left the nest for the first time. But he was a capable young man and he wrote well.[12]

52. Two Proclamations

More important than the inventory of these characters, who were of interest to me only as a painter, is an account of the events that occurred in the course of Santa Anna's revolution of 1832.

After the fruitless negotiations in Puente Nacional, there appeared in Jalapa a proclamation of the new general-in-chief, Don José Antonio Facio, dated July 14, 1832:

> Comrades in Arms!
> The government has attempted every means of reconciliation to prevent the further spilling of Mexican blood. It sent commissioners to Puente Nacional to save the republic additional suffering and to negotiate with Don Antonio López de Santa Anna. The war, which is beginning anew, will have no other outcome than the destruction of the man who has always been the cause of tragedy in the fatherland. You shall be the victors because you are fighting for a most just cause, and because no one can equal your courage. Never try to reach an understanding with such people, for the Mexican people demand that you liberate them from such monsters. All negotiation will be not only useless, but even harmful. If they do not submit unconditionally, then may the sword of justice prevail over them. Soldiers, the new campaign that is just beginning shall bring you glory. Soon you shall see order restored and the fatherland will owe it all to you. When you have returned to your homes after restoring life to this nation, you will remember with pride that you belonged to the division that fought against [the rebels of] Veracruz.[1]

A bit of printed folly that made the rounds in Puebla went as follows:

> Praise be to almighty God, the Creator, and the original Lawgiver of our fatherland, namely of all Mexicans. Praise be to the Holy Virgin of Guada-

lupe, the Most High Empress of the Mexicans! Long live all Mexicans—
none excepted! Long live the friends of Mexicans! May their enemies die!
Long live the constitution! Long live our just laws! Such were my wishes,
as I defied Don Antonio López [de] Santa Anna. "Reason or the sword!"
said Anzures to S[anta] Anna, as I solemnly resolved to sacrifice my life
on the battlefields of the fatherland if this man did not listen to my proposals. Jalapa is a witness to my firm resolve, and to carry it out, I have
requested permission from the supreme government to go and to speak
with that rabble-rouser of the revolution as his true friend.
Jalapa, July 22, 1832

Manuel María Anzures
Printed by Blanco and Aburto

This person Anzures runs around in Puebla, handing out copies of
his broadside, but of course, everyone just laughs at him.[2]

53. *Progress of the Revolution*

July 25

According to *La Egide de la Ley* of July 19, the insurgents of
Teziutlán [Kühne: Tozintlau] were beaten by Maj. D[on] Félix Merino
in an engagement that lasted two hours. Of the government troops, five
were killed and fifteen wounded. A hundred rebels were captured,
several killed, and they lost to the enemy their only two cannons, their
munitions park, their rifles, and the village.[1]

It seems that a conference between the two sides had been called,
and Merino suddenly broke off the talks.

August 1

Santa Anna is with his troops in Córdoba and Orizaba, where for
several weeks he has been building fortifications. [General] Facio is in
Jalapa. It appears that an attack is planned for next week.[2]

August 8

Frequent visits, my painting in miniature, for which I have received several orders, correspondence with friends in Oaxaca, and
other things have kept me from writing anything [important] since July
9. The crisis that is building for the revolution, and my ideas and preparations to flee this place require that henceforth I keep this journal

current up to the last moment. At least I shall not leave any gaps in it until that long interruption that will probably come.

My painting of the *galería* is circulating even among the nuns.[3] My workroom has become renowned. Everybody comes by to see how I am immortalizing the deeds of the revolution on paper and canvas here, while outside, history takes its course as things change every day.

Today the news came that Gen. [Esteban] Moctezuma was attacked and repulsed by government troops in S[an] Luis Potosí, but that soon afterwards two thousand men joined Moctezuma's remaining forces, and they then destroyed the government division.[4] The vice-president [Bustamante] is supposed to have gathered together fifteen hundred men in Mexico City and has already received the permission of the senate to lead them to battle.[5] Santa Anna has fortified himself very well in Orizaba and is said to be occupying Puente Colorado and neighboring points.[6] Because of numerous desertions, [General] Facio is said to have withdrawn from the *cañada* [valley] of [San José] Ixtapa. Near Tlaxcala [Kühne: Flascula] there is one of Santa Anna's divisions with a thousand men.[7]

Everyone here appears indecisive; they seem to be merely awaiting the impending departure of the commanding general [Andrade] as the signal to start a commotion. He will take the fifth regiment with him. The mood of the other troops is promising. There seems to be no more doubt about the success of the endeavor. I expect to hear some important news in a few days.

August 10

Today several battalions arrived here from government headquarters [in Acultzingo]. The vice-president [Bustamante] summoned them to put into service against S[an] Luis Potosí and Zacatecas.[8] There are hardly two hundred survivors of the thousand men who fought in the campaign against Veracruz. Two light cannons were brought in here [today], too. In this manner, [General] Facio is dividing his forces and he will probably not be able to stop Santa Anna.

WITH SANTA ANNA'S ARMY

Since I have not been able to keep my journal current since my escape from Puebla on August 16, I must take the liberty of recording first of all my adventures of that period from memory. This sketch will enable me then to extract from my papers everything that has had a bearing on my story since my arrival in Orizaba. I have lost several papers, and the following one I just found again.

54. *Orizaba, General Santa Anna's Headquarters, Six Months after the Battle of Tolomé, or September 3, 1832*

I am free! I sit down now, hale and hearty, and I take my pen to describe my successful escape from Puebla on the sixteenth of last month. My surroundings have completely changed since then. Now I am sitting in a large, pleasant room on the first floor [of a house] on the main street of this friendly city, which is surrounded by luxuriant vegetation. Thick clouds already envelop the stately volcano of Orizaba (it is afternoon), which I can see from my window early every morning in all its serene beauty. It is surrounded by the picturesque peaks of smaller mountains. The streets are animated by the colorful crowds of Indians who have come to market day today, and by the soldiers of General Santa Anna, who has had his headquarters here for two months now. I am awakened every morning at four o'clock by the rattle of drums and by the ring of fifes and trumpets, for the troops conduct their drill right here in the streets. I have my drawing instruments laid out in beautiful order on an old table that has been made fairly sturdy again by nailing on some brace boards, transforming it into a rather tolerable drawing table. Clothes, mattresses, weapons, and a tea service are piled up all about the room as neatly as circumstances permit. What a change from the cell in Perote fortress and even from the barracks at Puebla! One can imagine how I feel. I have just completed copying a geographic map of the district of Orizaba that was found here. We intend to use my copy in our military operations. I am going to take the time to continue my journal and to relate first of all the story of my liberation.

55. *Escape from Puebla and Reception in Orizaba*

The pages following the above entry were lost through the various mishaps of my papers (which I recovered after the battle of Puebla from their hiding place behind a rafter).[1] Consequently, I can fill in the resulting hiatus only very roughly.

Upon my arrival in Orizaba, I was led as a victorious hero to the house of the General. He received me very cordially, welcoming me with the words, "We haven't seen each other since Tolomé! Well, how did the rascals treat you?" The British vice-consul, [Joseph] Welsh, took me in as a brother, bathed me with his own hands, and gave me underwear, some clothes, money, and everything I needed.[2] I was treated just as kindly by Lieutenant Colonel Becelli, chief of the engineers corps, and by Capt. [Juan José] Holzinger.[3] I rested for eight days. Then, after I had received from the General a brevet for the rank of colonel, I was assigned to the engineers corps under Becelli to help with the fortifications in Escamela.[4] When these were finished, the order came to draw up plans for a new artillery road over the Cuesta de Maltrata.[5] (Adventure while reconnoitering for this road. Becelli's and Holzinger's quarrels. The actual execution of the road work; description of this work. Becelli's and my adventures in reconnoitering San Antonio de Arniva where we were pursued by 150 lancers, etc.[6]— Facio's position in Ixtapa [Kühne: Jalapa] to protect Puente Colorado.)[7]

56. A March, Fortifications, and Combat

On September 23 or 24, Santa Anna finally broke camp in Orizaba. With all of his cavalry he went over the [Cuesta de] Maltrata by a different mountain road (the same one I had traveled on my flight from Puebla) to San Antonio de Abajo.[1] He halted there until [September] 26, when the whole division moved out. I was leading the artillery along the blue road [?] at night and in the rain, by torchlight with oxen and Indians. Creeping along almost on our hands and knees in the wind and rain (which extinguished our torches), we finally got the first cannon to the summit by midnight. Then I rode to San Antonio de Abajo to report to the General, who was waiting very impatiently for the artillery.

September 28

In San Antonio de Abajo, a hacienda, we fortified ourselves and were constantly on alert, awaiting an attack by Facio. Outwitted by us, he finally appeared, circled us once with his troops (like a cat that's been burned once before), encamped finally near Hacienda Blanca, and was going to attack us the next morning [September 29]. At midnight we decamped and left the hacienda surreptitiously, going toward San Agustín del Palmar. When Facio found our nest empty, he came after us. The following morning [September 30], he began firing grenades at us. We advanced and the notorious battle began—one that we at first were losing, then began winning. We overwhelmed his [artillery] battery, etc.[2]

The morning of the following day [October 1], we decamped, leaving all our baggage behind, and after two forced marches we came to the outskirts of Puebla.[3] (I was riding on the howitzer we had taken.) We demanded the surrender of the city within two hours. When Gov. [Juan José] Andrade refused to surrender, we immediately stormed the city, passing through the same *garita* through which I had made my escape on August 16. I crossed the canal with one cannon, and under a rain of fire, I pushed through the city until I was before the [municipal] palace—still occupied by [Gen. José María] Calderón.[4] I did not open fire, however, in order not to damage the palace. The doors were quickly broken open; the palace was plundered, and the city was ours. In a barracks the next day [October 4], [Governor] Andrade capitulated also.[5] We had won a total victory. We then found ourselves some lodgings. I moved into the *hotel de diligencias* [stagecoach inn], where I was quite comfortable finally. Instead of marching immediately on to Mexico City, where everyone was in a state of great alarm and disorder, the General remained here [in Puebla] for two weeks—in complete idleness. During this time I amused myself in the city as well as I could. Someone stole all of my freshly washed clothes, but I visited the museum, went for walks, etc.

October 12

Finally, we set out to lay siege to Mexico City. We left at four o'clock in the morning. The previous evening I had been given the [official] rank of lieutenant colonel. In San Martín [Texmelucán] it was raining, and I had trouble finding shelter for the night. The rain had made the roads a bottomless mire.[6]

October 13

A ride to Venta de Córdoba.[7] An adventure in the cabin. Bad weather. When the thick fog lifted, a splendid view. A terrible filthiness in the kitchen; one would have to be a chemist to swallow all the filth without some uneasiness. Greetings of the Indians among themselves. Optical illusions of lakes that appear to be real.

Upon our arrival in Venta [de Córdoba], there were fireworks and shooting to celebrate [José Antonio] Mejía's promotion to the rank of general.[8] At three o'clock that afternoon Santa Anna arrived. We decamped and marched first to Hacienda Buenavista [Kühne: Buenanita], then to Chalco, where four generals were united.[9] The weather was beautiful. I enjoyed very much the beautiful view of the volcano [Popocatépetl?]. Pleasure trips on the [Chalco] canal. *Te Deum* in the church. Frequent changes of lodgings. Arrival of the barks and on them several prisoners from Tolomé. There are three types of *canoa* [barge]; the first is six feet wide, one foot above the water, and sixteen paces long, with and without a cover that is supported on iron hoops.[10] Thoughts on cleaning the [Chalco] canal that in a few years will be blocked up if measures are not taken.[11] Gambling among the soldiers—[over] a pile of gold I saw lying there.

October 18

I was given the task of drawing a map of the valley of Mexico City as described to me by a colonel who knows the terrain. I worked on it without pause. Then that night I received orders suddenly to be ready to move out with half of the engineers' park. At four o'clock that morning the order was canceled.

October 19

Muster. Two battalions, numbers eight and nine, with four cannons; marched under [the command of Gen. Juan] Arago to Toluca for an expedition.[12]

October 20

I rode to Ayotla on leave to fetch my things, which were supposed to have arrived there with the diligence. By coincidence I found them, but not [Captain] Holzinger.[13] A delightfully good breakfast. I became lost on the return trip.

October 21

March of the second and third brigade via Ayotla to Ixtapalapa and Mexicalcingo [Kühne: Istalapa, Mejualcingo].[14] A ball, [with dancing] to Indian music. Lodgings at the schoolmaster's house. A thousand fleas. Several Englishmen invited me to go with them to their hacienda, but I was not able to do so.

57. Battle at Chapultepec

October 22

We marched over the causeway to Tacubaya [Kühne: Tammbaya], skirting Mexico City very closely and advancing our lines of siege or, as I should say, our lines of embarkation.[1] Tacubaya, the episcopal palace with a beautiful garden.[2] Monsieur Martens's hotel provided comfortable lodgings for us: Becelli, Arago, and myself. The enemy was shooting every day from Chapultepec [Castle]. We blocked up an aqueduct. Early on the morning of October 24 [*sic*], an enemy attack under Gen. [Luis] Quintanar [Kühne: Guintanaur]. After a two-hour cannonade, the enemy retreated. We stood ready at arms for a few hours more, and then we went home, too.[3] The cannonade from Chapultepec went on the whole day long; however, we were not especially mindful of it. Outpost duty was very neglected; otherwise the [above] attack would not have been possible. The composure of the General is admirable.

October 24

As ordered, I broke down the bridge toward Chapultepec [Castle] and was just advancing to reconnoiter when the enemy greeted me with a blast of case shot. Alerted then to my presence, our sentries began to shoot at me, so that for a while I had to conceal myself from my own men. Arrival of the large howitzer.

October 25

Suddenly, the order [came] to decamp at three o'clock in the morning; but for naught, for we were not being attacked after all. That afternoon the brigade came from Lerma and Toluca [Kühne: Lecina] under [the command of Generals] Arago and Mejía.[4]

October 26

The second brigade and the section of engineers (with the exception of [Captain] Holzinger, who has gone to Guadalupe) marched to Tacuba, past Chapultepec. Tacuba [Kühne: Tamba and Tacuca], a rambling village.[5] A romantic scene that evening in the cemetery where we camped among skulls and cooked on them.[6]

October 28
Yesterday was a day of rest; today fortifications and a terrific din. Santa Anna came in a quarrelsome mood.

October 29
We threw up fortifications around the cemetery. The enemy was throwing grenades over at us from Chapultepec.[7] Monsieur Groignart, the French cook, came with a meat pie and bottle of Burgundy. [Lieutenant Colonel] Becelli and I hired him as our cook; we set up his kitchen in the charnel house. Many visitors from the city.

November 1
A coach with many ladies. Alert. Camp under the olive trees.

November 3 and 4
Daily alerts. Transfer to Azcapotzalco [Kühne: Azcapusalco], to [the command of] Gen. [Juan Pablo] Anaya (Pablo).[8]

November 6
I rode to Tacubaya, past Chapultepec, where the enemy, against all rules [of warfare], was shooting his big fieldpieces at me, a lone rider.

58. Artillery in Combat

November 7
Just as I was sitting in a steambath trying to get rid of a throbbing toothache, an adjutant brought me the order to decamp. We all thought that we were going to attack Mexico City, but we marched a distance of five leagues [thirteen miles] during the night.[1]

November 8
Today was a day of rest. During the night we were suddenly ordered to decamp and to march to Lechería, where we stopped and

slept the whole night on the road.[2] Someone stole my food supplies. Early the next morning we marched back.

November 9
Rest. With the cavalry, Santa Anna chased the enemy troops pursuing [us] back into the city.[3] During the night we marched to Huehuetoca. At the canal we started back, then turned around again.[4]

November 10
Rest in Huehuetoca. Saltwater. A map of Tula, where Bustamante is said to be located.[5]

59. Developments at the Lake

November 11
Early in the afternoon, at two o'clock, we decamped and marched along past Lake Zumpango [Kühne: Zumpangemby] toward the hacienda of Casas Blancas [Kühne: Hac. blanca].[1] The cause for this march. A glorious dawn with golden clouds reflecting in the clear lake while the moon was still casting a pale shadow. The setting of the hacienda of Casas Blancas. Shortly after our arrival, alert and battle positions, because the enemy had come up unexpectedly. An artillery battle from three until six o'clock in the afternoon—very fierce; firing from twenty-four cannons and howitzers.[2] A spent ball knocked me down, but since it made only a contusion, I got up again and resumed command. A grenade landed in our artillery park, but it did no damage. We blasted a part of the enemy's park away. The enemy retreated and was being pursued [by our troops], but the approach of night and heavy rain saved him. I lost my beautiful pistol.

November 12
March back to Huehuetoca. An evening scene at the lake corresponding to the previous morning scene. Watchfulness during the night. An alert early the next morning. [Captain] Holzinger's cooking woman has [only] one foot. The golden key of Huehuetoca.[3]

November 13 and 14

Preparations to fortify Huehuetoca. The second brigade was sent to Zumpango [Kühne: Impagno].[4]

November 15

The whole division was following [us]. So, we marched past the lake for the third time. Description of Zumpango: tall cactus, palms, etc.

November 16

Rest and entrenchments.

November 17

The enemy ([General] Quintanar from Mexico City) passed us on his way to Huehuetoca. We went after his rear guard, *para picar* [just to harass him], and took twenty women prisoners. The enemy has united his forces.[5]

November 18

Four days' work to establish the *fortín* [small fort] of Matamoros [Kühne: Matamores].[6] I camped in it with my cannons in the intense cold. I do the work of two men.

60. A Cavalry Engagement

November 25

An outpost engagement.

November 26

Very early in the morning, just as I was reconnoitering the lake, the enemy was withdrawing; he abandoned his position and went around the lake toward San Andrés.[1]

November 27

In the afternoon, a sudden alert. The dike was cut through.

November 28

I was ordered to accompany General Anaya and the cavalry to meet the *conducta* from Puebla.[2]

November 30

Hacienda [de] Nanacamilpa.[3] Yesterday was a remarkably unlucky day. [First of all], we rode out of Zumpango the evening of the day before yesterday with fifteen hundred cavalry troops.[4] A nocturnal march took us near Otumba [Kühne: Otemba] (NB *mala noche* of Cortés) and through enormous pulque [agave] plantations.[5] At one o'clock in the afternoon, as we were marching peacefully across the plain, near Hacienda [de] San Lorenzo, the enemy came along—also only cavalry. As quickly as possible we fell into battle formation. Attack—disastrous results—a general rout.[6] My *retirada* [retreat] via Calpulalpan [Kühne: Capulacpa]. Scenes with [Captain] Holzinger, with the blue dragoon, and with the authorities in Calpulalpan.[7] I was appointed commander of the artillery there, at which the people of the village were extremely pleased and they played for me a *diana* (morning salute, reveille). I have also been busy here drafting a plan of fortification. While I was working, Holzinger came, too.

Our position [was] critical, for we feared an assault almost any hour. Many detached and scattered troops arrived. This morning a staff meeting; the command was given to [General?] Palafox.[8] It is rumored that [General] Anaya is dead, that [General] Andrade was shot, etc. Pedro José Rico from Buenos Aires.[9] Several alerts. The poor position of the hacienda [de Nanacamilpa].

In the meanwhile, Bustamante's and Santa Anna's divisions had also set out to secure for themselves the "golden apple," the *conducta* with eighty thousand dollars. But since Santa Anna was faster, he gained the lead, although Bustamante was pressing hard on his heels, and we were saved.[10] We have been camping for two or three days in this little fort that we built. It is bitterly cold.

61. A Horseback Ride to Puebla

December 4

We broke camp to go to San Martín [Texmelucán], and then on to Puebla.[1] After a difficult march, during which we broke an axle on one of the cannons, we finally arrived there [San Martín Texmelucán].

December 5

I was given leave by the General to ride on ahead to Puebla, while the troops were supposed to wash their shirts today. I had ridden several leagues along the road when I was met by messengers, [some] officers, the sick, and by arms carriages going back the other way with the news that Bustamante had taken a shortcut through the mountains and was already advancing on Puebla.[2] His *avanzadas* [outposts] were already occupying the roads. I was not frightened by this news, so I rode on along. Soon I met [Captain] Holzinger, too. By going through Cholula, we skirted Bustamante's troops, whom we saw advancing on the city. We arrived in Puebla by this detour, through the same *garita* that I had passed [once] before, just as Bustamante was attacking the city.[3] We presented ourselves immediately to the commanding general, where, to my amazement, I found [Adolf] Hegewisch, too.[4] I was sent first to the artillery depot to join Lieutenant Colonel Ortiz in defending it.[5] Then the next morning I was sent as commander of the artillery to Fort Loreto.[6] [Captain] Holzinger remained in the city to erect barricades in the streets. We were saved by a violent rainstorm. I had some men carry hand grenades up onto the roof, etc. Bustamante's assault was unsuccessful. He overran a few of our positions, but in the meantime Santa Anna had come up behind him.[7]

62. A Battle and [Gómez] Pedraza as President

December 6

The battle of "Puente de México" is under way and remains fairly undecided so far. There have been losses enough on both sides; among our losses were my friend, Colonel Medina, and my comrade from Perote prison, Lieutenant Frías.[1] From my stronghold I have been bombarding the city, firing grenades and twenty-four pounders at the positions occupied by the enemy.[2]

December 9

Cease-fire and surrender. Cessation of hostilities. Bustamante has pulled out [of Puebla], and we entered [the city] triumphantly. Recognition of [Manuel Gómez] Pedraza as president.[3]

December 14

Holiday of the Purísima [Virgin Mary].[4] In the evening, music in the cathedral. A beautiful organ.[5] If I could choose the way I would die, then it would have to be from a cannonball, or while listening to beautiful music.

December 16

High Mass in [the church of] Santo Domingo to celebrate the arrival of [Gómez] Pedraza. A blind musician was playing by striking tuned sticks on the ground. A large fireworks display. A *coloquio* [conference] in the *coliseo* [coliseum].[6]

December 19

Mass at three o'clock in the morning in the convent of Santa Clara. A small, pretty church. Music to the singing of young nuns and the chirping of birds. Warm sulfur baths of San Pablo, about fifteen degrees Reaumur.[7]

December 20 and 21

I went to Cerro de San Juan, which, if fortified well, would be very strong.[8] Acknowledgment of [Gómez] Pedraza as president.[9]

December 22

[I spent] this evening at the home of a Spaniard—sweetmeats, little flowers, and flags, according to the native custom. A good piece of roast would have been better than all the sweets. Decorative lights.

63. *Entrance into Mexico City*

December 28

We are finally breaking camp for Mexico City. On January 3, the anniversary of the revolution [in Veracruz], we shall march into the city amid great ceremony.[1]

(End of the Revolution of 1832 and of my notes.)

PART 3
Letters

Letters

1. To Professor Breithaupt in Freiberg

Colima, February 9, 1834

Finally, respected friend, I seem to have found a haven here, near the great Pacific Ocean.[1] It is my intention to remain here a few months at least—if heaven wills it and if the political troubles of this country allow it. Now, finally, I can fulfill a wish I have nurtured so long and perform a pleasant duty at the same time, namely, to furnish Herr Lampadius, Herr Kühn, and you with some news about myself.[2] I would like also to assure you and all the others in Freiberg that it was only the extraordinary and bizarre turns of my fate over the last two years that have prevented me from writing earlier. You shall receive a cursory report on my experiences now, and then you shall certainly forgive me for my negligence—even more so when you know that I have not at all given up my mining research. I have frequently and diligently sought out news of Freiberg and I have heard a great deal that interested me very much. The most detailed reports I have from Mr. Kilaley, who attended the academy there and who came to Zacatecas a short while ago, where I met him and where he told me a lot about things [over] there.[3] Furthermore, I have received several enjoyable letters from you, from Herr Lampadius, and from Herr [E. G.] Müller, as well as from my brother in Leipzig.[4] But I cannot answer any of these letters specifically, since I do not have them here with me. Therefore, I shall proceed directly to my narrative, which in places may strike you as rather fantastic, but I assure you on my honor as a *caballero* [gentleman], that everything is the literal truth.

You know, esteemed Herr Professor, that for many years while I was in the service of the Mexican Company, I tried to improve the company's mining enterprise in the state of Oaxaca. I believe that I can even say that the firm owes its continuing existence to me. In a foreign country where things are so different from one's expectations, it is very natural that one finds great obstacles before him and that one frequently even makes blunders. But after all those toilsome years of meager compensation, I know that I have a clear conscience—notwithstanding the hundreds of thousands of dollars that passed through my hands, but over which I had no control. This is probably not always so strictly the case among Mexican mining enterprises.

Whenever I had the time and my travels permitted it, I took pleasure in indulging my penchant for geographical studies; and I had collected many data already toward the production of a special map of the state of Oaxaca, where the mining works of the Mexican Company are located. Then my successor, Mr. Obicini, arrived from London. I could not get along well with him, and since my contract with the company had almost expired, I negotiated with the government of Oaxaca for completion of the map of the state and left the service of the [Mexican] Company to devote myself completely to my topographical studies. I was doing my scientific work and leading a pleasant life in Oaxaca, when on January 3, 1832, the revolution of General Santa Anna interrupted my pursuits and gave the government of Oaxaca reason not to keep the contract promised me. I had the map already half finished, but had received nothing yet for it. Everything so far had been done at my own expense. I had also given lectures on mineralogy at the Institute [of Sciences and Arts in Oaxaca].[5] I had also organized a mineral collection there according to your system. In return, I was appointed as a member and cofounder of the Society for Natural History founded there.

Under such circumstances, I had no other choice than to offer my services to General Santa Anna, which he gladly accepted. Only a few days later I participated as his adjutant in the battle of Tolomé, where, after a fray with three dragoons, I was left for dead on the battlefield. I was then taken captive, stripped of my belongings, and twice I was supposed to be shot, but I escaped each time by a miracle. I then spent three months (part of it in the hospital) in Perote fortress, whereupon I was finally sent to Puebla as a prisoner of war. After about a month, I had the daring to make my escape in disguise from that prison. I traveled about eight *leguas* [leagues] on foot, wandering through the mountains and encountering all sorts of difficulties, until I finally rejoined General Santa Anna in Orizaba. He appointed me captain for my deeds.[6] As an officer of engineers, I was now chiefly responsible for laying out the infamous Artillery Road that goes by the volcano of Orizaba. Generally, I was involved with engineering projects besides managing my cannons in the battles. From then on, I participated in the whole campaign of 1832. I was in the battle of San Agustín del Palmar, in the storming of Puebla, in the engagements at Tacubaya, at Casas Blancas, and at San Lorenzo, and in the last battle of Puebla, until we entered Mexico City on January 3, 1833. Through these battles I had gradually advanced to the rank of lieutenant colonel and, as the people here tell me, had acquired a certain fame for my intrepidity.

Then I thought that I would be able to live quietly in Mexico City for some time, for I had received together with Col. [Ignacio] Mora [y Villamil] of the engineers a commission to draft a new general map of the Republic of Mexico.[7] I had been working on this project in the palace at Mexico City for three months when a new revolution broke out, incited by the clergy and the aristocrats.[8] Then I received from the *ministerio* [Ministry of War?] the order to join the campaign against Querétaro as chief of engineers under Gen. [José Antonio] Mejía.[9] I did so, and had the opportunity to see there the mining operations of the German[-American] Mining Company at Angangueo.[10] After we had taken Querétaro, I left General Mejía and for a few weeks I went to the mining district of Zimapán [Kühne: Cimapan] to study it.[11] Earlier, while I was in Mexico City, I had already gone to visit the Real del Monte [district] and the ironworks at Zacualpan [Kühne: Jucualpan].[12] I left Zimapán [then] to go to the famous *mineral* [mines] of Guanajuato for that same purpose [to study them]. There I was taken ill with cholera and I almost became one of its victims.[13]

During my illness, Gen. [Mariano] Arista of the new revolution came to Guanajuato, too; and after three days of captivity, I escaped finally through the state of San Luis [Potosí] to Zacatecas.[14] There I had an engagement to work on some joint geographical projects with a German gentleman, Herr [Carl] de Berghes.[15] But no sooner had I arrived there [Zacatecas], when I was commandeered by the state governor for service in his state militia. For five weeks I was also in charge of fortifications in Zacatecas. I also drafted the [general] plan of defense. Then as a *general mayor*, I marched [with General Santa Anna] against Guanajuato, and, after we stormed the city, I remained there as the local commandant.[16]

From Santa Anna, who is president now, I received the commission to make paintings and maps of his military operations. They were completed, and I rode to Mexico City to present them to him.[17] By now I had already become (by legislative decree) a citizen of [the states of] Zacatecas and Guanajuato, and I had advanced to [the rank of] colonel. Then, just as I was about to return to Zacatecas, fortune intervened, and I committed myself first to accompany [Johann] Moritz Rugendas on several scientific expeditions. He is extremely famous for his work on Brazil.[18] So, since that time we have been together. We have visited Angangueo several times, as well as the city of Morelia [Kühne: *den Staat von* Morelia] (Valladolid).[19] Near Morelia are Lakes Araron and Pátzcuaro and Jorullo volcano, which we both ascended.[20] Then we went to Lake Chapala, a large lake that even today is still not well known.[21] We explored its entire length on one side. [From there we went] to Guadalajara, thence again to Lake Chapala (the other side), and finally [we came] here to Colima, near the southern coast [of Mexico]. A week ago we (of all mortals!) successfully ascended the famous volcano of Colima for the first time. It erupted the last time in 1829.[22]

Herr Rugendas made some sketches and paintings on these travels; I made some geographic and geological studies. Then, as luck would have it, the government of Colima commissioned me to prepare (for fair compensation) an accurate map of the small state. I accepted this commission with even more pleasure, since it would enable me to have for several months a home base and the opportunity to explore a part of the local coast as well as several interesting districts nearby, e.g., the iron mines and copper mines of Coalcomán, the saltworks on the coast, pearl fishing, and many other things.[23]

I am most delighted, however, that this enterprise will enable me finally to organize somewhat my numerous sketches, observations, and notes, and to begin work on a book that I want to put together from these notes, etc. There is no doubt that with my many and varied travels, incidents, and adventures, I have amassed a wealth of most interesting knowledge about this country. My information should also be worth publishing—even more so, since it is both accurate and complete, because where it was at all possible, I kept a journal and tried [always] to note everything accurately. My own adventures are certainly strange enough. [The record of] my wartime adventures and my studies of mining practices and geography contain a great deal that is new, interesting, and useful. I just wish that I had a publisher with whom I could negotiate about the publication of this work that I plan to illustrate with several maps and drawings. May I please solicit your advice about this idea, Herr Professor?

I have already about three hundred subscribers among the Germans [currently living] in Mexico. This demonstration of interest in my book can probably persuade a publisher to accept it on terms that would assure me of some compensation for my many years of peril and sacrifice. My plan would be to publish the book in serial or booklet form under the title, "Episodes in the History of the Republic of Mexico." These episodes would contribute to the knowledge of this country, especially knowledge of the most recent events here (i.e., since 1832), for in my personal narrative I would interweave information about popular customs, the military, topography, geognosy, mining, etc. Once the series has aroused some interest, then I can see how long that interest warrants a continuation of the reports, and I shall agree to send an installment with each packet ship. Please be so kind and tell me your helpful opinion of my plan and initiate negotiations for me, if you think the project is a good one. If an advertisement for subscriptions among my friends there seems advisable, then I leave that to you, also. I shall send you the original list of my subscribers here. Perhaps my reports would be of interest to a journal; but it would be difficult to locate a suitable one, since the subjects covered in my reports are so numerous, and many of them cannot be treated well separately from others.[24]

February 11, [1834]

It is strange, but since writing the above, I have been at the scene of fighting again. I earned a few new laurels, too. You see, we were attacked last night by a superior number of enemy forces. Fortunately, however, we were able to repel the attack and to kill their leader with a cannon shot; he was the head of the revolutionary activity in the administrative district of Colima. For that reason, things have quieted down here for the moment, so that for the time being I can continue my surveys.

I forgot to note that at present the revolution of the clergy and the aristocracy has not been suppressed at all. Gen. [Nicolás] Bravo, especially, is still playing a role in the opposition. He carried on his mischief in the neighboring state of Michoacán [Kühne: Morelia].[25] It was one of his partisans who caused the trouble here and, as I said, who attacked us with 150 cavalry troops. My plans to stay here for a longer period of time may be disrupted by more of these incidents—perhaps even before I finish this letter and mail it. I am awaiting orders every day to return to Guadalajara and to take command of the artillery there—especially if the enemy's progress remains unchecked. If that should be the case, then later on I shall return here anyway to complete the work I have begun. Then I shall probably go to the United States for a couple of months. This digression, of course, should be explained more fully.

I have already told you that President Santa Anna had commissioned me in Guanajuato to prepare the maps of his military campaigns there and that he had given me permission to publish them.[26] Consequently, I advertised for subscriptions to them. They have attracted so much interest that at present I have already nearly three thousand subscribers and I can easily get five thousand. My profit [from this project] is certain to be between eight thousand and ten thousand dollars.[27] I have the maps completed, but I cannot have an engraving made of them here in Mexico. Hence, I must have it done either in the United States or in France. I cannot let the originals out of my hands [either]; and to make copies of them would delay production at least three or four months. Therefore, I would do much better to go there myself and to see to the engraving of the originals personally. In that way, I save some time and I have the pleasure of a nice trip. I shall travel from here, you see, to Zacatecas (the state governor has promised me an advance for the necessary expenses), from there to San Luis [Potosí], and on to Tampico, where I shall embark for New Orleans. I shall return perhaps via Veracruz with the whole shipment of the printed copies. I shall probably append these maps to my book or send a number of copies to Europe. If I return successfully from that journey and if everything goes according to plan, then I shall go either to Oaxaca to finish my map of that state, which should earn me another five thousand dollars, or I shall draw one in Guadalajara. Then I am going to find for myself a nice little place where I can complete my notebooks on Mexico, which by that time will have proliferated again. Then I shall not be able to resist the temptation to see my home and Saxony once more. I shall return [here] again perhaps to undertake the preparation of a new map of the Republic of Mexico. I have already gathered a lot of data for the project. So, there you have my future for several years to come, as far as my intentions go. But will it all work out that way? ¿Quién sabe? [Who knows?] says the Mexican, and I say in German, Gott weiss es! [Only God knows!].

At the present time I am in Colima—that much is certain. I have a small house in this very romantic but hot town. During the day I work, or I relax in my nice hammock from Guayaquil.[28] Early every morning I drink my [cup of] chocolate coffee. Whenever I want, I also drink palm wine or coconut milk. For relaxation I go horseback riding in the groves of plantain, coconut, orange, or cacao trees. Unfortunately, I must spend the nights (by my own choice) in the garrison, where I have a detachment of soldiers. There I am bitten terribly by certain jumping insects. Otherwise the nights are very pleasant, which is why I always love the coastal regions. A flute is still my constant companion.

Of all my trips, the most recent ones in the company of my talented friend Rugendas were the most enjoyable. Our ascent on the volcano of Colima was very laborious; it took us a whole day just to climb the last cone. Right now I am working on a survey and a drawing of the volcano. Its approximate geographic position is: 19°29′ N[orth] L[atitude] and 97°31′ from Cádiz [Kühne: Cadix], [Spain]. However, as I said, I am working on its dimensions myself and I have (preliminarily) determined its height to be 12,780 Spanish feet above sea level.[29]

Please tell Professor Kühn that I have become something of a volcanologist as far as porphyry and basalts are concerned. It is almost impossible not to be, when one sees for hundreds of leagues nothing but large and small volcanoes, nothing but lava flows, porphyry of all sorts, trachyte, and basalts. From my topographical and geognostical map I have set up a geological system on the formation of the whole district of Mexico down to the coast here.[30] My system will be set out in greater detail in my aforementioned book. Incidentally, I have also investigated the area around Zacoalco [Kühne: Zatoalco] (twenty-five leagues from here), which is on an old lakebed.[31] Last year they unearthed some very well preserved mammoth skeletons there. One of them is nearly perfect (only a few vertebrae are missing) and is in Guadalajara now. I shall send some drawings of it.

February 13, 1834

What I feared has happened. Yesterday I received by messenger from Guadalajara the order to go there immediately and to take command of the entire section of artillery. This comes at a very bad time for me, and the local government is going to propose that I remain here, where I am indispensable under such critical conditions. Therefore, I shall put aside this letter to you for a while to await the outcome. Before I mail it, I can report my decision to you or write a little something every day if I have time.

February 15

I am still here and shall remain here until my work is finished. I have been appointed chief of defense preparations here. I intend to close this letter, therefore, and to give it to a friend for delivery, for it could get lost [here] in an uprising. That would distress me all the more, since I want very much for you to learn something about my activities and my work. I cannot refuse my participation in the political struggles, for I am committed now. I am a colonel now, and I would like to become a general, which will perhaps come soon.

Although I have come through all the battles successfully so far, it is very possible that a bullet, a lance, or something else will cost me not just the use of an arm and hand in my work, but will even drill me through my soft heart. If that should happen, then you know in general at least how I have been doing until now, and you can correct an article about me that (according to a German friend) has appeared in the Leipzig general encyclopedia.[32] In that event [i.e., his death], then you can also demand on my behalf my portrait that Rugendas painted in oil. It is in the hands of Dr. Adolf Hegewisch in Mexico City, and portrays me in the full uniform of a lieutenant colonel in the [artillery] battery of Orizaba, in the act of completing a military map.[33] "That is just vanity," you will say, but when one's life is subject to the powers of chance that lurk in every bullet and cannonball, then one is content to come to terms with oneself, and to have his family and friends remember him no differently than he was. "All is vanity," saith Solomon the Wise.[34]

The friend to whom I am giving this letter is Herr Heinrich Virmont from Düren on the Rhine.[35] He is the owner of three ships in the South Seas [South Pacific]. He has been waiting here for some time for one of his ships, and, like a true compatriot, he has been a real friend to me. Please address your answer in care of the Prussian consul in Mexico City, Herr [Friedrich] von Gerolt, to whom I report my whereabouts from time to time.[36] I shall be very grateful to my friends for their letters; they may consider this letter to be directed to them all in common. They should forgive me, too, that I do not write to them individually, which is impossible under the present circumstances. Greet them all and also my brothers in Leipzig from your [devoted friend], etc.[37]

2. To Johann Moritz Rugendas

Colima, February 10, 1834

Dear Friend Rugendas,[1]

You will be surprised that I am writing you the news of a battle that we fought this morning at eight [o'clock]. The enemy came to attack us, but we beat him back, and the leader of the main rebels, Salazar, was left [dead] on the river.[2] So, the revolution seems to be at an end here, and I shall continue with my [geographic] measurements; and I hope to see you soon. A courier is going from here to Guadalajara, [that is,] the bearer of this letter, whom you know as our dinner host. I would ask you to give him those of my things that you can or want to bring with you, or better yet, [give him] all of them. In this way I will get them very quickly and safely. Don't forget to include drawing paper, for I have to make four copies of the map [of the Colima territory], for which I am getting 700 $ [pesos], besides a gratuity.[3] The [battle] scene here was ugly; it deserved to be painted by you. Perhaps the *ayuntamiento* will commission a painting [of it] to commemorate this glorious day, and then you can really be called the Liberals' battlefield artist. In this day of patriotism you could easily earn a few thalers for your trip [home].

Eternally yours,

E. Harcort

P.S. Greetings [to you], too, Blume.[4]

3. To Johann Moritz Rugendas

Perote Fortress (in the Republic of Mexico),
August 2, 1835

Dear Friend Rugendas,

You will be astonished when you receive this letter and learn that your traveling companion, who had the pleasure of accompanying you on your expedition, namely, the undersigned *Colonel Tramp* (as you graciously used to call him), has been captured for the third time and is imprisoned once again in this fortress.[1] I am also facing deportation, but I am not so free as was the prince of Naples with the long legs back then.[2] Just listen now how that happened.

After you had embarked for the second time [May, 1834] in the port of Colima (actually Manzanillo), and *really did not* return, I finished my map [of the territory of Colima] and was outfitting myself for a planned pearl-fishing trip.[3] Then the political agitation started again, and I was secretly warned that my position in the territory of Colima was not secure. These and other signs that I had become aware of, and warnings that I had received from Guadalajara, persuaded me to take French leave. I followed the road through the mountains *west* of the volcano, around which I traveled in a large circle. From this side the *Nevado* has exactly the same shape, however, as the volcano. For this reason I suspect that it has a crater, too.[4] When I arrived in Guadalajara, they were arming themselves against [the town of San Juan de los] Lagos, which was rebelling in favor of the Catholic religion. Gov. [Pedro] Tamés had to hide me because of all this, so I went along [with it] and took charge of the cannons.[5] The campaign was not a bloody one, however. We went only as far as Tepatitlán, where, with the enemy only 4 leagues [10.4 miles] away, we amused ourselves every evening with dances and games of forfeits.[6] But we did not attack the enemy, for we unexpectedly received the order to pull back, which was also carried out without difficulty. The clerical troops *tried* only once to besiege us in Zapotlanejo, but I raked them with a good many cannon shots, and we returned unhindered to Puente [Grande] and Guadalajara.[7] I was so annoyed about this outstanding campaign that, instead of taking leave, I simply left to spend some time with my friend [W.] Spangenberg in the large barranca of Bolaños. The very next day after my arrival there, I rode with several friends (Spangenberg had been for some time in Zacatecas, which I had not known) to the company forester's house, called la Berbería, situated five thousand feet above the [Bolaños] River and the valley.[8] After my return, I was met by a courier from the government of Guadalajara with a *despacho* [dispatch], naming me as general commander of the artillery and of the military engineers in that state, which now was threatened by an invasion of government troops under [Gen. Luis?] Cortázar and [Gen. Miguel]

Barragán.[9] I should have liked to refuse the urgent invitation to return immediately to the capital [Guadalajara]. But I arrived there again just as the intruders, who in the meantime had advanced into the city, were being engaged in *battle*. We gave them a sound thrashing, as did Saul the Philistines, and took all of their artillery from them.[10] Gen. [José Antonio] Mejía had arrived there just four hours ahead of me, and I was made general commander [of the artillery] against the national government.[11] Now our plan (Mejía's and mine) was to defend the crossings over the Santiago River, primarily the bridge at Puente [Grande] p.p.[12] I went there intermittently, directing the [construction of] entrenchments, and in fourteen days, I had set up an artillery battery completely in the Prussian manner with twenty-two fieldpieces. Everybody who saw it admired it. I had enough to do just rushing and riding back and forth, as you can imagine, if you really want to try. [Anyway], the enemy came, our positions held fast, and once again I was getting tired of the sight and sound of cannon and musket fire, p.p. But then nothing came of it, anyway, for Mejía and Cortázar unexpectedly made peace [with each other]. Our troops were enraged. They wanted to shoot Mejía and they offered me the general command. I rejected it, however, and the *tratados* [treaties] and *convenios* [agreements] were ratified by the state congress. As a result, nothing was to be changed, and nobody was supposed to be molested, but the underlying conditions were (1) the recognition of S[anta] Anna [as president] (against whose presidency we had issued a *pronunciamiento*); and (2) the entry of the government troops [into the city]. During this campaign I had been given lodgings at the home of F. H. [*sic*] Blume and Weiskopf, where, with [General] Mejía, we had several (very splendid) balls, and we often thought of *you*.[13] The same morning that [General] Cortázar entered the city, I had to leave Guadalajara, going again to Bolaños, but I took a detour to see the *mineral* [mine] of Mesquital, El Oro.[14] I arrived at Spangenberg's place (who had returned in the meanwhile [from Zacatecas]) exhausted from all the martial goings-on, and we decided that I should spend several weeks with him. Incidentally, Bolaños is situated in an enormous barranca, compared with which those [barrancas] of the Colima volcano are insignificant. I had never before seen a valley of such gigantic dimensions. I had decided that I wanted to record trigonometrically the dimensions of the entire valley, but then one day, as I was sitting quietly at breakfast, a soldier asked for me and presented an official letter from the commandant of Bolaños. It contained the order for me to leave the town and the district within two hours, pursuant to an order received from Guadalajara. So, I was led out of there, going from one village to another, until I came to the state of Zacatecas, where I was left alone until I reached the city of Zacatecas. An order had been sent there already from Mexico City to arrest me and to send me to Tampico. I went into hiding, however, as the bishop of Puebla had done, and did not let myself be lured out, living instead with friends in the mining district.[15] Finally, I became tired of playing hide-and-seek, and turned myself in, whereupon I was confined in a barracks, but after four weeks I had a fresh attack of cowardice again. . . .

Now for a couple of months I lived quietly and happily. I gave an English lady drawing lessons, set up an assay laboratory, and in association with other friends I began operating a mercury testing laboratory. Then the devil, who in this country never takes a holiday, ignited the flames of revolution in the formerly peaceful [state of] Zacatecas. All of the state's financial and political means were applied [to the war effort] and really, the most favorable outcome was in prospect.[16] The government was able to commit me [to its cause], and I was given the position of quartermaster general and chief of ordnance, and the command of all the artillery. Santa Anna himself was leading his army against us, and on May 10, the two armies sighted one another on the plains of Guadalupe, for [Francisco] García, the former governor who had been elected commander-in-chief, insisted stupidly (asinaliter) on our forces meeting the enemy in open terrain. The battle plan that I had drawn up was rejected by him, and I had to organize and position our forces according to his notions.[17] I still believed [at the time] that he would pass on the command to me for the day of the battle, but the pride of the Mexicans does not admit of such [modesty]. It so happened then that on May 11, before dawn, we were attacked from all four sides and were thoroughly (totaliter) defeated. Our loss was due in no small part to the cowardice of [Governor] García, who ran away at the first shot, and to the cowardice of the troops, who by entire battalions threw away their weapons in the darkness before even seeing an enemy soldier.[18] Two of my adjutants lost their lives. A third one (the wild little Frenchman, whom you know from Colima) was seriously wounded. I survived in spite of myself, and was captured with 150 other officers. I lost all of my gear; I was put *in chains*, and with other prisoners, I was made to march to Mexico City.[19] Over half of the way we had to carry the *grillos* [shackles] on our backs—at the *express order* of Santa Anna!! In Mexico City I was locked up in the Inquisition [prison], where they allowed me just enough freedom so that my friends could visit me. Among the compassionate Samaritans who did visit me was your friend, Dr. [Christian] Schiede, who from time to time poured good wine not in my wounds (for I had none), but in my stomach, which gave me refreshing comfort.[20] May heaven recompense our faithful friend for that, and send him many patients.

On June 23 the day of freedom dawned for all the prisoners—except for me and a Frenchman in the artillery, Captain Legoff, who always shared a common fate with me. In the meantime, we expected to be set free within a few days, too, when early on the morning of June 25, we were hauled off to Puebla. Under an escort of seventy-five dragoons, and on foot, we set off down the road to Puebla. We were given neither the time nor the opportunity to take anything with us, not even to bid our friends farewell. In Puebla we were locked up for days (both day and night) in the *calabozo* [jail] of a cavalry barracks (*cuartel*). They took even our knives from us and, giving us only the soft earth to sleep on, they granted us not the slightest convenience. Through the goodwill of several soldiers who knew me from the defense of Puebla, *año* 1832, we were given some brandy, which we *slugged* down like *derelicts.* [21] Then we were led off again, but riding this time (i.e., on horses), and on July 4, we arrived in good spirits at this fortress. Here at last, we have been treated with honor and kindness by the governor, Gen. [Antonio de?] Castro and his family, and by Arago, the young man who is the *mayor de la plaza* here.[22] I live with these good people, give my companions lessons in music and drawing, and await calmly the things to come, e.g., the great warrantor, letters from my friends, the *continuation of our march*, etc.[23] I have finally learned here that I am supposed to go on to Veracruz to emigrate as an undesirable. They were supposed to have marched me off already, but the governor has held me back under various pretenses, to ensure that the fever season in Veracruz is completely past.[24] So, I shall still spend at least the entire month of August here; then in God's name may I continue my trip— stowed on the first ship leaving port. Hurrah, to sail merrily away to other ports!!

There you have the brief but factually true story of my life since we bade farewell to each other on the coast of the great Pacific Ocean. Now, I would also like to learn your story, which I am sure is interesting enough, but it will be difficult for you to address a letter to me without the kind services of Dr. Schiede as intermediary, whom I shall write of my whereabouts. If I was difficult to find in the Republic of Mexico, then it will be even more difficult once I am aboard a floating house of wood. But please do try! With the capture of Zacatecas I lost everything I owned in the way of equipment, splendid horses p.p., but my maps and manuscripts were saved. I expect them to arrive here soon, and I shall perhaps take them with me to Germany, to publish them there. [I hope that] you will allow me to speak about you also in my writings—of course, with all the respect due you as an artist, and with the greatest fondness for my former traveling companion. In it I shall compose also an epitaph to your [horse] Babir, for unfortunately, as I was leaving Bolaños and was letting him follow along loose behind me, to be easy on him, he got lost and *injured* himself in a fall. I saved a lock of his hair for you, but after the battle at Zacatecas the devil took that too—very probably.

I still have heard nothing from Colima. I know only that [Carl] Benesky [de Beaufort] is commandant there.[25] I have received letters from [H. F.] Blume and Whitehead, and they are well.[26] I have heard *here* that [our] friend [Heinrich] Virmons has gotten married in Mexico City; hence, he did not marry the runaway bride.[27] I had firmly anticipated this last turn of events. I don't know what else could be of interest to you, but . . .

There were once three geese, p.p.[28]

The weather is always bad here in Perote, but this week I had hoped for pretty weather, on account of an expedition that we had planned on the *Cofre* [de Perote]. There I want to measure all the angles between the other volcanoes that I do not have yet. The points shall be the Pico de Orizaba, Pizarro, the volcano of Tuxtla, Malinche, the snow-covered peaks [Popocatépetl and Ixtaccihuatl] near Mexico City, Cempoaltepec in Oaxaca (where I have already measured the angles), and many other points, including some on the coast, too, I hope.

Now, my dear itinerant battle-landscape-animal-and-portrait-painter, I wish you well in your valley of paradise, or wherever you are. Don't climb too much on the volcanoes there, either, and when you write to friends in Europe, please greet them from me, albeit as a stranger.

Your topographer resigned to suffering and deportation,

Eduard Harkort

PS. If I had been given the choice of my itinerary, then I probably would have followed you.

Notes

Part 1. Introduction

1. The complete citation of these works can be found in the bibliography. See also Garold Cole, *American Travelers to Mexico, 1821–1872: A Descriptive Bibliography;* and Drewey Wayne Gunn, *Mexico in American and British Letters: A Bibliography of Fiction and Travel Books, Citing Original Editions.*

2. Eduard Harkort, *Aus Mejicanischen Gefängnissen: Bruchstück aus Eduard Harkorts hinterlassenen Papieren,* pp. ix, 105. For more on Kühne and Junges Deutschland, see Henry Garland and Mary Garland, *The Oxford Companion to German Literature* (Oxford: Clarendon Press, 1976), pp. 442–43, 498; and *Allgemeine Deutsche Biographie* LI, 431–35.

3. Letters, Gertrud Herrmann-Kühne to Louis E. Brister (June 8, and Sept. 14, 1980); letter, Deutsche Staatsbibliothek, East Berlin, to LEB (July 22, 1980); letter, Stadtarchiv Leipzig to LEB (Mar. 31, 1979).

4. Harkort, *Aus Mejicanischen Gefängnissen,* p. 105. For more on Rugendas in Mexico, see Gertrud Richert, *Johann Moritz Rugendas: Ein deutscher Maler des XIX. Jahrhunderts,* pp. 29–38.

5. A certified excerpt from the baptismal records of the Lutheran church at Hagen, Germany, supplied by the Gesamtverband der Evangelischen Kirchengemeinden Hagen to LEB (June 19, 1979). Much of the information in this biographical introduction to Harkort's journal first appeared in Louis E. Brister, "Colonel Eduard Harkort: A German Soldier of Fortune in Mexico and Texas, 1832–1836," *Southwestern Historical Quarterly,* 88 (Jan., 1985); 229–46 (hereafter, *SHQ*). Quotations from that article are reprinted here by permission of the Texas State Historical Association.

6. Eberhard Winkhaus, *Wir stammen aus Bauern- und Schmiedegeschlecht: Genealogie eines süderländischen Sippenkreises und der ihm angehörenden Industriepioniere,* pp. 17–22, 62. See also "Eduard Harkort—'der schwarze Prinz,'" *Westfalenland,* 23 (1932): 109; and Kurt Klotzbach, "Eduard Harkort: Pionier und Abenteurer in Mexiko und Texas," *Heimatbuch Hagen + Mark: Hagener Heimatkalender 1981,* 22 (1980): 63.

7. Winkhaus, *Bauern- und Schmiedegeschlecht,* pp. 62–63.

8. Typed one-page excerpt from Henriette Kühne-Harkort's "Lebensgeschichte," supplied by Eduard Harkort's great-granddaughter, Gertrud Herrmann-Kühne, of East Berlin, Germany, to LEB; Winkhaus, *Bauern- und Schmiedegeschlecht,* p. 63.

9. Winkhaus, *Bauern- und Schmiedegeschlecht,* p. 63. Unfortunately, Eduard Harkort's German military service records were destroyed in 1945, along with the military archives containing those records. Letter, Geheimes Staatsarchiv, Preussischer Kulturbesitz, West Berlin, to LEB (June 29, 1979); Akademisches Archiv der Bergakademie Freiberg, Saxony, Oberbergamt (OBA) File 9980, Vol. 14, fol. 165 (hereafter AABF, OBA).

10. AABF, OBA File 9980, Vol. 14, fols. 166, 171–172.

11. Winkhaus, *Bauern- und Schmiedegeschlecht,* p. 63; J. Erik Jorpes, *Jac. Berze-*

lius: His Life and Work, trans. Barbara Steele (Berkeley & Los Angeles: University of California Press, 1970) pp. 87–89.

12. Johann C. Poggendorf, comp., *Biographisch-Literarisches Handwörterbuch zur Geschichte der exacten Wissenschaften* I, col. 1,019; C[arl] Schiffner, *Aus dem Leben alter Freiberger Bergstudenten und der Lehrkörper der Bergakademie* III, 11–12; Eduard Harkort, *Die Probirkunst mit dem Löthrohre* . . . , p. 2.

13. Historisches Staatsarchiv (Bergarchiv) Freiberg, Oberbergamt (OBA) Freiberg, Rep. H, sec. 91d, no. 10,881/1, fols. 1–5 (Oct. 3, 1826); fols. 9–10 (Dec. 15, 1826); fols. 20–21 (July 4, 1828); fols. 24–28, 36 (July 23, 1828) (hereafter HSF, OBA); Schiffner, *Aus dem Leben alter Freiberger Bergstudenten* I, 57–58, III, 11–12; Charles Coulston Gillispie, ed., *Dictionary of Scientific Biography* XI, 33–34.

14. AABF, OBA File 9904, Vol. 2, fols. 205–10. Translation of this quote and others from all German sources cited in English are mine; emphasis is Breithaupt's own. Ibid., AABF, OBA, File 9904, Vol. 2, fol. 208.

15. Ibid., fol. 212.

16. Harkort, *Die Probirkunst mit dem Löthrohre,* pp. v–vii, 2. In English the entire title is "The Art of Assaying with the Blowpipe, or an Attempt to Demonstrate How One Can Analyze with Reasonable Accuracy the Metal Content of Ores, Minerals, and Smelter Products with the Aid of the Blowpipe. Booklet I: Assaying Silver." The book contained 113 pages, and the different phases of the procedure were illustrated with ink drawings.

17. HSF, OBA, Rep. H, Sec. 91d, no. 10,881/1, fols. 24–28, 36 (July 23, 1828).

18. Winkhaus, *Bauern- und Schmiedegeschlecht,* pp. 58–59, 63–64; Schiffner, *Aus dem Leben alter Freiberger Bergstudenten* III, 13; Hans Kruse, ed., *Deutsche Briefe aus Mexiko, mit einer Geschichte des Deutsch-Amerikanischen Bergwerkvereins 1824–1838,* pp. ii–iv.

19. The "mining mania" of the 1820s in England is described by Newton R. Gilmore, "British Mining Ventures in Early National Mexico," pp. 2–27; he lists no less than twenty-eight companies formed for the purpose of working mines in Mexico and Latin America (p. 23). See also J. Fred Rippy, "Latin America and the British Investment 'Boom' of the 1820's," *Journal of Modern History* 19 (June, 1947): 122–129. For an account of the establishment of German mining interests in Mexico, see Kruse, ed., *Deutsche Briefe aus Mexiko,* pp. i–iv, xvii–xxix.

20. Gilmore, "British Mining Ventures," p. 112; Mexican Company, *Report of the Directors of the Mexican Company, Presented at the Third Annual General Meeting of the Proprietors,* . . . p. 10; Harkort, *Aus Mejicanischen Gefängnissen,* p. 14; Winkhaus, *Bauern- und Schmiedegeschlecht,* p. 64.

21. According to his daughter, who claimed to have later read her father's letter, Eduard Harkort did write his wife after his departure, begging her forgiveness for his churlish behavior toward her. Henriette Kühne-Harkort, excerpt from "Lebensgeschichte."

22. Harkort, *Aus Mejicanischen Gefängnissen,* p. 50.

23. Winkhaus, *Bauern- und Schmiedegeschlecht,* pp. 63, 67.

24. Ibid., p. 64; Harkort, *Aus Mejicanischen Gefängnissen,* 14; Mexican Company, *Report of the Directors of the Mexican Company, Presented at the Second Annual General Meeting of the Proprietors,* . . . p. 11; Mexican Company, *Report of the Directors of the Mexican Company, Presented at the Third Annual General Meeting of the Proprietors,* . . . p. 10 (quotation).

25. Harkort, *Aus Mejicanischen Gefängnissen,* p. 16; Mexican Company, *Extracts*

from the Report of Mr. Justus Ludwig von Uslar, . . . Relative to the "Negociacion" of Yavesia, in the State of Oaxaca, Dated San Antonio de Padua, (Oaxaca) 6th January 1828, pp. 72–79.

26. Gilmore, "British Mining Ventures," pp. 111–13; Mexican Company, *Extracts,* pp. 23–25. The first group of forty German mining specialists and craftsmen was sent to Mexico in February, 1827. Mexican Company, *Second Annual General Meeting*, pp. 8, 10–11. With Harkort's party of twenty, which sailed ten months later, in December, 1827, the total number of German workers employed by the Mexican Company in Mexico increased to about sixty. Mexican Company, *Second Annual General Meeting*, p. 11; Mexican Company, *Third Annual General Meeting*, p. 10.

27. See the letters appended to the translation of Harkort's journal, Harkort to Rugendas, Aug. 2, 1835.

28. Harkort, *Aus Mejicanischen Gefängnissen*, pp. 24–25.

29. The details of Harkort's departure from the Mexican Company and of his subsequent career in the Mexican army are recounted by Harkort himself in his journal and letters, annotated by me.

30. Harkort (written as Arcourt) and five other men, two Germans, one Frenchman, and two Spaniards, were the sole passengers aboard the ship. All six listed their occupation as merchant and indicated an intent to become inhabitants of the United States. National Archives, *Passenger Lists of Vessels Arriving at New Orleans 1820–1902*, no. 320.

31. Wilfrid Hardy Callcott, *Santa Anna: The Story of an Enigma Who Once Was Mexico*, p. 122; Oakah L. Jones, Jr., *Santa Anna*, p. 64; James A. Magner, *Men of Mexico*, pp. 325–27.

32. Harkort, *Aus Mejicanischen Gefängnissen*, pp. 97, 108; letter, Harkort to Rugendas, Aug. 2, 1835.

33. Mejía had returned to New Orleans from Texas by the end of December, 1835. Eugene C. Barker, "The Tampico Expedition," *Quarterly of the Texas State Historical Association* 6 (Jan., 1903); 185–86.

34. John H. Jenkins, ed., *The Papers of the Texas Revolution 1835–1836* IV, 110. It should be noted that in all extant records of Harkort's service in the Texas Revolution, his name is spelled Harcourt.

35. Ibid., IV, 410–12; see also Eugene C. Barker, "Don Carlos Barrett," *SHQ* 20 (Oct., 1916): 143–44.

36. Jenkins, ed., *Papers of the Texas Revolution* IV, 411–12. Barrett did not identify any of the Germans with Harkort by name, and Harkort's letter has evidently been lost, for I could find no other record of it. I know its general content only from Barrett's statements about it.

37. Letter, Thomson and Pattillo to Robinson, Feb., 1836, Governor's Correspondence, Nov. 18, 1835–Mar. 6, 1836, Secretary of State Record Group (Archives Division, Texas State Library, Austin) (hereafter SSRG). In the letter, reproduced also in ibid., IV, 472, the phrase "two gentlemen" should probably read "ten gentlemen." The poor condition of the original letter, however, did not permit positive verification of this discrepancy.

38. The emphasis in the quotations is Harkort's. Edward Harcourt, "*Pro Memoria or a* Representation . . . ," Memorials and Petitions Series, SSRG; also in Jenkins, ed., *Papers of the Texas Revolution* V, 76–77; *The General Convention at Washington, March 1–17, 1836* (Houston, 1838), p. 76, reprinted in H. P. N. Gammell, comp., *The Laws of Texas, 1822–1897* . . . I, 896; and Jenkins, ed., *Papers of the Texas Revolution* IX, 362.

In his representation, Harkort names besides Dr. Jaeger three others of the ten Germans who had come with him to Texas from New Orleans: Orderly Sgt. of Artillery Christian Hansen, 1st Lt. F[riedrich] W[ilhelm] Huesman (later anglicized to Houseman), and 1st Lt. F. C. Scheling. The identities of the other six Germans in the group remain unknown. It is interesting to note, however, that Christian Hansen had preceded Harkort to New Orleans, arriving there on July 21, 1835, aboard the brig *Orion* from Campeche, Mexico. National Archives, *Passenger Lists*, no. 227. I could locate no records of Hansen's or of Scheling's military service in Texas at this time. More will be said about Jaeger and Huesman later in this introduction.

39. Hubert H. Bancroft, *History of the North Mexican States and Texas* II, 75, 158; Callcott, *Santa Anna*, pp. 122–23; Jones, *Santa Anna*, p. 64; Magner, *Men of Mexico*, p. 326.

40. Jenkins, ed., *Papers of the Texas Revolution* V, 79; Brister, "Colonel Eduard Harkort," p. 242.

41. H[enderson K.] Yoakum, *History of Texas from Its First Settlement in 1685 to Its Annexation to the United States in 1846* II, 105–107, 114; Amelia W. Williams and Eugene C. Barker, eds., *The Writings of Sam Houston 1813–1863* I, 385–86; Jenkins, ed., *Papers of the Texas Revolution* V, 216, 234, IX, 144.

42. Jenkins, ed., *Papers of the Texas Revolution* V, 257–58. On Mar. 16, the convention had elected Potter secretary of the navy in the *ad interim* government. Yoakum, *History of Texas* II, 73–74.

43. Jenkins, ed., *Papers of the Texas Revolution* V, 257.

44. Ibid., V, 384–85. Morgan had been commandant of Galveston Island only since Mar. 20, 1836. Walter Prescott Webb, H. Bailey Carroll, and Eldon Stephen Branda, eds., *The Handbook of Texas* II, 234.

45. Jenkins, ed., *Papers of the Texas Revolution* V, 467.

46. Eugene C. Barker, ed., *Readings in Texas History*, pp. 306–307.

47. Jenkins, ed., *Papers of the Texas Revolution* VI, 26. The same day Rusk drafted a brief dispatch to General Houston from Zavala's house concerning the need for more men to guard about five hundred Mexican prisoners. Jenkins, ed., *Papers of the Texas Revolution* VI, 32. The proximity of Zavala's house to the San Jacinto battleground can be seen in William C. Pool, *A Historical Atlas of Texas*, p. 60.

48. Jenkins, ed., *Papers of the Texas Revolution* VI, 408, 418, 481; Gerald S. Pierce, *Texas under Arms: The Camps, Posts, Forts, & Military Towns of the Republic of Texas 1836–1846*, p. 48.

49. Pierce, *Texas under Arms*, p. 49. On May 29, Harkort issued to Lt. L. B. Raymond a receipt for 121 Mexican prisoners "for the Fortification works of this Island." Jenkins, ed., *Papers of the Texas Revolution* VI, 408; see also Harkort's inventory of the fort of June 1, 1836. Jenkins, ed., *Papers of the Texas Revolution* VI, 476.

50. Joseph O. Dyer, *The Early History of Galveston: Centenary Edition Part I*, p. 23. In a letter of August 23, 1836, Henry M. Morfit described Fort Travis as "a mud fort . . . [with] a few cannon." Jenkins, ed., *Papers of the Texas Revolution* VIII, 301.

51. Pierce, *Texas under Arms*, p. 49; a map on the front flyleaf of this book depicts the location of the camp and fort. On May 31, Dr. Jaeger submitted a request to Colonel Morgan to be transferred from Camp Travis to the Galveston hospital. Jenkins, ed., *Papers of the Texas Revolution* VI, 440.

52. On June 20, President David G. Burnet wrote to the commander of the schooner *Invincible* to be alert to a fleet fitting out at Veracruz; on the same day he wrote to Commissioners Peter W. Grayson and James Collingsworth in Washington, D.C.,

pleading for artillery reinforcements at Galveston against the rumored assault. Jenkins, ed., *Papers of the Texas Revolution* VII, 206–207; Yoakum, *History of Texas* II, 176.

53. See Harkort's letters to Morgan of May 9, and May [30], concerning the shortage of axes and labor in the fort, and his inventory of the fort of June 1, 1836. Jenkins, ed., *Papers of the Texas Revolution* VI, 195, 418, 476.

54. Letters, Harcourt to Morgan, May 1, and May 2 (quotation), 1836, James Morgan Papers (Rosenberg Library, Galveston).

55. Dyer, *Early History of Galveston*, p. 26.

56. Letter, Harcourt to Morgan, May 1, 1836. For an account of the capture of the brig *Pocket*, see Claude L. Douglas, *Thunder on the Gulf: Story of the Texas Navy*, pp. 36–43.

57. Jenkins, ed., *Papers of the Texas Revolution* VI, 417.

58. Ibid., VI, 480.

59. First Lt. William S. Stilwell was originally in the infantry and listed as an officer in the regular army, appointed by the General Council on March 10, 1836. Ibid., V, 42, IX, 345.

60. Ibid., VI, 480.

61. Ibid., VII, 208–209.

62. Ibid., VII, 281–82. It was rumored already in June that a Mexican force of thousands was preparing to invade Texas again from Matamoros and Veracruz. Joseph Milton Nance, *After San Jacinto: The Texas-Mexican Frontier, 1836–1841*, pp. 10–11, 14; Jenkins, ed., *Papers of the Texas Revolution* VII, 206, 280–81.

63. Jenkins, ed., *Papers of the Texas Revolution* VIII, 44. The proprietor of the sawmill was Lt. Col. David B. Macomb, an artillery officer in the regular army, appointed by the General Council on March 10, 1836. Jenkins, ed., *Papers of the Texas Revolution* V, 42, IX, 345.

64. Harkort mentioned Huesman by name in his *pro memoria* of Mar. 14, 1836, to the Texas convention; see note 38. Huesman served a little over a year in the Texas army, beginning May 26, 1836, and ending August 23, 1837. For his term of service he was issued Bounty Warrant no. 617 for 1,280 acres of land. Thomas Lloyd Miller, comp., *Bounty and Donation Land Grants of Texas 1835–1888*, p. 360. Almost a decade later, on January 27, 1844, Huesman (also written Hüsman) was named a trustee of the ill-fated Herman University. Gammel, comp., *Laws of Texas*, II, 948; see also Webb, Carroll, and Branda, eds., *Handbook of Texas* I, 801–802.

65. The only information about the cause of Harkort's death is supplied by his son-in-law, F. Gustav Kühne, the editor of the prison journal, who states merely that Harkort succumbed to "a fever." Harkort, *Aus Mejicanischen Gefängnissen*, p. xi.

66. *Telegraph and Texas Register* (Houston, Sept. 13, 1836). For information about David L. Kokernot, see *Memorial and Genealogical Record of Southwest Texas, Containing Biographical Histories and Genealogical Records of Many Leading Men and Prominent Families*, p. 300; and Webb, Carroll, and Branda, eds., *Handbook of Texas* I, 972, III, 484.

67. See note 73.

68. Edward Harcourt file, Audited Military Claims, Comptroller of Public Accounts Record Group (Archives Division, Texas State Library, Austin).

69. Pierce, *Texas under Arms*, p. 51.

70. *Telegraph and Texas Register* (Houston, July 22, 1837).

71. Eugene Maissin, *The French in Mexico and Texas (1838–1839)*, p. 182.

72. Jenkins, ed., *Papers of the Texas Revolution* VI, 480, V, 42. My efforts to deter-

mine the identity of the second individual mentioned were fruitless. Harkort's letter to Morgan of May 31, 1836, is not included in the Morgan Papers collection; its present location is unknown. Letter, Robert Stevens, assistant archivist, Rosenberg Library, to LEB (June 17, 1980).

73. The complete probate records of the Edward Harcourt estate, including the correspondence of both Dr. C. Hermann Jaeger and John S. Lindner, can be found in File 243, Brazoria County Probate Records (Brazoria County Courthouse, Angleton). Other pertinent records in the Brazoria County Courthouse include Bond Record Book A, p. 127; Land Certificates, Book B, p. 30, no. 181; Transcribed Minutes of the Brazoria County Probate Court, Book B, p. 26; Book C, p. 77; Book D, pp. 81, 93. Notices of Jaeger's administration appeared in the *Telegraph and Texas Register* (Houston, June 16 and July 21, 1838).

Harkort's heirs received land patents for one-third league headrights and for 1,920 acres bounty lands. General Land Office, Stephen F. Austin Bldg., Austin; File Bexar First Class 984, and File Bexar County 1270; Miller, comp., *Bounty and Donation Land Grants*, p. 323.

Part 2. Puebla Journal

PEROTE

1. [San Carlos de] Perote Fortress

1. The fortress, San Carlos de Perote, known also as Perote prison, was built during the reign of Charles III of Spain (1759–1788). Located near the town of Perote in the state of Veracruz, the fortress was used in the 1800s chiefly as a prison. In Texas history it gained notoriety as the prison for the captives from the Santa Fe expedition in 1841 and from the capture of San Antonio and the Mier expedition in 1842. J. J. McGrath and Walace Hawkins, "Perote Fort—Where Texans Were Imprisoned," *SHQ* 48 (Jan., 1945): 340–45; Joseph D. McCutchan, *Mier Expedition Diary: A Texan Prisoner's Account,* p. 5; George F. Lyon, *Journal of a Residence and Tour in the Republic of Mexico in the Year 1826* . . . II, 173.

2. Harkort's description of the prisoners' cell is corroborated by the published accounts of the Mier captives who just ten years later were also imprisoned in Perote fortress. See Thomas W. Bell, *A Narrative of the Capture and Subsequent Sufferings of the Mier Prisoners in Mexico,* . . . p. 55; Thomas J. Green, *Journal of the Texian Expedition against Mier,* . . . p. 241; McCutchan, *Mier Expedition Diary,* p. 121; William Preston Stapp, *The Prisoners of Perote,* . . . p. 154.

3. Cofre de Perote is one of the highest peaks in the Sierra Madre Oriental range of Mexico; see *Diccionario Porrúa de historia, biografía y geografía de México* I, 459; and T. Philip Terry, *Terry's Guide to Mexico: The New Standard Guidebook to the Mexican Republic,* p. 504.

4. Mexican Company, *Third Annual General Meeting,* p. 10.

5. *Die Schildbürger,* a *Volksbuch* printed in 1597, is a collection of humorous anecdotes about the inhabitants of the town of Schilda. See Garland and Garland, *Oxford Companion to German Literature,* p. 758.

6. In Part 2 of his narrative Harkort names and describes briefly thirteen of his prison comrades. See Eduard Harkort, *Aus Mejicanischen Gefängnissen,* pp. 86–88.

7. Green, *Journal of the Texian Expedition*, p. 240, estimated the prison courtyard to be "about five hundred feet square," whereas McCutchan, *Mier Expedition Diary*, p. 105, estimated the area at "about one hundred yards square." Evidently, Harkort and his fellow captives were allowed to exercise only in a small corner of the large courtyard.

8. Bell, *Mier Prisoners in Mexico*, p. 58, complained, too, of "the putrid air of a room in which thirty men were confined."

9. *El Constitucional* was, until June 15, 1832, a daily newspaper published in Jalapa. After June 17, 1832, it appeared three times a week. Steven M. Charno, comp., *Latin American Newspapers in United States Libraries: A Union List* p. 293.

10. The *jarana* (spelled *garana* by Harkort) is a medium-sized instrument of the guitar family, usually with five double courses of strings. It is associated with the regional song and dance of the Yucatan peninsula and with the Veracruz region (*son jarocho*) of Mexico. Stanley Sadie, ed., *The New Grove Dictionary of Music and Musicians*, 20 vols. (London: Macmillan, 1980), IX, 555, XII, 232–34. Hereafter, Spanish words and proper nouns from the original German edition, that I have corrected will be cited parenthetically in the text as follows: [Kühne: *garana*].

11. Ernst Friedrich Adolf Hegewisch (1802–1868) was a native of Hanover, Germany. After earning the doctorate of medicine in 1825 at the University of Göttingen, he was sent to Mexico in February, 1827, as company physician for the Mexican Company. After only a year or two, however, he left the company and established a private practice in Oaxaca. During the Federalist revolt of 1832, Hegewisch was first adjutant in Santa Anna's army medical corps. After a distinguished medical career in Mexico, including an appointment as inspector general of the military medical corps in 1854, he died in Veracruz on June 28, 1868. Photocopy, Birth Record Book (1802), p. 81, no. 62, of the Aegidienkirche in Hanover, supplied by the Evangelisch-lutheranischer Kirchenverband, Hanover (July 16, 1982); letter, Archiv der Georg-August-Universität Göttingen to LEB (July 13, 1982); Mexican Company, *Second Annual General Meeting*, pp. 8, 10–11; photocopy, "Extracto de antecedentes militares . . . de Inspector General del Cuerpo Médico Militar Adolfo Hegewisch," Archivo Militar, Secretaría de la Defensa Nacional, Mexico City (Feb. 26, 1945), supplied by Adolf Hegewisch's great-grandson, A. E. Hegewisch, of Mexico City; José A. López, "El Dr. D. Adolfo Hegewisch," *El Progreso* (June 30, 1868); Wilhelm Pferdekamp, *Auf Humboldts Spuren: Deutsche im jungen Mexiko*, pp. 224–25.

12. I could locate no record of the Freiberg Literary Society (Litterarischer Verein zu Freiberg). The director of the municipal library in Freiberg could corroborate only that an organization by that name had once existed. Letter, Leiterin der Städtischen Bücherei Freiberg to LEB (Feb. 15, 1982).

13. The expression "Glück Auf!" or "Glückauf!" is an idiomatic variation on the noun *Glück* (luck, fortune, good luck; success; happiness), which has been a traditional greeting among miners since about 1700. Friedrich Kluge and Walther Mitzka, *Etymologisches Wörterbuch der deutschen Sprache*, 20th ed. (Berlin: Walter de Gruyter, 1967), p. 262; *Brockhaus Enzyklopädie*, 17th ed., 20 vols. (Wiesbaden: F. A. Brockhaus, 1966–1974), VII, 414.

2. Mr. Obicini's Insults

1. Ambrosio Obicini is not named in the Mexican Company's *Report of the Directors* for either 1827 or 1828. I could not locate a subsequent report.

2. I could locate no record of Harkort's map of the state of Oaxaca.

3. According to the company report submitted by Justus Ludwig von Uslar, chief director of mines for the Mexican Company, and presented to the directors of the company at their meeting in May, 1828, there was a mine called Santa Ana in the company's northern district of Oaxaca, north of the Yavesía River, and a smelting establishment by the same name directly on the Yavesía River. Evidently, construction of the Santa Ana reduction establishment had begun just before Harkort's arrival in Oaxaca, around April, 1828, for von Uslar included in his report, dated January 6, 1828, a detailed plan for its development. Mexican Company, *Extracts*, pp. 23–24, 77–79.

The Yavesía River is minor tributary of the Río Grande de Quiotepec. Mexican Company *Extracts*, p. 6. Both Harkort and von Uslar use a colloquial abbreviation of the name, Río Grande de Quiotepec, and this river does, in fact, flow in a northerly direction immediately before joining the Río Salado. At their confluence the Quiotepec and Salado rivers form the Río Santo Domingo, which flows in an easterly direction and becomes the Río Papaloapan as it crosses the southern end of the state of Veracruz and empties into the Laguna de Alvarado on the Gulf of Mexico. Harkort's longitudinal and latitudinal coordinates agree generally with those on recent maps of the area. See Enriqueta García de Miranda and Zaida Falcón de Gyves, *Atlas: Nuevo atlas Porrúa de la república mexicana*, pp. 66–67; American Geographical Society, "Ciudad de México" (NE-14), and "Istmo de Tehuantepec" (NE-15), *Millionth Map of Hispanic America* (Baltimore: A. Hoen and Company, 1959). The maps in these two sources, as well as American Geographical Society, *Index to Map of Hispanic America, 1:1,000,000: Mexico*, and the *Diccionario Porrúa*, were invaluable aids in identifying and locating many of the villages and rivers mentioned by Harkort in his journal and letters. Unless some additional explanation is required, I shall not cite these sources each time they were consulted to corroborate Harkort's information or to correct the German editor's spelling of a proper noun.

4. Socorro was another reduction establishment that was to be used for the preparation of concentrated ore, see Mexican Company, *Extracts*, pp. 74–79.

5. In England the name Webster had been associated with fine timepieces since the early eighteenth century. Harkort's chronometer was probably a product of the firm Webster and Son in London; see G. H. Baillie et al, *Britten's Old Clocks and Watches and Their Makers . . .* , 7th ed. (New York: Crown, 1956), p. 495. I could find no information about a British manufacturer of sextants by the name of Carry.

6. The meeting of May, 1829, was the fourth annual general meeting of the proprietors of the Mexican Company. I could not corroborate the presentation of a sword to Harkort at that meeting, however, for I could not locate a published report of the meeting. As Harkort states later in his journal, he did travel to England on company business between January and July, 1829. Harkort, *Aus Mejicanischen Gefängnissen*, pp. 24–25.

Aristides F. Mornay was a management consultant to the proprietors and directors of the Mexican Company. From a "Memoir to the Chairman and Directors of the Mexican Company," dated April 14, 1827, it is evident that Mornay had a first-hand knowledge of silver mining practices in Germany and in Mexico. Mexican Company, *Second Annual General Meeting*, pp. 13–36.

7. Von Uslar evidently was dismissed from the company's service sometime between May, 1828, when the directors published his report on operations in Mexico, and May, 1829, when Harkort traveled to London for a personal report to the proprietors and directors; see note 6. I could not corroborate the salaries reported here by Harkort in any of the company reports.

8. I could not verify this figure. The "General Budget of the Mexican Company"

contained in von Uslar's report of January, 1828, shows only a salary total for all the company's skilled employees in Mexico. Mexican Company, *Extracts*, pp. 164–65.

9. Harkort's records and documents concerning the Mexican Company have been lost—either while he lived in Mexico or later by his descendants in Germany. Letter, Gertrud Herrmann-Kühne of East Berlin, Germany, to LEB (Sept. 14, 1980).

3. Ascent on Cempoaltepec

1. The Breithaupt system, named after its inventor, Johann Friedrich August Breithaupt, amounted to the "natural classification" of minerals into classes, orders, genera, and species. Gillispie, ed., *Dictionary of Scientific Biography* II, 440–41.

The Institute of Arts and Sciences in Oaxaca was founded on January 8, 1827. However, I could locate no record of Harkort's activities there.

2. The district of Zaachila is about eight kilometers southwest of the city of Oaxaca.

3. The village San Pedro Yólox is about sixty kilometers north of the city of Oaxaca. Cempoaltepec is, with an altitude of 3,396 meters (11,140 feet), the highest peak in the Cempoaltépetl region in the state of Oaxaca. José Rogelio Alvarez, ed., *Enciclopedia de México* . . . II, 238; Terry, *Guide to Mexico*, p. 541.

4. Harkort's data and experiences on Cempoaltepec are corroborated by Terry, *Guide to Mexico*, p. 541.

William Glennie was temporarily on leave from the British navy in 1827 to the United Mexican Company and was working as superintendent of some of that company's mines in Zacatecas and Sombrerete. It is reported that in 1827 he ascended Popocatépetl also. Gilmore, "British Mining Ventures," pp. 59–60; Kruse, ed., *Deutsche Briefe aus Mexiko*, p. xciv.

The volcano San Martín Tuxtla is in the Sierra de los Tuxtlas range in the state of Veracruz.

5. Among the western Mixes of Oaxaca, such offerings were made to the spirits of lightning and the wind to secure rain and good crops. This ceremony is described in detail by Frances Toor, *A Treasury of Mexican Folkways*, p. 36.

6. Unfortunately, Harkort's blue flower on Cerro Cempoaltepec could not be identified, for the name *Cempoaltepecana* indicates neither the plant family nor the species of the flower in question. For this information, I am indebted to C. H. Muller, professor emeritus of botany at the University of California, Santa Barbara. Letter, C. H. Muller to LEB (Feb. 2, 1983).

7. Harkort appears to have come across some colonial *lienzos*, historical-cartographical Indian documents delineating native land boundaries. See Alvarez, ed., *Enciclopedia de México* VIII, 72–92.

4. Excursion into the Mountains

1. The revolution in Piedmont, the region in northwest Italy bordering on France and Switzerland, broke out on March 10, 1821. The leaders of the revolt, which was more like a pronouncement than a popular uprising, were military officers and members of court circles. George R. Potter et al., eds., *The New Cambridge Modern History*, 14 vols. (Cambridge: Cambridge University Press, 1957–1970), IX, 433–34.

2. The silver peso or *piaster* was in Harkort's time the monetary unit of Mexico. The Mexican peso and the American dollar were approximately equal in value. Joseph Burkart, *Aufenthalt und Reisen in Mexico in den Jahren 1825 bis 1834: Bemerkungen*

über Land, Produkte, Leben und Sitten der Einwohner . . . I, x; Robert W. Randall, *Real del Monte: A British Mining Venture in Mexico*, p. xv.

3. The noun *topil* is derived from the Aztec word *topilli* and was the title given to an Indian who performed minor civil and judicial duties in his village. Francisco J. Santamaría, *Diccionario de mejicanismos*, p. 1073.

4. The villages San Andrés Zautla and Santo Tomás Mazaltepec are located northwest of the city of Oaxaca.

5. I could not find Kühne's word in any Germany dictionary, contemporary or modern. Harkort probably wrote *Rohrenstaken*, which would mean "palisade fence of bamboo," and which seems appropriate to the scene he describes.

Village feuds over territorial boundaries were evidently common in Mexico—even into the twentieth century. See Anita Brenner, *Idols behind Altars*, p. 121.

5. Nocturnal Indian Ceremonies

1. Harkort possibly witnessed an Indian variation on the fiesta of Candlemas, which is celebrated in the churches of Mexico on February 2, with the blessing of candles, seeds, and sometimes even animals. Toor, *Mexican Folkways*, p. 193.

6. Outbreak of the Revolution

1. The Gulf of Tehuantepec and the Bay of Acapulco are on the Pacific coast of Mexico, in the states of Oaxaca and Guerrero, respectively.

2. The Tehuantepec River originates southeast of the city of Oaxaca.

The Río Coatzacoalcos originates in the state of Oaxaca on the northern slope of the Sierra Atravesada range. It is joined from the west by the Jaltepec River, which originates in the Sierra de los Mijes, near the Tehuantepec River. It is the proximity of the Jaltepec River and the Tehuantepec River that Harkort probably wished to investigate, and which in later years prompted some interest in constructing a canal across the Isthmus of Tehuantepec to connect the Atlantic and Pacific oceans.

3. The region between Tehuacán, in the state of Puebla, and Oaxaca is very mountainous, characterized by rocky canyons, deep gorges, and high cliffs. Today the two cities are connected both by rail and by a major highway. See Terry, *Guide to Mexico*, pp. 526–28.

4. A *pronunciamiento* was issued on January 2, 1832, not by Santa Anna, but by Col. Pedro Landero, commander of the military garrison at Veracruz. The same day, Santa Anna was invited to join the revolt, but he declined at first, preferring to play initially the role of mediator between the government and the rebels. The pronouncement is reproduced in full in José María Bocanegra, ed., *Memorias para la historia de México independiente, 1822–1846* II, 265–68. For a complete account of Santa Anna's role in the revolt, see Hubert Howe Bancroft, *History of Mexico (The Works of Hubert Howe Bancroft)* V, 104–108; Callcott, *Santa Anna*, pp. 86–90; Manuel Rivera Cambas, *Historia antigua y moderna de Jalapa y de las revoluciones del estado de Veracruz*, 2nd ed. (17 vols; Mexico City: Editorial Citaltépetl, 1959–1960), VI, 107–16; Juan Suárez y Navarro, *Historia de México y del General Antonio López de Santa Anna* . . . I, 262–67.

At the time of the revolt in Veracruz, Anastasio Bustamante was no longer vice-president, but in fact president of Mexico. Callcott, *Santa Anna*, pp. 84–88; Jones, *Santa Anna*, pp. 52–53.

5. There were four ministers in Bustamante's cabinet: Alamán was minister of domestic and foreign relations; Mangino y Mendívil, minister of the treasury; Facio, minister of war and the navy; and José Ignacio Espinoza Vidaurre, minister of justice and ecclesiastical affairs. The proclamation demanded chiefly (1) a renewal of the government's obligation to observe faithfully the federal constitution and laws and (2) the dismissal of the ministers who were perceived to be promoting centralism and tolerating abuses of civil liberties. Bancroft, *History of Mexico* V, 107–108.

Harkort refers to a plan, allegedly developed in 1830 in Europe, to enthrone in Mexico a prince of the Orleans family. Bancroft, *History of Mexico* V, 76; Lorenzo de Zavala, *Ensayo crítico de las revoluciones de México desde 1808 hasta 1830*, pp. 486–88.

6. On January 4, Santa Anna wrote Bustamante offering his services as mediator and included copies of the *pronunciamiento*. By January 11, these dispatches had been received in the capital and the ministers had submitted their resignations, which were not accepted. Bustamante's endorsement of his minsters, who were supported also by the congress, amounted to a complete rejection of the rebels' demands. The same day, José Antonio Facio departed for Jalapa to organize his forces of resistance. As late as January 25, Santa Anna sent a second letter to Bustamante, repeating his ostensible desire to mediate and urging negotiation. Bancroft, *History of Mexico* V, 108–109; Callcott, *Santa Anna*, pp. 89–90.

7. See note 4. Veracruz, Mexico's chief port of commerce with Europe and the United States, appears to have been fiercely loyal to Santa Anna and the other rebels. Facio tried to bribe the commandant of San Juan de Ulúa fortress, Lt. Col. José María Flores, to issue a counterpronouncement against Santa Anna, Landero, and the other insurgents, but the offer was rejected. Bancroft, *History of Mexico* V, 109.

8. Harkort refers here to the political maneuvers of Vice-President Bustamante between December, 1829, and February, 1830, to force Vicente Guerrero from the presidency. After his overthrow and until his death in February, 1831, Guerrero tried unsuccessfully to launch a general revolution against Bustamante from the region near Acapulco in the present state of Guerrero. Ibid., pp. 88–96. The region was near but not in the state of Oaxaca, as Harkort seemed to think.

9. Harkort's account is completely correct. Cuilapa is now called Ciudad Guerrero. For a complete account of the entire incident, see Bancroft, *History of Mexico* V, 96–101. The term *picaluganos* appears in ibid., p. 131. The eponym *picalugada* appears, however, to have passed out of use in Mexico. It is not listed in Santamaría, *Diccionario de mejicanismos*.

10. Harkort refers to Santa Anna's support of Vicente Guerrero from September to December, 1828, in the latter's struggle for the presidency against Manuel Gómez Pedraza, the president-elect and former minister of war in the administration of Guadalupe Victoria; see Callcott, *Santa Anna*, pp. 64–70; Jones, *Santa Anna*, pp. 46–48.

11. See note 6. On January 11, Bustamante's minister of war, José Antonio Facio, left Mexico City for Jalapa to organize a strong division, which was placed under the command of Gen. José María Calderón. Bancroft, *History of Mexico* V, 109.

12. By "northern coast," Harkort means the Gulf of Mexico; the southern coast is, of course, the Pacific coast.

Juan Alvarez (1790–1867), a hero of the struggle for independence, was a staunch republican and a vigorous defender of federalism. In 1830, while Vicente Guerrero was president, Alvarez was given the rank of brigadier general. In December, 1830, after being forced from the presidency by Bustamante, Guerrero found a ready ally in

Alvarez. After Guerrero's execution in 1831, Alvarez energetically opposed Bustamante. *Diccionario Porrúa* I, 87; Alberto María Carreño, ed., *Jefes del ejército mexicano en 1847: Biografías de generales de división y de brigada y de coroneles del ejército mexicano por fines del año de 1847,* pp. 57–59; Manuel García Purón, *México y sus gobernantes: Biografías,* pp. 194–95.

13. The Mixtec region, in Spanish la Mixteca, is the linguistic and anthropological designation for the area in the northern and western parts of the state of Oaxaca inhabited by the Mixtec Indians. Robert Ravicz and A. Kimball Romney, "The Mixtec," *Handbook of Middle American Indians,* ed. Robert Wauchope, 16 vols. (Austin: University of Texas Press, 1964–1976), VII, 367–69.

7. Harkort Meets Santa Anna

1. The revolt of 1828 began ten days after the presidential elections of September 1, 1828, in which Manuel Gómez Pedraza, the centralist candidate, had defeated the federalist candidate, Vicente Guerrero. The revolution was led by Santa Anna, who in a *pronunciamiento* issued at Perote fortress, called for the substitution of Guerrero for the president-elect, Gómez Pedraza. Bancroft, *History of Mexico* V, 42; Callcott, *Santa Anna,* pp. 64–66; Jones, *Santa Anna,* pp. 46–47.

2. The town of San Andrés Chalchicomula is now called Ciudad Serdán. Concerning Harkort's trip to England in 1829, see episode 2.

3. Harkort's account is essentially correct; see note 1. Vastly outnumbered by the combined government forces of Generals Manuel Rincón and José María Calderón advancing on his position at Perote fortress, Santa Anna had fled south to the city of Oaxaca about the middle of October, 1828. With his small force of about eight hundred men, he had then seized Oaxaca and fortified his position in the convent of Santo Domingo. The pursuing army, now led by Calderón, lay siege to the city. The following January the siege was lifted after a revolt in Mexico City had resulted in Vicente Guerrero's becoming president. Hence, Santa Anna held off Calderón's forces for about three months. Callcott, *Santa Anna,* pp. 67–69; Jones, *Santa Anna,* pp. 47–48; Magner, *Men of Mexico,* pp. 316–17; Fay[ette] Robinson, *Mexico and Her Military Chieftains, from the Revolution of Hidalgo to the Present Time, . . .* pp. 156–59.

4. Duke Friedrich Wilhelm von Braunschweig-Oels (1771–1815) was an officer in the Prussian army during the Napoleonic Wars. Upon the outbreak of the Austrian revolt in 1809, he raised a regiment of cavalry and, with the support of Austrian troops, succeeded in capturing Leipzig and Dresden. *Meyers Konversations-Lexikon,* 4th ed., 19 vols. (Leipzig: Verlag des Bibliographischen Instituts, 1889–1892), VI, 701; Ernest F. Henderson, *Blücher and the Uprising of Prussia against Napoleon, 1806–1815* (New York: G. P. Putnam's Sons, 1911), p. 48.

Harkort is no doubt referring to the surrender of Lt. Col. Timoteo Reyes at Etla on November 1, 1828. The Etla valley and the district by the same name are directly north of the city of Oaxaca. Suárez y Navarro, *Historia de México* I, 116–18.

5. Gebhard Leberecht Blücher (1742–1819) was the dynamic commander of the Prussian army in the Napoleonic Wars. Indeed, in 1815 Blücher captured the minds and hearts of the Germans with his feats and became almost overnight a national hero. David I. Eggenberger, ed., *The McGraw-Hill Encyclopedia of World Biography,* 12 vols. (New York: McGraw-Hill, 1973), II, 26–27; Henderson, *Blücher,* pp. 283–309, 333.

Ferdinand von Schill (1776–1809) was a major in the Prussian army who, upon the outbreak of Austrian opposition to Napoleon in 1809, tried to draw Prussia into the conflict by riding out of Berlin with his regiment of hussars and personally declaring war on France. Henderson, *Blücher,* p. 49; *Meyers Konversations-Lexikon* XIV, 473.

In the army of Frederick the Great there were ten hussar regiments. They wore green, red, blue, and white uniforms, although the officers generally wore a red-lined panther skin. Preben Kannik, *Military Uniforms in Color* (New York: Macmillan, 1968), p. 165; I. T. Schick, ed., *Battledress: The Uniforms of the World's Great Armies 1700 to the Present* (Boston: Little, Brown, 1978), pp. 42, 114.

6. Harkort's new friend and fencing opponent was Mariano Arista (1802–1855), who in 1828 held the rank of lieutenant colonel. In 1828 Arista still had a successful military career ahead of him, becoming in 1848 secretary of war and the navy, and from 1851 to 1853 president of Mexico. Miguel Angel Peral, *Diccionario biográfico mexicano,* pp. 65–66; Carreño, ed., *Jefes del ejército mexicano,* pp. 44–53; García Purón, *México y sus gobernantes,* pp. 189–90.

7. Harkort means July, 1829, for if he had been in London at a meeting of the proprietors of the Mexican Company in May, as he stated earlier (see episode 2), he would have scarcely had time to return to Mexico in less than a month. Moreover, the Spanish expeditionary force under Brig. Gen. Isidro Barradas did not sail from Havana until the sixth or seventh of July, and Santa Anna did not even begin preparations to repel the invaders until July 16. The Spanish landed on July 27 at Cabo Rojo, near Tampico. Bancroft, *History of Mexico* V, 72–73; Jones, *Santa Anna,* pp. 49–50; Miguel A. Sánchez Lamego, *La invasión española de 1829,* pp. 26–27.

Encero was a small village three leagues (eight miles) southeast of Jalapa, on the road to Veracruz; see Edward Thornton Tayloe, *Mexico 1825–1828: The Journal and Correspondence of Edward Thornton Tayloe,* p. 25; and Lyon, *Journal of a Residence* II, 205.

8. Harkort fails to mention that while Santa Anna was sailing with about six hundred or seven hundred infantry troops to Tuxpán, a village on the coast south of Tampico, his cavalry was advancing by land to the same destination. In all, Santa Anna raised an army of about two thousand men. From Tuxpán they marched north to Puebla Viejo, a village on the Pánuco River, just opposite the Spaniards' position in Tampico. The circumstances and conditions of Barradas's surrender to Santa Anna on September 11, 1829, can be found in Callcott, *Santa Anna,* pp. 74–75; Jones, *Santa Anna,* pp. 50–51; Sánchez Lamego, *La invasión española,* pp. 59–63; Zavala, *Ensayo crítico,* pp. 436–46.

9. The Plan of Jalapa was a proclamation issued in December, 1829, and devised by then-vice-president Anastasio Bustamante to force President Vicente Guerrero from office. The plan called for the reinstatement of the Constitution of 1824, which had been violated by the selection of Guerrero to replace Manuel Gómez Pedraza as president. Although it ostensibly sought the installation of Gómez Pedraza in the presidency, the Plan of Jalapa was Bustamante's instrument to put himself in the executive office. Callcott, *Santa Anna,* p. 82.

I could not establish the identity of Harkort's friend Don Vicente.

10. Lieutenant Colonel Ortiz is probably Ignacio Ortiz, who served in Santa Anna's rebel army in September, 1828, as commander of artillery; see Rivera Cambas, *Historia antigua* V, 124–27; and note 1 above.

8. Departure for Veracruz

1. See episode 2, note 3, and episode 3, note 3.
2. Valentín Canalizo (1794–1850) supported the conservative centralist party dur-

ing the federalist-centralist struggles in Mexico after the fall of Iturbide in 1823. For his part in helping Bustamante force Guerrero from the presidency in 1830, Canalizo was given the rank of general and the command of the district of Oaxaca. Bancroft, *History of Mexico* V, 258; Carreño, ed., *Jefes del ejército mexicano*, p. 89; García Purón, *México y sus gobernantes*, pp. 180–81.

3. Harkort is probably referring to *cacalosúchil* (derived from the Aztec noun *caclotl*), which is an apocynaceous plant and a member of the dogbane family. Santamaría, *Diccionario de mejicanismos*, pp. 170–71.

4. Harkort is in error here. He is probably referring to the surrender of a unit of government forces under the command of Lt. Col. Timoteo Reyes on November 1, 1828. The main body of government troops under General Calderón subsequently pursued Santa Anna into the city of Oaxaca; see episode 7, notes 3 and 4.

5. Ohnewitz is the name of a fictitious village in the mock-heroic verse epic by Carl Arnold Kortum, *Leben, Meynungen und Thaten von Hieronimus Jobs.* . . . The epic was published in 1784, and in 1799 it was continued in two parts under a new title, *Die Jobsiade.* In chapter 30 of the first part, the young schoolmaster Hieronimus Jobs is driven from the village of Ohnewitz for introducing several innovations in the school curriculum. Like the Indians in Harkort's experience, the farmers of Ohnewitz are hostile to what they do not understand and arm themselves with clubs and flails to repel the intruder. Carl Arnold Kortum, *Die Jobsiade*, 7th ed., 3 vols. (Leipzig: F. A. Brockhaus, 1854), I, 138–39; see also Garland and Garland, *Oxford Companion to German Literature*, p. 489.

9. *Lerche's Troubles*

1. The mine formerly supervised by Lerche was in the northern district of mines worked by the Mexican Company and was called Nuestra Señora de Guadalupe or simply Plomosa. Mexican Company, *Extracts*, p. 24.

2. The main base of the Tlalpujahua Company was located in the village by that name on the eastern boundary of the present state of Michoacán, adjacent ot the state of Mexico. This company, which was formed in 1825, had succumbed by the end of 1828 to the financial and physical hazards of mining in Mexico. Vicente Rivafinoli was the company's managing director in Mexico. The chief director of mining operations was Joseph Burkart, who later became director of the Bolaños Company. Gilmore, "British Mining Ventures," pp. 101–108; Burkart, *Aufenthalt und Reisen in Mexico* I, 75–101; Randall, *Real Del Monte*, p. 40.

3. Lerche must have been dismissed in early September, 1828, for by the end of the month, Rincón had left the capital for Perote. Callcott, *Santa Anna*, pp. 65–67; Rivera Cambas, *Historia antigua* V, 129.

Harkort's information about the course of events following Santa Anna's *pronunciamiento* on September 11, 1828, seems to be slightly confused. I could find no record of a battle at Jalapa. Perhaps he is referring to Santa Anna's retreat early in October to a position in the *mal país* about ten miles east of Perote before the advance of Rincón, and where he intercepted government dispatches indicating the approach of General Calderón. See Callcott, *Santa Anna*, pp. 67–68; Rivera Cambas, *Historia antigua* V, 129–36; and episode 7, note 3.

4. Santa Anna returned to Jalapa victorious in February, 1829. Callcott, *Santa Anna*, p. 70.

5. Justus Ludwig von Uslar was chief director of mines for the Mexican Company

from February, 1827, to sometime after May, 1828. Harkort held that position after von Uslar's dismissal until his own resignation in October, 1831. Von Uslar evidently found employment with another mining company near Oaxaca after leaving the Mexican Company. Mexican Company, *Second Annual General Meeting*, pp. 8, 10–11; Harkort, *Aus Mejicanischen Gefängnissen*, pp. 16–18; episode 2, note 7.

6. Wiedu is possibly Lerche's variation on the Germanic name Wido. Lerche is perhaps paying mock homage to the Westphalian chieftain Widukind, who about the year 775 led the Saxons against Charlemagne. Adolf Bach, *Deutsche Namenkunde*, 3 vols. (Heidelberg: Carl Winter Universitätsverlag, 1952–1956), vol. 1, pt. 2, pp. 8, 61; *Brockhaus Enzyklopädie* XX, 300.

10. Churches of the Indians

1. For a contemporary description of Etla and San Juan del Estado, see Eduard Mühlenpfordt, *Versuch einer getreuen Schilderung der Republik Mexiko* II, 187–89.

2. Others shared Harkort's observations on the Mexicans' musical sense. See Calderón de la Barca, *Life in Mexico*, pp. 169, 441, 472; and Carl Sartorius, *Mexico about 1850*, p. 125.

3. This view is expressed also by Waddy Thompson, *Recollections of Mexico*, pp. 107, 189; and Sartorius, *Mexico about 1850*, p. 76.

4. The Indians' apparent indifference to Christian dogma and their devout worship of Christian representations of native Indian deities are described also by Calderón de la Barca, *Life in Mexico*, pp. 430–31.

5. Harkort's analogy is sheer hyperbole, of course, but Fanny Calderón de la Barca was moved also to write of such "human sacrifices" in Mexico City. Ibid., pp. 258, 263, 267.

6. The Indians' covert worship of their native images and deities was reported also a little over a decade later in 1847 by Thompson, *Recollections of Mexico*, p. 189. For a thorough discussion of the unique blending of the Christian and native Indian religions in Mexico, see Brenner, *Idols behind Altars*, pp. 127–56.

11. Corruption among the Clergy

1. Waddy Thompson expressed the same low opinion of the clergy in Mexico, noting also that many of the priests "have several nephews and nieces in their houses or, at least, those who *call them uncle.*" Thompson, *Recollections of Mexico*, pp. 115, 247.

2. These villages are all in the state of Oaxaca.

Harkort's description of the Catholic church's extreme neglect of its Indian parishioners in Mexico could not be corroborated in other contemporary sources. Indeed, one of the Texan prisoners in Perote fortress a decade later had only praise for the rural clergy, while deploring the licentiousness of the clergy in Mexico City. Stapp, *Prisoners of Perote*, p. 195.

3. These Indian rituals, which Harkort knew only from hearsay, perhaps, are similar to those performed by the western Mixes of Oaxaca; see Toor, *Mexican Folkways*, p. 36.

4. Vicente Rocafuerte (1783–1847) was a native of Ecuador. He was educated at Madrid and Paris and became a career diplomat first in 1812 as Guayaquil's representative to the Spanish Cortes, and then in 1824 as secretary to the Mexican legation in London. He went to Mexico in 1830 to serve in the foreign ministry under Lucas

Alamán. A reformer at heart, Rocafuerte published, in 1830 and 1831, respectively, two proposals for reform, the first on the judicial system in Mexico, and the second on religious freedom. It is to the latter, the *Ensayo sobre la tolerancia religiosa* (Mexico City, 1831), that Harkort refers. The publication of this work, which called for the deletion of that article in the constitution prohibiting in Mexico all religions but the Roman Catholic faith, immediately unleashed a storm of controversy. Rocafuerte was formally accused by the Catholic church of subverting the constitution. The entire affair is described in great detail by Carl Wilhelm Koppe, *Mexicanische Zustände aus den Jahren 1830 bis 1832.* . . . I, 322–27; William J. McDonald, et al., eds., *The New Catholic Encyclopedia*, 16 vols. (New York: McGraw-Hill, 1967–1974), XII, 539–40; and Charles A. Hale, *Mexican Liberalism in the Age of Mora, 1821–1853*, p. 165.

5. A Spanish foot was a lineal unit in the old Castilian system of weights and measures. There were 3 feet (*pies*) in one *vara*, which was equivalent to 2.784 feet in the British system. Hence, one Spanish foot was equivalent to 0.909 feet in the British system.

12. A Previous Trip to Oaxaca

1. In 1826 it was reported that the mines of Zomelahuacán were being worked by the Mexican Company. Lyon, *Journal of a Residence* II, 173–75.

2. The Río Frío is also called the Río San Martín.

3. According to an American traveler on this route in the 1820s, the distance between Mexico City and Puebla was twenty-six leagues, or about seventy miles. Hence, Harkort's coach would have been traveling at the rate of about seven miles an hour. A good rate of speed in those years for that particular route was a mere five miles an hour. Tayloe, *Mexico 1825–1828*, p. 199; Joel R. Poinsett, *Notes on Mexico, Made in the Autumn of 1822*, p. 38.

4. The city of Tehuacán is today about eighty miles from the city of Puebla. Hereafter, following each of Harkort's references to distance in leagues, I shall supply in brackets within the text of the journal the approximate equivalent distance in miles, based on the ratio of 2.633 English miles to the league; see Tayloe, *Mexico 1825–1828*, p. 22.

5. The *armas de agua* or *armas de pelo* was, as Harkort states, a protective blanket made of cured goat pelts and was attached to the rider's waist or to the saddlebow to cover the rider's legs and feet. It could also be spread on the ground for sleeping. Santamaría, *Diccionario de mejicanismos*, p. 80; Tayloe, *Mexico 1825–1828*, p. 80.

6. I could find no village by the name of Venta on the route between Puebla and Tehuacán. The German (and Harkort's) practice of capitalizing all nouns must have misled the German editor to think that *venta*, meaning a roadside inn or, here, a way station, was a proper noun.

13. A Marathon on Horseback

1. The village San Sebastián Nicananduta is about midway along the route between Tehuacán and the city of Oaxaca.

2. Don Dominguillo, according to Mühlenpfordt, *Schilderung der Republik Mexiko* II, 208, was a small village on the left bank of the Río de las Vueltas. On modern maps it appears as Santiago Dominguillo. American Geographical Society, "Ciudad de México" (NE-14), 18–97d.

3. The village of Aragón adjoined a sugar plantation. Mühlenpfordt, *Schilderung der Republik Mexiko* II, 209; and episode 14.

4. The distance by highway today from Mexico City to Oaxaca is about 300 miles. Harkort's estimate of 127 leagues, i.e., 300 miles, is correct. Frances Toor, *Frances Toor's New Guide to Mexico* . . . , pp. 200–202.

14. The Torrid Region

1. The village of San Juan del Estado is situated at an altitude of 1,670 meters (5,478 feet). Cuesta de San Juan must refer to a mountain ridge above the village.

2. Aragón's situation at an altitude of 3,862 feet would place it not in the torrid or tropic zone, but within the temperate zone, i.e., the *tierra templada*. The torrid zone, called the *tierra caliente* in Mexico, begins at the seacoast and extends inland to an altitude of about 3,000 feet.

3. Harkort lists these rivers in the order that he approached them, traveling south to north. The Río de las Vueltas is a tributary of the Río Grande de Quiotepec, which at its confluence with the Río Salado forms the Río Santo Domingo.

4. According to C. H. Muller, professor emeritus of botany at the University of California, Santa Barbara, Harkort's phrase *Cactus polygenetus* is apparently a *nomen nudum*, i.e., a Latin botanical binomial within the genus *Cactus* that was never published in conjunction with a suitable description of the species intended. Letter, C. H. Muller to LEB (Nov. 10, 1982). The name does not appear in Joseph D. Hooker and B. Dayton Jackson, comps., *Index Kewensis: An Enumeration of the Genera and Species of Flowering Plants from the Time of Linnaeus to the Year 1885*, 2 vols. (1895; reprint ed., Oxford: Clarendon Press, 1946, 1960), I, 367–69. According to Terry, *Guide to Mexico*, p. 527, the hillsides north of Oaxaca are "covered with many huge specimens of organ and candelabra cacti."

5. *Tepache* (from the Aztec noun *tepiatl*), is, as Harkort describes it, a fermented beverage prepared from the juice of several fruits, but commonly from the juice of sugarcane or pineapple. Santamaría, *Diccionario de mejicanismos*, p. 1031; see also Sartorius, *Mexico about 1850*, p. 75.

6. I could locate no village by the name of Atatlanta. San Juan Bautista Atlatlahuaca is located about fifty kilometers (thirty-one miles) north of the city of Oaxaca, on the Río de las Vueltas. Mühlenpfordt, *Schilderung der Republik Mexiko* II, 209, also mentions a village Atatlaúca at this location.

7. Don Dominguillo is now called Santiago Dominguillo; see episode 13, note 2.

8. I could locate no town or village by the name of Puente Colorado. From Harkort's description, it appears to be at or near the town of Esperanza. Terry, *Guide to Mexico*, p. 495.

9. In January, 1829, Harkort had accompanied Santa Anna from a point near the city of Oaxaca to San Andrés Chalchicomula, on the latter's return to Jalapa. See episode 7. I could not corroborate Harkort's report of a breakfast at Puente Colorado to honor Santa Anna, the leader of the revolt to place Vicente Guerrero in the presidency. There is no basis for doubting his story, however, for just a few days earlier Santa Anna had been similarly honored in Oaxaca. Ralph Roeder, *Juárez and His Mexico: A Biographical History* I, 50.

10. The gorge to which Harkort refers is probably Boca del Monte, the lowest point in the Cumbres del Maltrata, a part of the Sierra Madre Oriental range. See Terry, *Guide to Mexico*, pp. 494–95; *Diccionario Porrúa* I, 728, II, 1244.

11. The valley of Orizaba lies in the temperate region and is still reputed to produce some of the best coffee in Mexico. Terry, *Guide to Mexico*, pp. 489–90; *Diccionario Porrúa* II, 1,525.

12. Córdoba is located about thirty kilometers (nineteen miles) east of Orizaba. As in Harkort's time, coffee and tobacco are still two of the chief agricultural products of the region. Terry, *Guide to Mexico*, pp. 487–89; see also Sartorius, *Mexico about 1850*, p. 175; and Frederick A. Ober, *Travels in Mexico and Life among the Mexicans*, rev. ed. (Boston: Estes & Lauriat, 1887), pp. 202–209.

15. Traveling Companions in Orizaba

1. Medellín, or Medellín de Bravo, is sixteen kilometers (ten miles) south of the city of Veracruz.

2. The *pitorreal* is the name given to members of the family *Trogonidae* in Mexico. These tropical birds are noted for their colorful, lustrous plumage. Based on the noun *pito*, meaning whistle or horn, the name apparently derives from a reference to the bird's large beak, and not to its diet, as Harkort seems to think: Santamaría, *Diccionario de mejicanismos*, pp. 864–65; Alvarez, ed., *Enciclopedia de México* X, 618; Emmet Reid Blake, *Birds of Mexico: A Guide for Field Identification* (Chicago: University of Chicago Press, 1953), pp. 269–74.

16. The Outpost

1. The village of Pocitos, located just 1 league (2.6 miles) from the city of Veracruz, became well known during the so-called Pastry War with the French in 1838 as the site where Santa Anna lost his left leg to grapeshot from a French cannon. Callcott, *Santa Anna*, pp. 158–60; Rafael F. Muñoz, *Santa Anna: El que todo lo ganó y todo lo perdió* p. 155.

2. I could not locate a poem or prose narrative with the title "Scottish Highland Outpost," by Walter Scott. Harkort is referring perhaps to Scott's description of the Highlanders' camp in the novel *Waverly* on the day before the battle at the village of Preston, near Edinburgh. See Walter Scott, *Waverly; or 'Tis Sixty Years Since*, in *Waverly Novels* 25 vols. (Edinburgh: Adam & Charles Black, 1852–1871), I, 370–74.

3. A British traveler in Veracruz shortly before Harkort's arrival there described Santa Anna's troops in similar terms. See Henry Tudor, *Narrative of a Tour in North America . . .* II, 164–65.

Bell, *Mier Prisoners in Mexico*, p. 78, remarked also that every man in the region of Veracruz wore on his belt a "cutlas or short sword."

17. Reporting to the General

1. The gate called la Merced was located on the south wall of the city, on the road to Orizaba. A contemporary plan of Veracruz can be found in Bancroft, *History of Mexico* V, 443.

2. The *posada nacional* was apparently a popular lodging house in Veracruz, although I could find no reference to it by other visitors to the city in contemporary travel accounts.

3. Upon receiving the *pronunciamiento* of January 2, 1832, from Veracruz, the government had immediately begun preparations for resistance; see episode 6, note 6. A

division had been organized under the command of Gen. José María Calderón, who by the end of January, 1832, had begun slowly marching his troops to Veracruz. By February 21, Calderón had still not reached the village of Santa Fe, only twenty-five leagues (sixty-six miles) from Jalapa. Bancroft, *History of Mexico* V, 109; Rivera Cambas, *Historia antigua*, VI, 123; Suárez y Navarro, *Historia de México* I, 275.

4. See *El Censor* (Veracruz, March 3, 1832); Callcott, *Santa Anna*, pp. 90–91; and Suárez y Navarro, *Historia de México* I, 276, place the attack a day later, on February 25.

18. A False Alarm

1. The events of this episode occurred on February 26, i.e., "the next afternoon" after Harkort's arrival in Veracruz. The reference to Santa Anna's "victory two days ago" appears to confirm the date of that event as February 24.

19. New Entrenchments

1. For a history and description of the port fortress of San Juan de Ulúa, see Terry, *Guide to Mexico*, pp. 477–80.

2. Antigua is a village on the Gulf Coast where the Río de la Antigua empties into the Gulf of Mexico, about thirty kilometers (twenty miles) north of the city of Veracruz. Evidently, Harkort's plan was to be able to retreat to the coast, and from there back to Veracruz.

20. Arrival of the General

1. On March 1, General Calderón had begun a slow countermarch from Santa Fe back to Jalapa, progressing no farther, however, than Boquerón, a small village a couple of leagues north of Santa Fe. Santa Anna's successful attack on the government convoy recently had allegedly prompted Calderón to return to Puente Nacional to avoid being cut off from Jalapa by Santa Anna's highly mobile insurgents. Moreover, in Veracruz the season of the *vomito* (yellow fever) was just beginning, ·and it was starting to affect Calderón's troops. Callcott, *Santa Anna*, p. 91; Suárez y Navarro, *Historia de México* I, 276.

2. Manantiales, also called El Manantial, was a stagecoach stop 4 leagues (10.5 miles) north of Santa Fé. Tayloe, *Mexico, 1825–1828*, p. 22.

3. Harkort is inconsistent in describing the strength of Santa Anna's forces. Here he refers to "our division," whereas in the next episode he ponders "the sleeping soldiers of the battalion." According to one early source, Santa Anna had a total force of eleven hundred men, consisting of about six hundred infantry and five hundred cavalry troops, against thirty-six hundred government troops under General Calderón. Suárez y Navarro, *Historia de México* I, 277.

The strength of a battalion or division in the Mexican army at this time appears to have varied greatly, even from state to state. Koppe, *Mexicanische Zustände* II, 17–19.

4. Puente Nacional was located on the main highway from Veracruz to Jalapa, about midway between the two cities. Calderón de la Barca, *Life in Mexico*, p. 68; Tayloe, *Mexico 1825–1828*, pp. 22–23.

5. Nicolás de la Portilla (1808–1873) was a career officer in the Mexican army. By 1836, a mere four years after the events reported here by Harkort, he had achieved the rank of lieutenant colonel. He was the officer in charge of the captured Texans at Goliad who carried out Santa Anna's order for their execution. In 1856 Portilla was promoted to

the rank of brigadier general, a position he used to aid the French intervention in Mexico, and in 1867 he became minister of war and the navy under Emperor Maximilian. With the fall of Maximilian, Portilla fled into exile, but he was allowed to return to Mexico shortly before his death in 1873. Peral, *Diccionario biográfico mexicano*, p. 649; Alvarez, ed., *Enciclopedia de México* X, 407; Webb, Carroll, and Branda, eds., *Handbook of Texas* II, 396.

6. Harkort refers to an incident described in Genesis 28:11–12.

21. *Preparations for Battle*

1. The actual strength of Santa Anna's forces was about eleven hundred men; see episode 20, note 3.

2. Harkort is thinking of Edward Waverly's words to his friend Fergus Mac-Ivor on the eve of the battle at Preston, as the two men walked among the sleeping Highlanders; see Scott, *Waverly Novels* I, 386.

3. Although outnumbered three to one by the government forces, Santa Anna was preparing to meet Calderón's infantry, cavalry, and artillery in battle without a single fieldpiece of his own. Muñoz, *Santa Anna*, p. 103.

4. The village of Tolomé was between El Manantial, where Calderón's army was camped, and El Paso de Ovejas, a few leagues to the north. A few leagues beyond El Paso de Ovejas was Puente Nacional. Lyon, *Journal of a Residence* II, 209–211.

5. By encircling Calderón's position at El Manantial and placing the enemy between his own forces and his stronghold in Veracruz, Santa Anna thought perhaps that he had trapped Calderón in a vise to which he could apply gradual pressure to force Calderón's surrender. Obviously, Santa Anna seriously misjudged his adversary's willingness to fight. According to two accounts, Santa Anna halted in Tolomé because of intelligence he had received about the approach of seven hundred government troops from Jalapa, led by the minister of war, José Antonio Facio, and because he was still awaiting news of a surrender or revolt at Puente Nacional. Rivera Cambas, *Historia antigua* VI, 127; Suárez y Navarro, *Historia de México* I, 276–77. Facio did not arrive with the government reinforcements, however, until the following day, March 4. Muñoz, *Santa Anna*, p. 104.

6. The first body of government troops to approach the bridge at Tolomé was the vanguard of Calderón's army. The main body of infantry, with the cavalry and artillery, did not arrive until ten o'clock, as Harkort says, an hour or so later. Suárez y Navarro, *Historia de México* I, 277.

22. *The Battle Near Tolomé*

1. According to Rivera Cambas, *Historia antigua*, VI, 127, Col. Pedro Landero had assured Santa Anna that the garrison at Puente Nacional supported the federal cause. From Harkort's subsequent remarks, it appears that Santa Anna was still expecting some desertions among Calderón's forces, or at least some news of the troops' revolt at Puente Nacional.

2. Harkort's account of the headlong flight of Santa Anna's cavalry, and of the disastrous effect it had for the outcome of the battle, was corroborated by Calderón himself, who is said to have later attributed his victory to the lack of discipline among Santa Anna's cavalry. Those troops, which Harkort calls "cossacks," were mere farmers with no combat experience. Suárez y Navarro, *Historia de México* I, 277.

Notes to pp. 59–63   149

3. According to Suárez y Navarro, *Historia de México* I, 277, Andonaegui held the rank of colonel. He and Colonel Landero, who also died in this battle (see next episode), had served under Santa Anna in 1829 to repel the Spanish invasion. Bancroft, *History of Mexico* V, 110n. A brief list of the several units in both armies, with their respective commanders, can be found in Rivera Cambas, *Historia antigua* VI, 127–28.

23. Santa Anna's Defeat

1. Santa Anna had about eleven hundred troops; Calderón had approximately thirty-six hundred; see episode 20, note 3.

2. Squares, formed by ranks of infantry facing outward and at right angles to one another to form a square, sometimes two or three ranks deep, were the common defensive strategy in Harkort's time against charging cavalry: Henry Lee Scott, *Military Dictionary: Comprising Technical Definitions; Information on Raising and Keeping Troops,* . . . (1861; reprint ed., New York: Greenwood Press, 1968), pp. 565–66. The Mexican army must have had some knowledge of infantry squares, however, for in 1847 Waddy Thompson, *Recollections of Mexico*, pp. 170–71, described how the Mexican cavalry used the lasso to breach these squares.

3. The other European officers in Santa Anna's army who took part in this battle are not named by Harkort here or elsewhere.

4. The charge was led by Col. Juan María de Azcárate, commander of the 8th Cavalry Regiment. Rivera Cambas, *Historia antigua* VI, 128.

Colonel Landero was the commander of the garrison at Veracruz and the organizer of the group of army officers there who on January 2, 1832, had issued the pronouncement against Bustamante's government. Callcott, *Santa Anna*, p. 88. At Tolomé he commanded one of the three companies in Santa Anna's army. Rivera Cambas, *Historia antigua* VI, 127.

5. Harkort is possibly in error here. I could find no reference to a 10th Regiment in other historical accounts.

6. Harkort's daughter, Henriette, born in November, 1822, was only five years old when her father left Germany in 1827, bound for Mexico. Winkhaus, *Bauern- und Schmiedegeschlecht*, pp. 64, 67.

24. Captivity

1. The doubloon (*doblón*) was a gold Spanish coin, originally worth two escudos, but later it fluctuated in value. The coins that Harkort had in his pocket were probably eight-escudo pieces, minted either before Mexico's independence or during the short reign of Iturbide. *Enciclopedia universal ilustrado europeo-americana* XVIII, pt. 2, pp. 1700–1701; *Coin World Guide to Coins* (New York: Arco, 1965), pp. 86–87.

2. Evidence of the loss in men, animals, and equipment in this battle was described by a German traveler who passed through Tolomé a month after the engagement. Koppe, *Mexicanische Zustände* II, 312–13.

Suárez y Navarro, *Historia de México* I, 277, records that Calderón took 32 officers and 413 enlisted men prisoner that day. According to Muñoz, *Santa Anna*, p. 103, more than 700 of the rebel forces were captured, killed, or wounded.

3. Harkort appears merely to be repeating an opinion expressed by another prisoner.

4. Fortunately for Santa Anna, Calderón failed to follow up on his victory at Tolomé with the anticipated swift attack on Veracruz. Instead, he confidently reported to the

government that "General Santa Anna's division has been so thoroughly defeated that he alone is not under our control." By the time Calderón had leisurely planned his next move and did advance on Veracruz, Santa Anna had already recruited two thousand more troops and had fortified the walls for the awaited attack. The quote from Calderón's report (my translation) is taken from Suárez y Navarro, *Historia de México* I, 278. See also Bancroft, *History of Mexico* V, 110; Callcott, *Santa Anna*, p. 91; and Rivera Cambas, *Historia antigua* VI, 133.

25. Fever and Delirium

1. Wermelskirchen and Hückeswagen, located about forty kilometers southwest of Harkort's home near Hagen, are in the present state of North Rhine–Westphalia, in the Federal Republic of Germany.

2. In Harkort's time Wermelskirchen and Hückeswagen were in the Prussian province of Westphalia.

26. Causes of the Defeat

1. The "public account" to which Harkort refers was probably the self-congratulatory article that appeared on March 7, 1832, in the government-owned newspaper in Mexico City, *Registro Oficial del Gobierno de los Estados Unidos Mexicanos*. The article is cited in part by Suárez y Navarro, *Historia de México* I, 277–78. Unfortunately, I could not locate a copy of *Registro Oficial del Gobierno* for March 7, 1832. See Charno, comp., *Latin American Newspapers*, p. 404.

2. Harkort's estimate of the strength of Calderón's army is also supported by later historians. See Bancroft, *History of Mexico* V, 109–10; Muñoz, *Santa Anna*, p. 103; and Suárez y Navarro, *Historia de México* I, 277.

3. Santa Anna's total lack of artillery is corroborated by Muñoz, *Santa Anna*, p. 103.

4. Harkort refers to the government convoy captured by Santa Anna on February 25 (see episode 17). Suárez y Navarro, *Historia de México* I, 276, records that the escort troops under the command of [Lt. Col. José] Pérez Palacios joined the ranks of the insurgents.

5. Harkort's source for this information was probably Santa Anna himself; see episode 22, note 1.

6. In episode 20, Harkort reports that Santa Anna had confided to his officers his plan to skirt Calderón's position and to take Puente Nacional. Santa Anna put this plan aside, apparently in favor of the ambush at Tolomé. Indeed, the bridge at Puente Nacional would probably have been more easily defended than the bridge at Tolomé, but only with artillery. Harkort probably did not know what Santa Anna knew, namely, that Facio was approaching from Jalapa with reinforcements. If Santa Anna had continued on beyond Tolomé, he would likely have been caught between Calderón to the south and Facio's troops on the north. Suárez y Navarro, *Historia de México* I, 277.

27. A Death Sentence (and a Reprieve)

1. The lines are from Friedrich Schiller's ballad, "Der Gang nach dem Eisenhammer" ("The Errand to the Foundry"), first published in 1798. Friedrich Schiller, *Sämtliche Werke*, ed. Gerhart Fricke and Herbert G. Göpfert, 5 vols. (Munich: Carl Hanser Verlag, 1962–1963), I, 385, 903; my translation.

2. The reference here is to Jonah 4:8.

3. The officer in charge of the prisoners was Capt. Esteban Mora. Rivera Cambas, *Historia antigua* VI, 129. Harkort means Mexican pesos, but the Prussian thaler and the peso were at this time about equal in value. Burkart, *Aufenthalt und Reisen in Mexico* 1, xii.

4. First Lt. Mariano Veitia was one of the signatories to the *pronunciamiento* in Veracruz. Bocanegra, ed., *Memorias* II, 268.

5. See episode 20, and episode 26, note 6.

6. Harkort is referring to the Spanish dramatist and poet, Pedro Calderón de la Barca (1600–1681).

7. See episode 17, and episode 26, note 4.

28. The Journey Continues

1. El Paso de Ovejas was about midway between Tolomé and Puente Nacional on the highway from Veracruz to Jalapa; see episode 21, note 4.

2. José Antonio Facio (1790–1836) was born in Mexico, but was educated in Spain and had served in the Spanish army before Mexico's independence. He served President Bustamante loyally, and in January, 1832, when the government received news of the revolt in Veracruz, Facio hurried to Jalapa to organize an army. After Santa Anna's defeat at Tolomé, Facio personally took part in the siege on Veracruz. Bancroft, *History of Mexico* V, 88–89n; *Diccionario Porrúa* I, 749; Rivera Cambas, *Historia antigua*, VI, 137.

3. This remark is in German, a play on words. Harkort's comment in German, "Ende schlecht, alles schlecht," is the negative counterpart to the common adage, "Ende gut, alles gut," i.e., "All's well that ends well."

29. Arrival in Jalapa

1. Santa Anna's popularity in Jalapa, his birthplace, appears to have vacillated greatly during the first two decades of Mexico's independence and generally paralleled his political maneuverings between the liberal and conservative parties; see Callcott, *Santa Anna*, pp. 23, 32–33, 105, 110.

The date of the prisoners' arrival in Jalapa, as well as a collection among the inhabitants for them, is corroborated by Rivera Cambas, *Historia antigua* VI, 129.

2. The Plaza del Rey in Jalapa, in Harkort's time probably called Plaza de la Constitución, is depicted in C. F. Poyet, *Monografía de Xalapa*, p. 24 (facing page).

3. Hieronimus Jobs is the hero of the popular mock-heroic verse epic by Carl Arnold Kortum, *Die Jobsiade;* see episode 8, note 5. In chapter 30 of the second part of the work, Jobs becomes the pastor of the village of Ohnewitz. His inaugural sermon there is so stirring that the villagers welcome him by completely furnishing the parsonage with household furniture, utensils, and food. The parallel to Harkort's situation is obvious. Kortum, *Die Jobsiade* II, 142–43.

4. Friedrich Becher was the son of Carl Christian Becher, a director of the Rhenish West Indian Company who had come to Mexico on an inspection tour of his company's mining operations there. On March 7, 1832, Friedrich happened to be in Jalapa on a business errand from Mexico City when he met Edward Harkort. Carl Christian Becher, *Mexico in den ereignissvollen Jahren 1832 und 1833, und die Reise hin und zurück aus vertraulichen Briefen . . .* , pp. 74, 76–78; Kruse, ed., *Deutsche Briefe aus Mexiko*, p. lxii; Pferdekamp, *Auf Humboldts Spuren*, pp. 49–52.

5. According to most reports, General Calderón took more than a month to prepare for the siege on Veracruz, which he finally commenced on April 12. Bancroft, *History of Mexico* V, 110; Suárez y Navarro, *Historia de México* I, 280.

30. A Scientific Expedition

1. This group was the expedition led by Jean Frédéric Waldeck to explore the Mayan ruins at Palenque and in the Yucatán. Supported by Lucas Alamán and the National Museum, the group left Mexico City in early March, 1832. Robert L. Brunhouse, *In Search of the Maya: The First Archeologists* (Albuquerque: University of New Mexico Press, 1973), pp. 65–66; Jean Frédéric Waldeck, *Voyage pittoresque et archéologique dans la province d'Yucatán (Amérique centrale) pendant les années 1834 et 1835*, p. 108.

2. This member of the group could possibly be the German mining specialist, Franz Schmitz; see Pferdekamp, *Auf Humboldts Spuren*, p. 131.

3. Harkort evidently subscribes to the popular theory of his day, possibly overheard during his brief encounter with the Waldeck expedition, that Palenque and other such ruins were the remains of pre-Hispanic colonization in Central America by the Chinese, the Phoenicians, the Greeks, the Egyptians, or the Carthaginians; see Charles Gallenkamp, *Maya: The Riddle and Rediscovery of a Lost Civilization* (New York: David McKay Co., 1959), pp. 50–59.

4. Harkort is traveling through the *mal país*, so called because of the bleak landscape dominated by great masses of volcanic scoria. Las Vigas, La Cruz Blanca, and Los Molinos are villages between San Miguel del Soldado and Perote. Calderón de la Barca, *Life in Mexico*, pp. 74–75; Poinsett, *Notes on Mexico*, p. 31; Tayloe, *Mexico 1825–1828*, pp. 32–33.

31. Perote Fortress

1. According to Terry, *Guide to Mexico*, p. 502, San Carlos de Perote fortress is about a mile from the town of Perote. See also Mühlenpfordt, *Schilderung der Republik Mexiko* II, 84; Stapp, *Prisoners of Perote*, p. 153; Tayloe, *Mexico 1825–1828*, p. 33.

2. An excellent ground plan and description of the fortress, including the surrounding moat and palisade of "squared cedar timbers," can be found in Green, *Journal of the Texian Expedition*, pp. 238–240.

3. I could not determine the full name of Lieutenant Escanís.

4. The hospital inside the fortress was evidently only a makeshift facility. One of the Texans who were imprisoned in Perote fortress in the 1840s stated that there was no suitable hospital in the prison for the care of ill prisoners. Stapp, *Prisoners of Perote*, p. 159. A detailed floor plan of the fortress drawn by another of the Texan prisoners shows no hospital space, either, but only a row of cells on the north side used as storerooms, which in Harkort's time were probably used as hospital quarters for prisoners. Green, *Journal of the Texian Expedition*, p. 238 (facing page).

32. The Hospital and Its Staff

1. The first work Harkort read was possibly the story of Napoleon by Louis Antoine Fauvelet de Bourrienne, *Mémoires de M. de Bourrienne, ministre d'état: Sur Napoléon, le directoire, le consulat, l'empire et la restauration* . . . ,10 vols. (Paris: L'advocat,

1829). The diary of Saint Helena was by Emmanuel Comte de Las Casas, *Esprit du Mémorial de Ste.-Hélène: Extrait de l'original et reproduit sans commentaires avec l'agrément de l'autres*, 3 vols. (Paris: A. Boucher, 1823).

2. The two lawyers, Schluck and Schlauch, are characters in Carl Arnold Kortum's *Die Jobsiade*. Their names are epithets for gourmands, meaning literally "Gulp" and "Gullet," respectively. In the eighth chapter of the second part of this richly illustrated work, the two figures are characterized and depicted in silhouette. Kortum, *Die Jobsiade*, II, 37–42.

3. According to Rivera Cambas, *Historia antigua*, VI, 135, 138, Santa Anna's forces made frequent guerrilla raids on Calderón's outposts, and from ambush his cavalry robbed Calderón's munitions convoys.

33. Puebla de los Angeles

1. The city of Puebla is noted for its mild climate and picturesque situation on the central plateau of Mexico.

34. Departure from Perote Fortress

1. One of the signatories to the *pronunciamiento* in Veracruz on January 2, 1832, was Lt. Col. Ramón Hernández. Bocanegra, ed., *Memorias* II, 268. Concerning Lieutenant Portilla, see episode 20, note 5. The other officers are mentioned by Rivera Cambas, *Historia antigua* VI, 127, 130.

2. On June 13, after General Calderón had retreated from the siege on Veracruz, an armistice was drafted at Corral Falso, near Jalapa, to begin negotiations for peace. Bancroft, *History of Mexico* V, 113; Bocanegra, ed., *Memorias* II, 282–83; Callcott, *Santa Anna*, p. 92; Rivera Cambas, *Historia antigua* VI, 160–61.

3. Perote was about ninety-six miles from Puebla. Stapp, *Prisoners of Perote*, p. 153; Calderón de la Barca, *Life in Mexico*, p. 74.

4. Santa Gertrudis appears to have been a way station for coaches. Calderón de la Barca, *Life in Mexico*, p. 78.

For a brief description of El Cerro de Pizarro, see Poinsett, *Notes on Mexico*, pp. 33–34; and Tayloe, *Mexico 1825–1828*, p. 35.

5. Mount Malinche (Matlalcuéye) is southwest of Mount Pizarro, on the border between the states of Puebla and Tlaxcala.

6. According to Tayloe, *Mexico 1825–1828*, p. 35, the village of Tepeyahualco was about seven leagues (nineteen miles) from Perote.

35. The New Rifle Model

1. There are twelve lines to an inch; hence, the ball was about a quarter inch in diameter. Louis DeVries, ed., *German-English Science Dictionary*, rev. Leon Jacolev, 4th ed. (New York: McGraw-Hill, 1978), p. 558.

2. The fame of Johann Friedrich Benzenberg (1777–1846) rests mainly on his work in astronomy, physics, and geodesy. In his later years, however, he occupied himself with ballistics. As a surveyor, Harkort was no doubt familiar also with Benzenberg's several textbooks on surveying. Gillispie, ed., *Dictionary of Scientific Biography* I, 615–16; *Allgemeine Deutsche Biographie* II, 348–49.

36. Arrival in Vireyes

1. For a contemporary description of the village of Vireyes, see Poinsett, *Notes on Mexico*, p. 34.

2. The Mexican horseman's skillful use of the lasso was noted also by Calderón de la Barca, *Life in Mexico*, p. 351; Albert M. Gilliam, *Travels over the Table Lands and Cordilleras of Mexico during the Years 1843 and 44;* . . . pp. 350–51; and Lyon, *Journal of a Residence* I, 246–47.

3. Harkort's account of Santa Anna's escape to Veracruz appears to be unique. None of the other sources consulted narrate his flight from Tolomé in such detail. See Rivera Cambas, *Historia antigua* VI, 133; and Suárez y Navarro, *Historia de México* I, 279–80.

Harkort appears to be in error about the rank of his comrade. Two other sources mention in connection with the pronouncement and the battle at Tolomé a certain Lt. Col. Ramón Hernández. Bocanegra, ed., *Memorias* II, 268; Rivera Cambas, *Historia antigua* VI, 130.

37. The Third Day of Travel

1. I could not determine Colonel Franco's full name and identity.

2. I could find no information about the hacienda San Antonio de Tamaris.

3. In the epic poem *Temora*, there arose from the Lake of Lego a mist in which the souls of the dead resided in the interval between their death and their funeral song. James Macpherson, trans., *The Poems of Ossian* (Boston: Phillips, Sampson, [1840]), pp. 460–61.

4. In a later revision of his journal, Harkort probably intended to elaborate on the Indians' condition of semiservitude expressed in his term, *Fronarbeiter*. See Calderón de la Barca, *Life in Mexico*, p. 384; and Sartorius, *Mexico about 1850*, pp. 167–68.

38. A Hazardous Region

1. Venta del Piñal was the inn or way station for travelers by coach. See Poinsett, *Notes on Mexico*, p. 37; Tayloe, *Mexico 1825–1828*, p. 36; Tudor, *Narrative of a Tour in North America* II, 199–200.

For more on Acajete, see Calderón de la Barca, *Life in Mexico*, p. 81; Tayloe, *Mexico 1825–1828*, p. 37.

2. Harkort's remarks about this region are corroborated by Poinsett, *Notes on Mexico*, p. 36; and Tayloe, *Mexico 1825–1828*, p. 36.

3. After descending the Piñal, travelers found themselves on the extensive cultivated plain of Puebla. Tayloe, *Mexico 1825–1828*, p. 37.

4. The Corpus Christi festival is celebrated in honor of the Eucharist on the Thursday following Trinity Sunday.

5. The villages Las Animas and Chachapa are not mentioned in the other contemporary accounts cited in these notes.

At each gate to a large city in Mexico at this time, there was a checkpoint for internal customs. See Poinsett, *Notes on Mexico*, p. 38; Tayloe, *Mexico 1825–1828*, pp. 27, 38; Tudor, *Narrative of a Tour in North America* II, 103.

6. For a detailed description of the pyramid of Cholula as it appeared in Harkort's

time, see William Bullock, *Six Months' Residence and Travel in Mexico, Containing Remarks on the Present State of New Spain,* . . . pp. 111–112; Calderón de la Barca, *Life in Mexico,* pp. 403–404; Poinsett, *Notes on Mexico,* pp. 42–43; Tayloe, *Mexico 1825–1828,* pp. 42–43.

7. A contemporary plan of the city of Puebla showing the location of the presidio there can be found in Bancroft, *History of Mexico* V, 121.

8. For his success in repelling the Spanish invasion at Tampico in 1829, Santa Anna received the official title Benemérito de la patria, and he was popularly called El Vencedor de Tampico. Callcott, *Santa Anna,* pp. 76–77; Jones, *Santa Anna,* pp. 51–52.

39. An Imminent Parting

1. Cuautitlán is in the state of Mexico, about eighteen miles northwest of Mexico City.

2. On July 5, before peace negotiations between Santa Anna and Bustamante's delegates had actually begun, the garrison at Veracruz, with the support of the authorities of Jalisco and Zacatecas, had issued a pronouncement calling for the restoration of Manuel Gómez Pedraza as the legitimate president of Mexico. Hence, even as Harkort was writing these words, the so-called peace negotiations had already broken down. Bancroft, *History of Mexico* V, 113–14; Callcott, *Santa Anna,* p. 92; Rivera Cambas, *Historia antigua* VI, 162–63.

3. Harkort refers to Anastasio Bustamante, who, as vice-president, forced President Vicente Guerrero from office and in January, 1830, had himself installed in the presidency; see episode 6, notes 4 and 8.

4. Harkort describes his friend Felipe Alvarez in the journal entry of July 19; see episodes 49 and 51.

40. Cooking for Ourselves

1. In Harkort's time a real was worth about twelve cents; hence, each prisoner was paying about fifty cents a day for his rations. See Tayloe, *Mexico 1825–1828,* p. 20.

2. This officer is Capt. Francisco Macín. See Rivera Cambas, *Historia antigua* VI, 130.

3. *Chilmole* or *chimole* is defined by Santamaría, *Diccionario de mejicanismos,* p. 387, as a sauce or stew made with chile, and as a common mixture of tomatoes and chile peppers.

41. Corporal Punishment

1. Flogging for relatively minor offenses was evidently not uncommon in the Mexican army at this time. See Stapp, *Prisoners of Perote,* p. 117. By contrast, in the U.S. military, by law enacted in 1812, flogging could be inflicted only for desertion during peacetime. Scott, *Military Dictionary,* pp. 236, 577.

2. Harkort refers to the oligarchies that ruled the republic of Venice and several other Italian republics during the late Middle Ages and early Renaissance. See Frederic C. Lane, *Venice: A Maritime Republic* (Baltimore: Johns Hopkins University Press, 1973), pp. 251–73.

42. News from Veracruz

1. Juan José Andrade (1796–1843) began his military career in 1809 in the Spanish colonial army. At different times in his career he was commanding general of Puebla, then of San Luis Potosí, México, and finally of Sinaloa. Carreño, ed., _Jefes del ejército mexicano_, pp. 82–83; _Diccionario Porrúa_ I, 106.

2. There was a business firm in Veracruz by the name of Berman y Weber at the time. Carl Weber was perhaps the partner in that firm. See _El Censor_ (Veracruz, Mar. 3, 1832). The circumstances of Weber's murder are narrated by Becher, _Mexico in den ereignissvollen Jahren 1832 und 1833_, p. 115.

43. Music in Mexico

1. The Italian city of Cremona in the Lombardy region has been famous since the sixteenth century for the manufacture of excellent musical instruments, especially stringed instruments. Sadie, ed., _Grove Dictionary_ V, 30–31.

2. Ignace Joseph Pleyel (1757–1831) was an Austrian composer, music publisher, and piano maker. His compositions, including concertos with solo parts for flute, clarinet, and cello, achieved widespread popularity in Europe and North America. Ibid., XV, 6–10.

3. The distinctive features of these musical compositions, the capriccio, adagio, rondo, overture, and the sonata, respectively, can be found in ibid., III, 758–59, I, 88–89, XVI, 172–77, XIV, 33–35, XVII, 479–97.

4. Similar observations were made by Calderón de la Barca, _Life in Mexico_, pp. 169, 287, 411.

44. Important Dispatches

1. José Esteban Moctezuma (1779–1838) had been appointed to the command at Tampico by Bustamante himself. The revolt in Tamulipas was initiated in March, 1832, by the governor of that state, Francisco Vital Fernández, with the support of General Moctezuma. On May 13, after all attempts at negotiation with the rebels had failed, General Mier y Terán attacked Moctezuma at Tampico and met with a disastrous repulse. Bancroft, _History of Mexico_ V, 110–11; Peral, _Diccionario biográfico mexicano_, p. 537; Rivera Cambas, _Historia antigua_ VI, 154–55.

2. Manuel Mier y Terán (1789–1832) was in 1832 one of Mexico's most capable and high-minded leaders. After his disastrous attack on Tampico, he depaired of bringing about peace in the region under his command. His defeat, together with family troubles, apparently drove him to commit suicide on July 3, 1832, on the plaza of Padilla, a town north of Tampico. Bancroft, _History of Mexico_ V, 111; Bocanegra, ed., _Memorias_ II, 212–14; _Diccionario Porrúa_ II, 1346–1347; Peral, _Diccionario biográfico mexicano_ pp. 531–32; Rivera Cambas, _Historia antigua_ VI, 157–59.

3. The armistice of June 13, 1832, was terminated one month later, on July 13. Bancroft, _History of Mexico_ V, 113; Rivera Cambas, _Historia antigua_ VI, 166.

4. The proclamation that Harkort attributes to Gómez Pedraza was probably the declaration issued by the authorities of Zacatecas on July 10. A similar declaration, calling for the restoration of legitimacy to the government with the installation of Gómez Pedraza as the constitutionally elected president of Mexico, had already been issued by

the garrison at Veracruz on July 5. Bancroft, *History of Mexico* V, 114; Callcott, *Santa Anna*, p. 92; Rivera Cambas, *Historia antigua* VI, 166–67; Suárez y Navarro, *Historia de México* I, 309–10.

5. Harkort is mistaken about the state of Tabasco. Early in July, the states of San Luis Potosí, Michoacán, Chihuahua, Puebla, México, and Tabasco declared their support of Bustamante's government. Bancroft, *History of Mexico* V, 114; Rivera Cambas, *Historia antigua* VI, 167.

In June, 1832, Col. José Antonio Mejía had organized a small fleet of about five schooners and six hundred men in Tampico. He then sailed north to seize the port of Matamoros. With the seizure of Matamoros, Santa Anna's forces controlled the three major ports on the Gulf of Mexico: Veracruz, Tampico, and Matamoros. See Bancroft, *History of Mexico* V, 114; Rivera Cambas, *Historia antigua* VI, 156–57, 174; Suárez y Navarro, *Historia de México* I, 314–16.

45. An Unexpected Visit

1. The town of Tepotzotlán is in the state of México, about forty kilometers (twenty-five miles) north of Mexico City.

2. The story of the widow who gave two mites to the church treasury is told in the gospel of Saint Mark 12:41–44.

46. News and Prospects

1. By July 13, when the armistice in Puente Nacional was broken off, the states of Zacatecas, Durango, and Jalisco had declared their opposition to Bustamante's government. In this connection, a revolt in Campeche is mentioned neither by Bancroft, *History of Mexico* V, 114, nor by Rivera Cambas, *Historia antigua* VI, 174.

Between May 13, when General Calderón had abandoned the siege of Veracruz, and June 13, 1832, the date of the armistice at Corral Falso, Santa Anna had gained control of Puente Nacional, Bancroft, *History of Mexico*, V, 110, 113; Rivera Cambas, *Historia antigua* VI, 141–42; see also episode 34, note 2.

2. Harkort's source for this report of General Bravo's death is probably mere hearsay and without substance. Of the four brothers, Leonardo, Máximo, Miguel, and Víctor Bravo, who all gained national fame during Mexico's struggle for independence, only Máximo died during the 1830s, and the year of his death is generally thought to be 1835, not 1832. See Alejandro Villaseñor y Villaseñor, *Biografías de los héroes y caudillos de la independencia* II, 71–74, 77–80, 87–90, 96–98; *Diccionario Porrúa* I, 290, 292.

In May, 1832, after repulsing the attack on Tampico by General Mier y Terán, Gen. Esteban Moctezuma had marched his troops into the interior in the direction of San Luis Potosí. Bancroft, *History of Mexico* V, 111; Rivera Cambas, *Historia antigua* VI, 154.

3. See episode 42.

47. Painting Portraits

1. Harkort's reference to doubloons is figurative; no doubt he expected payment in Mexican pesos.

2. Till Eulenspiegel is the hero of a German *Volksbuch* by the same name that enjoyed widespread popularity in the sixteenth century. The book is a collection of unconnected comic episodes in the life of its hero. See Garland and Garland, *Oxford Compan-*

ion to German Literature, p. 852. Harkort has paraphrased a line from the forty-second episode, in which Till is told by his employer, a shoemaker, to make shoes "large and small, like the swine that the swineherd drives out of the village." Richard Benz, ed., *Drei deutsche Volkbücher* (Köln: Verlag Jacob Hegener, 1969), p. 303; my translation.

3. Harkort is apparently referring to the deprivations suffered by some of the French nobility during the revolution in France. See Jean Robiquet, *Daily Life in the French Revolution*, trans. James Kirkup, 4th ed. (New York: Macmillan, 1971), pp. 140–41.

48. The Old Musician

1. I could locate no additional information about Cayetano Negrete.

2. I could find no other record of this defection at Puebla. I also assume, moreover, that Harkort refers to Gen. Nicolás Bravo. See Villaseñor y Villaseñor, *Biografías de los héroes* II, 54–64;

3. Harkort means Mexican pesos, not American dollars.

4. Lord Stanhope, earl of Chesterfield, wrote in a letter of October 19, 1748, to his son, "Never hold anybody by the button, or by the hand, in order to be heard out.". Philip Dormer Stanhope, fourth earl of Chesterfield, *Lord Chesterfield's Letters to His Son*, ed. Joseph P. Seabury (New York: Silver, Burdett, 1902), p. 84.

5. King Sputterbeard (König Sprussenbart) is apparently an epithet from Germany history or folk literature. Unfortunately, I could not determine the origin of the name.

6. This publication is a diagram in folio; the complete title is *Essai d'une distribution généalogique des sciences et des arts principaux selon l'explication détaillée du système des connaissances humaines dans le Discours préliminaire des éditeurs de l'Encyclopédie publiée par M. Diderot et M. D'Alembert, à Paris, en 1751, réduit en cette forme pour découvrir la connaissance humaine d'un coup d'oeil, par Chrétien-Frédéric-Guillaume Roth* (Weimar: Benard, 1769).

7. For centuries the flea has been the object of satire and comedy in German literature. See Franz A. Schmitt, *Stoff- und Motivgeschichte der deutschen Literatur*, 3rd ed. (Berlin: Walter de Gruyter, 1976), p. 88. Other travelers in Mexico at this time shared Harkort's complaint. See Calderón de la Barca, *Life in Mexico*, p. 591; Gilliam, *Travels over the Table Lands*, p. 236; Tayloe, *Mexico 1825–1828*, p. 24.

49. The Storyteller of Perote Fortress

1. Harkort is mistaken. Not all of his prison comrades were officers; nor had they all been captured in the battle at Tolomé. According to most accounts, only thirty-two officers were captured by General Calderón at Tolomé. See Callcott, *Santa Anna*, p.91; Rivera Cambas, *Historia antigua* VI, 128; Suárez y Navarro, *Historia de México* I, 277. Two or three of the thirty-five prisoners with Harkort in Perote fortress had been captured elsewhere and later placed with the captives from Tolomé. Harkort identifies one of these additions himself later in this episode: Felipe Alvarez, a civilian, was captured at Puente Nacional. See also episode 51.

2. "Schinderhannes" was the epithet applied to Johann Wilhelm Bückler (1783–1803), a young robber chieftain in the Rhineland area of Germany. Gerhard Taddey, ed., *Lexikon der deutschen Geschichte: Personen, Ereignisse, Institutionen . . .* (Stuttgart: Alfred Kröner Verlag, 1977), pp. 1073–74.

The literary works mentioned here and their authors can be found in Garland and

Garland, *Oxford Companion to German Literature*, pp. 328, 392–93, 614, 850–51, 852.

3. For more information about these plays by Schiller, see John D. Simons, *Friedrich Schiller* (Boston: Twayne Publishers, 1981), pp. 70–86, 124–32.

4. A description and history of the legend and song of the Nibelungen can be found in Garland and Garland, *Oxford Companion to German Literature*, pp. 634–36.

Friedrich Heinrich Karl, Baron de la Motte Fouqué (1777–1843) was the author of a number of romantic novels, tales, and plays. In Harkort's youth, Fouqué was probably the most widely read of all German romantic writers. *Der Zauberring*, Fouqué's most popular novel, was published in 1813, and *Die Fahrten Thiodolfs des Isländers* in 1815. Ibid., pp. 233, 966; *Allgemeine Deutsche Biographie* VII, 198–201.

For more information about Alxinger (1755–1797) and his Arthurian romance, *Bliomberis, ein Rittergedicht in zwölf Gesängen* (1791), see Garland and Garland, *Oxford Companion to German Literature*, p. 22.

5. Friedrich Baron von der Trenck (1726–1794) achieved a literary reputation in Germany and Europe through his autobiography, *Des Freiherrn von der Trenck merkwürdige Lebensgeschichte* (1787). Garland and Garland, *Oxford Companion to German Literature*, pp. 861–62.

The hero of *Der Freischütz* (The Freeshooter) is a young gamekeeper who uses magic bullets (*Freikugeln*) in a shooting contest for the hand of the girl he loves. Ibid., p. 244.

More about Friedrich Schiller's classical tragedy *Maria Stuart* (1801), can be found in Simons, *Friedrich Schiller*, pp. 114–24.

Karl Friedrich Hieronymus Baron von Münchhausen (1720–1797) was the popular hero and narrator of a number of extraordinary and absurdly improbable adventures that were first published in 1781 in the *Vademecum für lustige Leute*. Harkort probably knew Münchhausen's tales through Gottfried August Bürger's German translation of the expanded English version, *Baron Münchhausen's Narrative of his Marvellous Travels and Campaigns in Russia* (1785). Garland and Garland, *Oxford Companion to German Literature*, pp. 612–613.

Friedrich Wilhelm Baron von Kyau (1654–1733) was a general in the Saxony army who, because of his sharp wit, became a popular figure at the court of August the Strong, Electoral Prince of Saxony. Harkort knew of Kyau probably through the latter's biography, *Kyaus Leben und Schwänke* (1800). *Brockhaus Enzyklopädie* X, 834.

50. Escape Attempts

1. The cell walls of Perote prison were constructed of solid masonry several feet thick. For a thorough description of its construction, see MacGrath and Hawkins, "Perote Fort," p. 344; and Stapp, *Prisoners of Perote*, pp. 169–70.

2. In 1843 Perote fortress was manned by two companies of infantry and one company of artillery. In Harkort's time there it must have been similarly garrisoned. Stapp, *Prisoners of Perote*, p. 154.

51. The Prisoners of Perote

1. Manuel Fernández Castrillón later achieved the rank of brigadier general, and in 1836 he participated in Santa Anna's campaign in Texas. He was killed in the battle at San Jacinto on April 21, 1836. Antonio López de Santa Anna et al., *The Mexican Side of the Texas Revolution* [1836] *by the Chief Mexican Participants*, pp. 77–78.

2. Nicolás de la Portilla (1808–1873) served in the Mexican army more than thirty years, ascending finally to the post of minister of war and of the navy in 1867 under Emperor Maximilian; see episode 20, note 5.

3. Joaquín Arzamendi I could not further identify. Rivera Cambas, *Historia antigua* VI, 130, mentions only that the two captains Arzamendi fought valiantly at Tolomé and were taken prisoner by General Calderón.

4. .Francisco Macín's courageous service at Tolomé is noted also by Rivera Cambas, ibid. I could not locate additional information about him, however.

5. Harkort and Lieutenant Escanís were hospitalized together in Perote fortress; see episode 31. I could find nothing more about him.

6. I could locate Juan Arzamendi in no sources other than ibid.

7. Felipe Alvarez is also mentioned by Harkort in episode 49. I could locate no additional information about him.

8. Eusebio Flores and his brother, José María Flores, were both signatories to the pronouncement of January 2, 1832, against Bustamante's government. See Bocanegra, ed., *Memorias* II, 268. The minister of war, José Antonio Facio, had attempted unsuccessfully to bribe José María Flores on January 25, 1832, to surrender the fortress under his command, San Juan de Ulúa, and thus to subvert the revolt in Veracruz. Bancroft, *History of Mexico* V, 109; Suárez y Navarro, *Historia de México* I, 274–75.

9. I could not identify Lieutenant Barbagose further.

10. I could find nothing more about Daté.

11. According to Rivera Cambas, *Historia antigua*, VI, 127, Captain Robles commanded one of the three units of Santa Anna's forces at Tolomé. He was a captain of fusiliers.

12. I could find nothing more about Montamo.

52. Two Proclamations

1. This appeal by Facio evidently was published only as a broadside; I could not find it in the government newspaper, *El Constitucional*, published in Jalapa, for the period July 1–20, 1832.

Before the failure of the negotiations at Puente Nacional on July 13 (see episode 46, note 1), Facio had resigned as minister of war and had taken direct command of the armed forces in Veracruz. Bancroft, *History of Mexico* V, 118; Rivera Cambas, *Historia antigua* VI, 166, 176; Suárez y Navarro, *Historia de México* I, 289–93.

2. From July 6 to July 15, 1832, Manuel María Anzures had already published in *El Constitucional* (nos. 833–37), some poems and letters to Santa Anna, appealing to him to settle his differences with the government. These appeals, published in the "Remitidos" column, had also provoked some ridiculing responses from other readers. The poem that appeared in the issue of July 8, 1832 (p. 3), was entitled "Con la razón o la espada, Anzures dice a Santa Anna." In the issue of July 20, Anzures is identified as a lawyer and a district judge in the state of Veracruz (p. 5).

Blanco and Aburto were the publishers of the newspaper in 1832.

53. Progress of the Revolution

1. The daily newspaper *La Egide de la Ley* was established in 1830 in the city of Puebla. Charno, comp., *Latin American Newspapers*, p. 444. Unfortunately, I could not corroborate the details of Harkort's report by examining this issue.

In July, 1832, Lt. Col. Félix Merino was ordered by General Facio to march on Teziutlán. The insurgents at Teziutlán were commanded by Francisco Mejía. A brief description of this engagement can be found in Rivera Cambas, *Historia antigua* VI, 177; and Suárez y Navarro, *Historia de México* I, 323.

2. Santa Anna had been in Córdoba and Orizaba since the end of July, shortly after the negotiations at Puente Nacional had failed. Becher, *Mexico in den ereignissvollen Jahren 1832 und 1833*, p. 113; Rivera Cambas, *Historia antigua* VI, 177.

3. Harkort's reference to a gallery is unclear. It is possible that he had painted a picture of his barracks prison, depicting the colonnade outside where he was often allowed to work during the day; see episode 42.

4. After his repulse of General Mier y Teran's assault at Tampico in May, General Moctezuma had marched into the interior in the direction of San Luis Potosí. On August 3, at Pozo de los Carmelos, near San Luis Potosí, Moctezuma defeated the government forces. Bancroft, *History of Mexico* V, 111, 114–15; Rivera Cambas, *Historia antigua* VI, 175; Suárez y Navarro, *Historia de México* I, 316–18.

5. The occupation of San Luis Potosí by the insurgents in late July had prompted the Chamber of Deputies in early August to authorize Bustamente to take direct command of the army. Bancroft, *History of Mexico* V, 115; Suárez y Navarro, *Historia de México* I, 319–20.

6. See note 2.

7. In August General Facio had moved his headquarters from Jalapa to Acultzingo, a few miles southwest of Orizaba. In September he moved the major part of his forces again, positioning them this time in the defiles of San José Ixtapa, about thirty miles west of Santa Anna's main force in Orizaba. I could not corroborate the desertions reported here by Harkort. See Rivera Cambas, *Historia antigua* VI, 177, 179.

Tlaxcala de Xicohténcatl, the state capital of Tlaxcala, is about twenty-five miles north of the city of Puebla. I could not corroborate Harkort's report of one of Santa Anna's divisions being near Tlaxcala.

8. On August 5 the authorities in San Luis Potosí, followed by the states of Zacatecas, Jalisco, and Durango, had declared Manuel Gómez Pedraza the lawful president of Mexico. By August 10, when Harkort wrote this note, General Moctezuma was in control of San Luis Potosí, and Zacatecas had placed four thousand militiamen under arms for active service. Bancroft, *History of Mexico* V, 114–115; Suárez y Navarro, *Historia de México* I, 318–19, 328.

55. *Escape from Puebla and Reception in Orizaba*

1. I could find no record of a disturbance in Puebla on August 16, 1832, the date of Harkort's escape from prison there. See episode 54.

2. Joseph Welsh, the British consul in Veracruz, had allied himself in February, 1832, with the insurgents there. In March he was removed from that post. Tudor, *Narrative of a Tour in North America* II, 159; Rivera Cambas, *Historia antigua* VI, 172–73.

3. I could find no other record of Lieutenant Colonel Becelli. Juan José Holzinger (d. 1864) was a native German who, according to statements he made in 1836 to Herman Ehrenberg, had come to Mexico about 1825 with Real del Monte, a British mining company. Soon after his arrival, he met Santa Anna, who was so impressed by Holzinger's engineering skills that he made him an officer in the Mexican army. In 1836, during the Texas Revolution, Lieutenant Colonel Holzinger was one of the Mexican negotiators for Gen. José Urrea when Col. James W. Fannin surrendered after the battle of Coleto.

H[ermann] Ehrenberg, *Der Freiheitskampf in Texas im Jahre 1836*, pp. 145–46, 205; Santa Anna et al., *The Mexican Side of the Texan Revolution*, pp. 62–63, 105; Webb, Carroll, and Branda, eds., *Handbook of Texas* I, 829, III, 403.

4. El Cerro de Escamela was a few miles east of the city of Orizaba.

5. Cuesta de Maltrata is one of the summits in the Cumbres de Maltrata range, west of the city of Orizaba.

6. San Antonio de Arniva was probably a hacienda or village near El Cerro de Escamela.

7. Until September 29, the major part of Facio's forces were positioned in the defiles of San José Ixtapa. Rivera Cambas, *Historia antigua* VI, 179. Puente Colorado was probably a village near the present town of Esperanza, a few miles north of San José Ixtapa; see episode 14, note 8.

56. A March, Fortifications, and Combat

1. As Harkort notes later in this episode, San Antonio de Abajo was a hacienda a few miles east of Esperanza.

2. Detailed descriptions of this battle can be found in Bancroft, *History of Mexico* V, 179–180; and Suárez y Navarro, *Historia de México* I, 324.

3. Santa Anna's forces arrived at the village of Amozoc, three leagues (eight miles) east of Puebla, on October 3, 1832. Rivera Cambas, *Historia antigua* VI 180; Suárez y Navarro, *Historia de México* I, 335; Tayloe, *Mexico 1825–1828*, pp. 37–38.

4. Santa Anna's forces entered Puebla through the gate of Amozoc on the afternoon of October 4, 1832. General Calderón was in Puebla working on a plan to initiate peace negotiations with Santa Anna. Rivera Cambas, *Historia antigua* VI, 180–81; Suárez y Navarro, *Historia de México* I, 335–36. For a contemporary plan of the city of Puebla, see Bancroft, *History of Mexico* V, 121.

5. The terms of the capitulation, which was signed on the evening of October 4, can be found in Bancroft, *History of Mexico* V, 119; Rivera Cambas, *Historia antigua* VI, 181; and Suárez y Navarro, *Historia de México* I, 336.

6. For a contemporary description of San Martín Texmelucán, seven leagues (nineteen miles) northwest of Puebla, as well as the route thence, see Tayloe, *Mexico 1825–1828*, pp. 41–45.

7. On October 19, two brigades of Santa Anna's army, under the command of Cols. José Antonio Mejía and José María Jarero, advanced to Ayotla and nearby Venta de Córdoba. Ayotla was six leagues (sixteen miles) from the customs gate to Mexico City. Rivera Cambas, *Historia antigua* VI, 186; Suárez y Navarro, *Historia de México* I, 338; Tayloe, *Mexico 1825–1828*, pp. 46, 199.

8. Mejía was promoted to the rank of brigadier general. *Diccionario Porrúa* II, 1302.

9. Harkort's remark about the view suggests the name Buenavista over Buenanita. The town of Chalco is thirty-seven kilometers (twenty-three miles) southeast of Mexico City. In the pre-Hispanic era of Mexico's history, Chalco was the center of a confederation of towns, consisting of four seigniories. *Diccionario Porrúa* I, 581. Harkort is possibly referring to these four seigniories with his remark about the "four generals." For a contemporary description and map of the area, see Gilliam, *Travels over the Table Lands*, pp. 75–78.

10. The type of barge mentioned by Harkort was used for the transport of passengers and goods from Chalco across Lake Chalco and up the Chalco and La Viga canals

to Mexico City. *Diccionario Porrúa* I, 581, II, 1455; Calderón de la Barca, *Life in Mexico*, pp. 162, 180; Mühlenpfordt, *Schilderung der Republik Mexiko* II, 266–67; Tudor, *Narrative of a Tour in North America* II, 262–63.

11. Harkort's fears for the Chalco canal were echoed by Mühlenpfordt, *Schilderung der Republik Mexiko* II, 262–63.

12. For more information on Juan Arago (1788–1837), see *Diccionario Porrúa* I, 125. The town of Toluca was about fifteen leagues (thirty-nine miles) west of Mexico City.

13. It is not clear why Harkort expected to find Captain Holzinger in Ayotla. Holzinger, who was an engineer (see episode 55, note 3), had been left there perhaps the week before by General Mejía to erect fortifications.

14. These two villages were about four leagues (ten miles) east of Mexico City.

57. Battle at Chapultepec

1. The town of Tacubaya was about one mile south of Chapultepec, and about four miles from the gate to the capital. A portion of Santa Anna's army marched over the causeways south of the city and then to Tacubaya on the causeway of Chapultepec. Harkort's unit reached Tacubaya on October 22. Other units of Santa Anna's army occupied other towns surrounding the capital. Bancroft, *History of Mexico* V, 119; also Tayloe, *Mexico 1825–1828*, p. 64; H[enry] G[eorge] Ward, *Mexico in 1827, by H. G. Ward, Esq., His Majesty's Chargé d'Affaires in that Country during the Years 1825, 1826, and Part of 1827* II, 232.

2. Tacubaya was celebrated for the beautiful palace and garden of the Spanish archbishop of Mexico. See Calderón de la Barca, *Life in Mexico*, p. 153.

3. This skirmish took place on October 23, just outside of Tacubaya. General Quintanar, who had been commandant of the capital since it was placed under martial law, was simply testing the strength of Santa Anna's forces. Bancroft, *History of Mexico* V, 119; Suárez y Navarro, *Historia de México* I, 338–39.

4. General Mejía had evidently brought this brigade to join the main body of Santa Anna's forces in Tacubaya in anticipation of another attack by General Quintanar. For more on Lerma and Toluca, see Tayloe, *Mexico 1825–1828*, pp. 75, 200.

5. Harkort refers to the village, La Villa de Guadalupe Hidalgo, the site of the cathedral and shrine of Nuestra Señora de Guadalupe, then about a league (2.6 miles) north of the capital. See Calderón de la Barca, *Life in Mexico*, pp. 120–22; Lyon, *Journal of a Residence* II, 134–39; also Toor, *Mexican Folkways*, pp. 172–76.

The village of Tacuba was directly north of Chapultepec. Calderón de la Barca, *Life in Mexico*, pp. 162, 186.

6. A similar scene, with "hundreds of whitened skulls scattered at random upon the ground . . ." in the cemetery near the city of Veracruz, was reported by Lyon, *Journal of a Residence* II, 214.

7. By November 1, Santa Anna's circumvallating forces occupied the villages of Tacubaya, Mexicalcingo, Peñón de los Baños, and Guadalupe, and the causeways of Vallejo on the north and of San Cosme on the west. Chapultepec was about two miles south of Tacuba. Suárez y Navarro, *Historia de México* I, 339. For a description and a map of these places, see Calderón de la Barca, *Life in Mexico*, p. 162; Tayloe, *Mexico 1825–1828*, p. 64; Terry, *Guide to Mexico*, map facing p. 246.

8. Azcapotzalco is about two miles north of Tacuba.

For more on Juan Pablo Anaya (1785–1850), see *Diccionario Porrúa* I, 103; Peral, *Diccionario biográfico mexicano*, p. 53.

58. Artillery in Combat

1. On November 6, Santa Anna broke camp in Tacubaya and marched in the direction of Cuautitlán, a town north of Mexico City. This march was a deception, however, designed to lure Quintanar out of the capital. Quintanar was supposed to think that Santa Anna was advancing to meet Bustamante's army, which was returning to the capital from Querétaro. Rivera Cambas, *Historia antigua* VI, 188; Suárez y Navarro, *Historia de México* I, 340.

2. Lechería was a large hacienda about twelve miles north of the capital. Calderón de la Barca, *Life in Mexico*, pp. 162, 221–22.

3. Reacting to Santa Anna's feigned march to meet Bustamante's army, General Quintanar had led his forces out of the capital in pursuit of the enemy. When Santa Anna turned to face his pursuers, however, Quintanar quickly retreated to Mexico City. Rivera Cambas, *Historia antigua* VI, 188; Suárez y Navarro, *Historia de México* I, 340.

4. The village of Huehuetoca was eleven leagues (twenty-nine miles) north of the capital, on the highway to Querétaro. The canal was the *desagüe*, a drainage canal built to divert the waters of nearby Lake Zumpango into the Río Moctezuma and away from the capital. Calderón de la Barca, *Life in Mexico*, pp. 184–85; Poinsett, *Notes on Mexico*, pp. 124–25; Tayloe, *Mexico 1825–1828*, pp. 138, 201.

5. On November 10, General Bustamante was still near San Juan del Río, a village about thirty leagues (seventy-nine miles) northwest of Tula. Suárez y Navarro, *Historia de México* I, 344.

59. Developments at the Lake

1. While Santa Anna was camped at Huehuetoca, General Bustamante had continued his march south to the capital. Bustamante had left the main highway before Huehuetoca, however, to join General Quintanar's forces before Santa Anna could force an engagement. Suárez y Navarro, *Historia de México* I, 344.

2. According to Bancroft, *History of Mexico* V, 120, and Suárez y Navarro, *Historia de México* I, 344–45, this battle took place on or about November 12, as Harkort indicates. The engagement, according to these two historians, ended indecisively, however, with Bustamante retreating to Tequixquiac, where General Quintanar joined him on November 16.

3. The meaning of this remark is not clear. Perhaps Harkort had viewed a golden artifact in the village of Huehuetoca, or he uses the term "golden key" in a figurative sense for the strategic importance of the village.

4. The town of Zumpango, now Zumpango de Ocampo, is about three kilometers (two miles) east of Lake Zumpango.

5. General Quintanar's division joined Bustamante's forces at Tequixquiac, a village about six miles northeast of Huehuetoca, on November 16. See note 2 above.

6. I could locate no settlement by the name of Matamores or Matamoros in the vicinity of Lake Zumpango. Matamoros was possibly the name given to this *fortín* by Harkort or his commanding officer.

60. A Cavalry Engagement

1. As soon as General Quintanar's division arrived in Tequixquiac, Bustamante resolved to carry out a preconcerted plan to capture Puebla while Santa Anna was still

encamped at Zumpango. Hence, the enemy movement reported by Harkort was Busta-mante's attempt to skirt Santa Anna's position and to march to Puebla via San Andrés. See Bancroft, *History of Mexico* V, 120; Suárez y Navarro, *Historia de México* I, 345. I could not identify a village or hacienda by the name of San Andrés near Lake Zumpango.

2. Santa Anna feared that the convoy might fall into government hands. General Anaya led a brigade to intercept the convoy, which was approaching the town of Otumba. Suárez y Navarro, *Historia de México* I, 345; also see note 5 below.

3. The village of Nanacamilpa is in the state of Tlaxcala.

4. The brigade commanded by General Anaya left on November 28. Suárez y Navarro, *Historia de México* I, 345.

5. The plain of Otumba was the site of a battle between the Mexicans and the re-treating forces of Hernán Cortés on July 14, 1520, following the expulsion of the Span-iards from Tenochtitlán on June 30. The following night, Cortés wept over his losses, and that night was henceforth called *la noche triste*. Harkort probably means *la noche triste*, "the sorrowful night," instead of *la mala noche*, "the bad night." See Bancroft, *History of Mexico* I, 469–81, 496–503; and Bernal Díaz del Castillo, *The Bernal Díaz Chron-icles*, trans. and ed. Albert Idell (New York: Doubleday, 1957), pp. 251–54, 257–59.

6. I could not locate the Hacienda de San Lorenzo. According to Suárez y Navarro, *Historia de México* I, 345, this skirmish between General Anaya's brigade and a govern-ment brigade commanded by Gen. Gabriel Durán did not end in a decisive victory for either side, but Anaya's retreat left the convoy clearly in danger of falling into Busta-mante's hands.

7. Calpulalpan is directly north of Nanacamilpa, in the state of Tlaxcala.

Harkort's intent with the expression "scenes" (*Scenen*) is not clear. It seems likely that his meaning is disparaging, i.e., he had some disagreements with Captain Holzinger and the others persons mentioned.

8. I could not identify an officer by the name of Palafox in Santa Anna's army at this time.

9. These rumors with without substance. Anaya lived until 1850, and Andrade did not die until 1843. *Diccionario Porrúa* I, 103, 106. I could find no information about Pedro José Rico.

10. Harkort means eighty thousand pesos. When Santa Anna learned at Zumpango that Bustamante had abandoned his position at Tequixquiac and on his march toward Puebla was likely to intercept the convoy from that city (see notes 1 and 2 above), Santa Anna passed Bustamante's army with a rapid march of about sixty miles in less than thirty hours. Santa Anna met the convoy just as it was approaching Otumba. Bancroft, *History of Mexico* V, 120; Suárez y Navarro, *Historia de México* I, 345.

61. A Horseback Ride to Puebla

1. San Martín Texmelucán is about thirty kilometers (nineteen miles) southeast of Nanacamilpa. From San Martín Texmelucán it was an additional seven leagues (nineteen miles) to Puebla.

2. On December 4 Bustamante marched his forces from their camp near Nanaca-milpa to San Pablo Apetatitlán, a town about thirty kilometers (twenty miles) southeast of Nanacamilpa, and about the same distance north of Puebla. Early on December 5, the vanguard of Bustamante's army, commanded by Gen. Gabriel Durán, arrived on the out-skirts of Puebla and took up a position on the hill, Cerro de San Juan, west of the city. The main body of government forces arrived later the same day, but Santa Anna re-

mained in San Martín Texmelucán until December 6. Bancroft, *History of Mexico* V, 120–21; Suárez y Navarro, *Historia de México* I, 346.

3. Harkort entered the city probably through the gate of Cholula, on the west side of the city, and southeast of Bustamante's position on Cerro de San Juan. Harkort refers to a trip in February, 1831, from Mexico City to Oaxaca (see episode 12). A map of Puebla at this time, showing the gates of the city and Cerro de San Juan, can be found in Bancroft, *History of Mexico* V, 121.

4. Adolf Hegewisch served in 1832 as first adjutant in the military medical corps of Santa Anna's army; see episode 1, note 11.

5. This officer is possibly Francisco Ortiz de Zárate; see Carreño, ed., *Jefes del ejército mexicano*, pp. 233–34.

6. The fort, Fuerte de Loreto, was located on the northeast corner of the city; see Bancroft, *History of Mexico* V, 121.

7. By the morning of December 6, Santa Anna's forces had taken positions at a place called "el puente de México," with headquarters in the nearby house of the Rancho de Posadas, on the northwest corner of the city, and directly north of Bustamante's position on the Cerro de San Juan. Suárez y Navarro, *Historia de México* I, 346. For a map showing these positions, see Bancroft, *History of Mexico* V, 121.

62. A Battle and [Gómez] Pedraza as President

1. At eight o'clock in the morning of December 6, Bustamante led an all-out assault with artillery, cavalry, and infantry on Santa Anna's positions near the Rancho de Posadas, but the government forces were finally repulsed, with heavy losses. Bancroft, *History of Mexico* V, 120–21; Suárez y Navarro, *Historia de México* I, 346.

I could not identify Harkort's friends, Colonel Medina and Lieutenant Frías.

2. After their unsuccessful assault, Bustamante's forces fell back to several positions both inside and outside the city; see Bancroft, *History of Mexico* V, 121; and Suárez y Navarro, *Historia de México* I, 346.

3. Manuel Gómez Pedraza, who had been summoned from exile in Pennsylvania as the legitimate president of Mexico (see episode 44, note 4), had arrived in Veracruz on November 5, 1832. He had proceeded at once to the city of Puebla, and from there had attempted to mediate an end to hostilities. By December, only two states, Chihuahua and Oaxaca, still supported the central government. Hence, after the disastrous battle of December 6, Bustamante saw the futility of continued attempts to capture Puebla, and on December 8, an armistice was declared until the congress could take action on a peace plan proposed to Bustamante by Gómez Pedraza and Santa Anna. The plan, dated December 9, 1832, called for, among other things, the absolute cessation of hostilities, the restoration of Gómez Pedraza as the rightful president until April 1, 1833, and new elections. Bancroft, *History of Mexico* V, 122–23; Suárez y Navarro, *Historia de México* I, 341–44, 354–57; Florentino M. Torner, ed., *Resumen integral de México a través de los siglos: Historia general y completa* . . . IV, 210.

4. On December 12 in Mexico, there are many fiestas honoring the Virgin of Guadalupe, some of which last several days. Toor, *Mexican Folkways*, p. 245.

5. A contemporary description of the cathedral of Puebla can be found in Calderón de la Barca, *Life in Mexico*, pp. 410–11; Mühlenpfordt, *Schilderung der Republik Mexiko* II, 225–27; and Poinsett, *Notes on Mexico*, p. 39.

6. The peace proposal of Gómez Pedraza and Santa Anna was presented to the Mexican congress on December 13. The congressional deputies refused, however, to

sanction the articles of the proposal. At the news of their rejection, Bustamante resolved to act independently of the congress. Immediately, he, Santa Anna, and Gómez Pedraza met in conference, evidently the conference mentioned here by Harkort, to appoint commissioners to draft a treaty establishing peace between the two factions. Bancroft, *History of Mexico* V, 123; Rivera Cambas, *Historia antigua* VI, 190–95; Suárez y Navarro, *Historia de México* I, 358–62.

7. On the Reaumur thermometric scale, the freezing point of water was zero and the boiling point eighty degrees. Hence, fifteen degrees Reaumur would be about nineteen degrees Celsius, or about sixty-six degrees Fahrenheit.

8. On December 5, Bustamante had established a major position on this hill west of Puebla; see episode 61, note 2.

9. On December 21, the commissioners of the two opposing armies met at the Hacienda de Zavaleta, just outside of Puebla, and framed a peace treaty. The sixth article of the treaty, the Plan de Zavaleta, recognized Gómez Pedraza as president of Mexico until April 1, 1833. Bancroft, *History of Mexico* V, 123; Rivera Cambas, *Historia antigua* VI, 195–98; Suárez y Navarro, *Historia de México* I, 362–65; Torner, ed., *Resumen integral de México* IV, 211.

63. *Entrance into Mexico City*

1. Harkort's statement that the new government made its triumphal entry into the capital on January 3, 1833, is corroborated by Bancroft, *History of Mexico* V, 126. The actual anniversary of the *pronunciamiento* in Veracruz, and of the revolution, however, was January 2; see Callcott, *Santa Anna*, pp. 88–89. A German businessman in Mexico City at the time, whose son had aided Harkort soon after the battle at Tolomé (see episode 29, note 4), described the procession and festivities of the day, including Lieutenant Colonel Harkort in full uniform, "with a pair of heavy gold epaulets." Becher, *Mexico in den ereignissvollen Jahren 1832 und 1833*, pp. 162–65.

Part 3. Letters
1. *To Professor Breithaupt in Freiberg*

1. The city of Colima is about forty kilometers (twenty-five miles) inland from the Pacific coast of Mexico. For more on Johann Friedrich August Breithaupt, see episode 3, note 1.

2. Wilhelm August Lampadius (1772–1842) and C. A. Kühn were professors at the mining academy in Freiberg and are listed as subscribers to Harkort's booklet on the quantitative analysis of silver ore. See Harkort, *Die Probirkunst mit dem Löthrohre*, p. vi; and *Allgemeine Deutsche Biographie* XVII, 578–79. I could find nothing more about C. A. Kühn.

3. I could find no information about a Mr. Kilaley.

4. E. G. Müller was an amalgamation specialist at the mining academy in Freiberg. Harkort, *Die Probirkunst mit dem Löthrohre*, p. vi.

By 1834 two of Eduard Harkort's brothers, Carl and Gustav, operated an export business in Leipzig. He probably heard regularly from his brother Carl, who by then had custody of Eduard's daughter, Henriette. Winkhaus, *Bauern- und Schmiedegeschlecht*, pp. 58, 67.

5. These same events are recounted in greater detail in Harkort's journal; see epi-

sodes 2, 3, and 6. The Society for Natural History is probably the Instituto de Ciencias y Artes de Oaxaca, which was founded in 1827. *Diccionario Porrúa* I, 1073.

6. In his journal Harkort writes that he received at this time from Santa Anna a brevet for the rank of colonel. He was promoted to the permanent rank of lieutenant colonel in October, 1832; see episodes 55 and 56. The details of these events and the following ones, until the end of 1832, are recounted in Harkort's journal, episodes 56 to 62.

7. Ignacio Mora y Villamil was chief of engineers in the Mexican army from about 1830 to 1848. Alvarez, ed., *Enciclopedia de México* IX, 181. The map begun by Harkort and Mora y Villamil was apparently lost or never completed, for Manuel Orozco y Berra comp., *Materiales para una cartografía mexicana*, pp. 91–114, contains no reference to such a map.

8. The details of the conservative revolt against the liberal reforms undertaken by Santa Anna's vice-president, Valentín Gómez Farías, and the congress are recounted in Bancroft, *History of Mexico* V, 129–36; Callcott, *Santa Anna*, pp. 98–105; Wilfrid Hardy Callcott, *Church and State in Mexico, 1822–1857*, pp. 86–103.

9. Harkort had served with Mejía once before, in October, 1832, during Santa Anna's siege of Chapultepec (episode 57). Mejía continued to support Santa Anna until 1834, when the president abandoned the federalist party; see Webb, Carroll, and Branda, eds., *Handbook of Texas* II, 182.

10. The Mineral de Angangueo is in the state of Michoacán, about sixty miles west of Mexico City. The German-American Mining Company had purchased some mining rights in the district of Angangueo in 1825. Kruse, ed., *Deutsche Briefe aus Mexiko*, p. xxix.

11. Zimapán is in the state of Hidalgo, about eighty miles east of San Miguel de Allende. The German-American Mining Company had at least one mine near there. Ibid.; see also Tayloe, *Mexico 1825–1828*, p. 166.

12. The mining operations of Real del Monte were about thirty leagues (seventy-eight miles) northeast of Mexico City. Tayloe, *Mexico 1825–1828*, pp. 133–36, 202; Lyon, *Journal of a Residence* II, 146–57.

Harkort is probably referring to Zacualpan in the state of Mexico, about sixty miles southwest of Mexico City. Iron and other metals are mined in the region.

13. From June to September, 1833, an epidemic of Asiatic cholera raged throughout Mexico. Bancroft, *History of Mexico* V, 135; and Callcott, *Santa Anna*, p. 104.

14. Mariano Arista (1802–1855) had served with Santa Anna since the revolt of September, 1828 (see episode 7, note 6). In June, 1833, General Arista had pronounced in support of the conservatives who opposed Vice-President Gómez Farías's liberal reforms. The details of his defection can be found in Bancroft, *History of Mexico* V, 132–33; and Callcott, *Santa Anna*, pp. 102–103.

15. Carl de Berghes was a mechanical and mining engineer employed by the German-American Mining Company. Kruse, ed., *Deutsche Briefe aus Mexiko*, pp. xxxi, xxxiv. Apparently, he and Harkort were never able to collaborate on these geographical projects, as I found no record of any joint publications by him and Harkort. See Pferdekamp, *Auf Humboldts Spuren*, p. 102; and Marianne Oeste de Bopp, *Contribución al estudio de las letras alemanas en México*, p. 220.

16. The post of *mayor general* designated Harkort merely as a member of General Santa Anna's personal staff.

In June, 1833, General Arista had declared his support of General Durán's opposition to the government of Vice-President Gómez Farías. On July 10, Santa Anna left the capital with about twenty-four hundred men to put down this new agitation by the army. By September, Arista and his forces had been driven into the city of Guanajuato, where on October 8 they finally surrendered. Bancroft, *History of Mexico* V, 132–35; Callcott, *Santa Anna*, pp. 102–103; Antonio López de Santa Anna, *The Eagle: The Autobiography of Santa Anna*, pp. 46–48.

17. It becomes clear in the continuation of Harkort's letter on February 11 that Santa Anna wanted him to prepare sketches and maps of the campaign in 1833 against the rebels in Guanajuato. Unfortunately, these illustrations and maps appear to have been lost. Orozco y Berra, comp., *Materiales para una cartografía mexicana*, pp. 317–20, contains no reference to such maps.

18. Johann Moritz Rugendas (1802–1858) had accompanied a scientific expedition from Germany to Brazil in 1821, where he spent four years serving as the group's illustrator and traveling on his own. He returned to Germany in 1825 and began preparing an illustrated record of his travels for publication. The work appeared in German and in French: *Die malerische Reise in Brasilien*, and *Voyage pittoresque dans le Brésil* (Paris and Mühlhausen: Engelmann, 1827–1835). Six years later Rugendas sailed on his own initiative to Mexico. In July, 1831, he arrived at Veracruz. Richert, *Johann Moritz Rugendas*, pp. 7–11, 29–38, 139.

19. The German editor probably confused "die Stadt" (the city) in Harkort's handwriting for "den Staat" (the state). The colonial city of Valladolid was renamed Morelia in September, 1828, to commemorate the hero of Mexico's independence, José María Morelos y Pavón. It is the capital of the state of Michoacán.

20. Lake Araron, now Lago de Cuitzeo, and Lake Pátzcuaro are in the state of Michoacán. The name Araron for Lake Cuitzeo is also reported by Mühlenpfordt, *Schilderung der Republik Mexiko* II, 362.

The volcano of Jorullo is in the state of Michoacán, southwest of Morelia.

21. Lake Chapala is located chiefly in the state of Jalisco, about thirty miles south of Guadalajara.

22. The volcano of Colima is about fifteen miles north of the city of Colima. The peak of the volcano is about 3,900 meters (12,790 feet) above sea level.

23. Colima achieved the status of a federal territory in 1824, and in 1857 became a state. Francisco R. Almada, *Diccionario de historia, geografía y biografía del estado de Colima*, pp. 45–46.

Several lithographs of Harkort's map were published between 1835 and 1854. See Orozco y Berra, comp., *Materiales para una geografía mexicana*, pp. 118–19. The most recent reprint of Harkort's map can be found in José Luis Mirafuentes Galván and Arturo Soberón Mora, comps., *Mapas y planos antiguos de Colima y del occidente de México (1521–1904)*, map no. 33. During this time Harkort also wrote a brief monograph on the geography and economy of Colima as a companion text to the map. It was not published, however, until eight years later: *Noticias geográfico-políticas, del territorio de Colima, escritas por el coronel ingeniero d[on] Eduardo Harcort, en el año de 1834, y publicadas en 1842 por Ramón de la Vega.* A copy of this rare publication is available in the Benson Latin American Collection, the University of Texas at Austin.

The district of Coalcomán is in the state of Michoacán and is noted today for its gold, silver, and iron mines.

24. I could locate no records of this project, neither a manuscript nor correspondence with a publisher.

25. The state of Michoacán borders directly on the eastern boundary of the state of Colima.

Gen. Nicolás Bravo (1790–1854) had returned to Mexico in 1829 from exile in Ecuador. For more on his political activities at this time, see Bancroft, *History of Mexico* V, 134n; Magner, *Men of Mexico*, p. 324; Purón, *México y sus gobernantes*, pp. 177–78.

26. See note 17 above.

27. Harkort means pesos. At this time the American dollar and the Mexican peso were about equal in value. Randall, *Real del Monte*, p. xv.

28. Guayaquil is the major port of Ecuador.

29. In Harkort's time the Spaniards still used Cádiz, Spain, as the prime meridian for measuring longitude. Lloyd A. Brown, *The Story of Maps* (Boston: Little, Brown, 1949), p. 283. Harkort's measurement of the height of the volcano of Colima agrees with recent figures (see note 22). A Spanish foot was slightly less than a British foot (see episode 11, note 5).

30. The federal district of Mexico was created in 1824. Harkort probably means, however, the state of Mexico, which originally did extend down to the Pacific coast. See García de Miranda and Falcón de Gyves, *Nuevo atlas Porrúa*, p. 19.

31. The town of Zacoalco de Torres is in the state of Jalisco, about ninety miles north of Colima. For a contemporary description of Zacoalco, see Mühlenpfordt, *Schilderung der Republik Mexiko* II, 388.

32. I could not locate this article in any contemporary German encyclopedias.

33. I could find no record of this portrait. The descendants of neither Eduard Harkort in Germany nor Adolf Hegewisch in Mexico had any record or recollection of this painting. Letter, Gertrud Herrmann-Kühne to LEB (June 8, 1980); letter, A. E. Hegewisch to LEB (Mar. 3, 1982).

34. Harkort paraphrases from the book of Ecclesiastes 1:2: "Es ist alles ganz eitel," ("All is vanity").

35. The town of Düren is in the present state of North Rhine–Westphalia, about fifteen miles west of Cologne and the Rhine River. I could locate no information about Herr Virmont.

36. In April, 1832, Friedrich von Gerolt appears to have been secretary at the Royal Prussian Consulate in the Mexican capital. Becher, *Mexico in den ereignissvollen Jahren 1832 und 1833*, p. 91. In 1836 he became Prussian ambassador to Mexico. Bopp, *Contribución al estudio de las letras alemanas en México*, p. 244.

37. Eduard Harkort had two brothers in Leipzig, Carl Friedrich, and Gustav, who operated an export business there; see note 4.

2. *To Johann Moritz Rugendas*

1. The originals of this letter and of the following one, dated August 2, 1835, are preserved among the correspondence of Johann Moritz Rugendas in the Archiv des Historischen Vereins für Schwaben in the Municipal Archives of Augsburg, Germany. Photocopies of the originals (no. 271, fols. 357r-358v, 366r-367v) were generously supplied to me by the archivist, Dr. Helmut Rischert.

2. Harkort wrote this letter concurrently with the previous one to his professor in Freiberg. The rebels he mentions were conservative reactionaries opposed to the liberal policies of Vice-President Gómez Farías and the congress. I could find nothing more about the regional leader of the rebels, Salazar. In the continuation of February 11 of the letter to Professor Breithaupt, however, Harkort also mentions having killed with a cannon shot the leader of the rebels in the region of Colima. See Bancroft, *History of Mexico* V, 129–37; and Callcott, *Santa Anna*, pp. 99–109.

3. See letter 1, note 23.

4. Harkort is greeting a German friend in Guadalajara, H. F. Blume, who operated a business there. Pferdekamp, *Auf Humboldts Spuren*, p. 59.

3. To Johann Moritz Rugendas

1. I have italicized all Spanish words used by Harkort in this letter; all other emphasis is Harkort's own.

Harkort was captured the first time in March, 1832, by government forces after the battle at Tolomé, and for the second time in Zacatecas early in 1835, when he first arrived in that city after fleeing from Santa Anna. In May, 1835, he was captured for the third time after the battle at Zacatecas. The latter two incidents are described further in this letter. He was imprisoned in Perote fortress the first time from March 9 until June 26, 1832. See episodes 1, 24, 31, and 34 of the journal.

2. I could not elucidate this reference to the legendary situation of a certain prince of Naples.

3. Harkort had drawn a map of the territory of Colima in 1834; see letter 1, note 23.

4. The volcano of Colima lies directly south of the taller mountain, El Nevado, with its perpetually snow-covered peak, and just fifteen miles north of the city of Colima (see letter 1, note 22). For more information about El Nevado, see Almada, *Diccionario*, p. 49.

5. San Juan de los Lagos is about eighty miles northeast of Guadalajara. For a brief account of this revolt in May, 1834, see Alvarez, ed., *Enciclopedia de México* VII, 411.

6. Tepatitlán de Morelos is about forty miles northeast of Guadalajara.

7. Zapotlanejo is about twenty-five miles east of Guadalajara. The village of Puente Grande was six leagues (sixteen miles) northeast of Guadalajara. Mühlenpfordt, *Schilderung der Republik Mexiko* II, 385.

8. The mining district of Bolaños was about sixty-five miles northwest of Guadalajara. For a detailed contemporary description of the Bolaños valley, including the town of Bolaños and the adjacent mountains, see Lyon, *Journal of a Residence* I, 284–318.

Spangenberg was a reduction specialist who had come to Mexico in 1825 for the German-American Mining Company. In 1832 he left that firm and then found work with the British mining enterprise, the Bolaños Company. Pferdekamp, *Auf Humboldts Spuren*, pp. 102, 117; Kruse, ed., *Deutsche Briefe aus Mexiko*, pp. xxx, lxiii; Randall, *Real del Monte*, p. 117.

La Berbería was a *rancho* situated on a steep slope above the town of Bolaños and on the road to Tepic and the coastal city of San Blas. Mühlenpfordt, *Schilderung der Republik Mexiko* II, 392.

9. Harkort is possibly referring here also to Luis Cortázar's brother, Pedro, who was a high-ranking officer in the Mexican army at the time. See Peral, *Diccionario biográfico mexicano*, p. 189; and *Diccionario Porrúa* I, 532.

Miguel Barragán (1789–1836) was in 1834 the minister of war in Santa Anna's government. Peral, *Diccionario biográfico mexicano*, p. 91; Purón, *México y sus gobernantes*, pp. 174–75.

10. The story of Saul's defeat of the Philistines and of the ensuing taking of spoils is found in Samuel 1:14.

11. José Antonio Mejía (1800–1839) was a loyal Federalist with whom Harkort had served in 1832 at the siege of Chapultepec, and in 1833 in Querétaro (see episode 57 of the journal and the letter to Breithaupt). In 1834 Mejía was serving as a member of the

Mexican congress when Santa Anna repudiated his own government. From Mexico City he had fled to Jalisco. Webb, Carroll, and Branda, eds., *Handbook of Texas* II, 182.

12. The Río Grande de Santiago lies about twenty miles northwest of Guadalajara.

The letters "p.p." used by Harkort here and later in his letter appear to be an abbreviated reference in Spanish to a mention of the same subject on a previous page of the letter, meaning p[ágina] p[asada]. It could also be an abbreviation of the Latin term "*perge perge,*" meaning "continue on; et cetera." *Brockhaus Enzyklopädie* XV, 75.

13. Harkort means H. F. Blume, who operated a business in Guadalajara. See Kruse, ed., *Deutsche Briefe aus Mexiko,* p. cvii; and Pferdekamp, *Auf Humboldts Spuren,* p. 59. I could find no information about Weiskopf.

14. General Cortázar took the city of Guadalajara on August 12, 1834. Alvarez, ed., *Enciclopedia de México* VII, 411.

Harkort is referring probably to Santa María del Oro, a mine operated by the Bolaños Company. See Mühlenpfordt, *Schilderung der Republik Mexiko* II, 390, 395.

15. Early in 1834, before Santa Anna repudiated his own government and restored the secular powers of the church, the bishop of Puebla had become so prominent in the reactionary forces that he was forced to leave the country. See Bancroft, *History of Mexico* V, 141; and Callcott, *Church and State in Mexico,* p. 96.

16. Detailed accounts of the events leading to the revolt in Zacatecas can be found in Hubert Howe Bancroft, *History of the North Mexican States and Texas (The Works of Hubert Howe Bancroft)* II, 152–53; and Callcott, *Santa Anna,* pp. 114–16.

17. Harkort's remarks concerning his and García's opposing strategies are borne out by the anonymous author of a contemporary pamphlet, *Diario exacto de Zacatecas, remitido por un curioso a un amigo de esta capital,* p. 2. A copy of this brief but detailed account by one of Santa Anna's adherents is available in the Benson Latin American Collection, the University of Texas at Austin.

18. Harkort's actions, which almost saved the Zacatecans from defeat in this battle, became legendary in the city. His gallant command of the artillery was still being recounted eight years later, when Albert M. Gilliam visited Zacatecas. Gilliam appears also to have been the first to record the story of Harkort's heroic resistance. See Gilliam, *Travels over the Table Lands,* pp. 219–20. His account, which corroborates Harkort's own version, was later retold by Robinson, *Mexico and Her Military Chieftains,* pp. 173–74; and by Frank C. Hanighen, *Santa Anna: The Napoleon of the West,* pp. 77–78. Somewhat different views of the battle are presented by the anonymous author of the *Diario exacto de Zacatecas,* pp. 2–7, and by Santa Anna himself in a report published in English in *Niles' Weekly Register* (June 20, 1835), p. 274.

19. According to Gilliam, Santa Anna had "issued a command that all foreigners, belonging to the Zacatecan army, should be shot on the spot." But Santa Anna's own officers protested so loudly that the order was rescinded, and the prisoners, including Harkort, were marched to Mexico City. Gilliam, *Travels over the Table Lands,* p. 220.

20. Dr. Christian Schiede had come to Mexico about 1825 as company physician for the German mining enterprise Deutscher Bergwerksverein. In 1832 he left the company, but he remained in Mexico for some years, conducting botanical research for several German universities. Pferdekamp, *Auf Humboldts Spuren,* pp. 103, 117, 221.

21. See episodes 61 and 62 of the journal.

22. In June, 1844, the temporary governor at Perote fortress was Gen. Antonio de Castro. Harkort's benefactor in 1835 was possibly the same person. See McCutchan, *Mier Expedition Diary,* p. 130 (note). I could locate no information identifying Arago.

23. The intent of Harkort's remark about "the great warrantor" ("den grossen Ka-

venten") is not clear. He might have meant a courier with orders for his deportation, or even a visit by Santa Anna himself, whose hacienda, Manga de Clavo, was not far from Perote. See Callcott, *Santa Anna*, p. 56.

24. The fever season in Veracruz and elsewhere along the Gulf Coast in the *tierra caliente* was from July to October. Tayloe, *Mexico 1825–1828*, pp. 187–88.

In late October or early November, 1835, Harkort was placed aboard the schooner *Concepción*, which was bound for New Orleans. The passenger list of that vessel shows that Edward Arcourt [*sic*] arrived in New Orleans on November 23, 1835 (see my introduction).

25. Carl Benesky de Beaufort was a native of Poland who had come to Mexico in 1824 with Iturbide, when the former emperor returned from exile in Europe. In 1834 Santa Anna appointed Colonel Benesky commander of the government forces at Colima. Benesky held that post for almost two years. Almada, *Diccionario*, p. 30.

26. Whitehead is the English translation of Weiskopf. He is probably the same friend mentioned earlier in the letter who shared a house in Guadalajara with H. F. Blume.

27. This friend Virmons is probably the same Virmont mentioned in the letter to Breithaupt; see letter 1, note 35.

28. Harkort is apparently making a parodistic reference here to his three German friends in Mexico (Blume, Weiskopf, and Virmont), with the familiar opening line of many German fairy tales; "Once upon a time . . ."

Bibliography

This bibliography contains only those documents and printed works directly pertinent to Eduard Harkort's life and works, the Harkort family genealogy, the history of mining in Germany and Mexico in the early nineteenth century, Mexican history, and Texas history. Most general reference works and several other secondary sources of a technical or literary nature that were cited only once or twice in the explanatory notes to the journal have been omitted.

ARCHIVAL MATERIALS

Akademisches Archiv der Bergakademie Freiberg (AABF). Freiberg, Germany. Oberbergamt (OBA) File 9904, Vol. 2; File 9980, Vol. 14; File 10711, Vol. 1.

Archivale Stadtarchiv Augsburg. Augsburg, Germany. Archiv des Historischen Vereins für Schwaben. Johann Moritz Rugendas Letters.

Brazoria County Probate Court Records. Brazoria County Courthouse. Angleton, Texas.

General Land Office. Austin, Texas. File Bexar First Class 984, and File Bexar Bounty 1270: Edward Harcourt.

Historisches Staatsarchiv (Bergarchiv) Freiberg. Freiberg, Germany. Oberbergamt (OBA) Freiberg, Rep. H, Sect. 91d, No. 10,881/1.

National Archives. Washington, D.C. *Passenger Lists of Vessels Arriving at New Orleans 1820–1902.* Microfilm Roll 13: June 1, 1835–April 30, 1836.

Rosenberg Library. Galveston, Texas. James Morgan Papers.

Texas State Library, Archives Division. Austin, Texas. Comptroller of Public Accounts Record Group, Audited Military Claims.

———. Secretary of State Record Group, Memorials and Petitions File.

NEWSPAPERS

El Censor. Veracruz. March–April, 1832.

El Constitucional. Puebla. July, 1832.

Galveston Daily News. Centennial edition, August 15, 1839.

Gonzales Weekly Inquirer. August 17, 1878.

Niles' Weekly Register. . . . Baltimore. March–December, 1832, June 20, 1835.

Telegraph and Texas Register. Houston. September 13, 1836, June 16, July 21, 1838.

BOOKS AND ARTICLES

Alamán, Lucas. *Historia de Méjico desde los primeros movimientos que prepararon su independencia en el año de 1808 hasta la época presente.* 2nd ed. 5 vols. Mexico City: Editorial Jus, 1968–69.

Allgemeine Deutsche Biographie. Edited by the Historische Commission bei der Königlichen Akademie der Wissenschaften. 56 vols. 1875–1912. Reprint. Berlin: Duncker & Humblot, 1967–71.

Almada, Francisco R. *Diccionario de historia, geográfia y biográfia del estado de Colima.* Chihuahua: n.p., 1937.

Althaus, Richard. *Hagen in alten Bildern.* 2 vols. Gummersbach: Gronenberg Verlag, 1977.

Alvarez, José Rogelio, ed. *Enciclopedia de México* . . . 12 vols. Mexico City: Enciclopedia de México, 1966–77.

American Geographical Society. *Index to Map of Hispanic America, 1: 1,000,000:Mexico.* Edited by Earl Parker Hanson. Washington, D.C.: Government Printing Office, 1945.

————. *Millionth Map of Hispanic America.* Baltimore: A. Hoen, 1959.

Austin, Stephen F. "The 'Prison Journal' of Stephen F. Austin." Contributed by Guy M. Bryan. *Quarterly of the Texas State Historical Association* 2 (January, 1899): 183–210.

Bancroft, Hubert Howe. *History of Mexico (The Works of Hubert Howe Bancroft).* 6 vols. San Francisco: A. L. Bancroft and the History Companies, 1883–88.

————. *History of the North Mexican States and Texas (The Works of Hubert Howe Bancroft).* 2 vols. San Francisco: A. L. Bancroft and the History Companies, 1884–89.

Barker, Eugene C. "Don Carlos Barrett." *Southwestern Historical Quarterly* 20 (October, 1916): 139–45.

————. *The Life of Stephen F. Austin.* Nashville: Cokesbury Press, 1925.

————. "The Tampico Expedition." *Quarterly of the Texas State Historical Association* 6 (January, 1903): 169–86.

Barker, Eugene C., ed. *Readings in Texas History.* Dallas: The Southwest Press, 1929.

Becher, Carl Christian. *Mexico in den ereignissvollen Jahren 1832 und 1833 und die Reise hin und zurück aus vertraulichen Briefen mit einem Anhange über die neuesten Ereignisse daselbst aus offizieller Quelle* . . . Hamburg: Perthes & Besser, 1834.

Bell, Thomas W. *A Narrative of the Capture and Subsequent Sufferings of the Mier Prisoners in Mexico,* . . . Edited by James M. Day. Waco: Texian Press, 1964.

Bocanegra, José María, ed. *Memorias para la historia de México independiente, 1822–1846.* 2 vols. Mexico City: Imprenta de Gobierno Federal, 1892.

Bopp, Marianne Oeste de. *Contribución al estudio de las letras alemanas en México*. Mexico City: Universidad Nacional Autónoma de México, 1961.

Brenner, Anita. *Idols behind Altars*. New York: Harcourt, Brace, 1929.

Brister, Louis E. "Colonel Eduard Harkort: A German Soldier of Fortune in Mexico and Texas, 1832–1836." *Southwestern Historical Quarterly* 88 (January, 1985): 229–46.

Bullock, William. *Six Months' Residence and Travels in Mexico, Containing Remarks on the Present State of New Spain, Its Natural Productions, State of Society, Manufactures, Trade, Agriculture, and Antiquities, etc.* London: John Murray, 1824.

Burkart, Joseph. *Aufenthalt und Reisen in Mexico in den Jahren 1825 bis 1834: Bemerkungen über Land, Produkte, Leben und Sitten der Einwohner und Beobachtungen aus dem Gebiete der Mineralogie, Geognosie, Bergbaukunde, Meteorologie, Geographie etc.* 2 vols. Stuttgart: E. Schweizerbart's Verlagshandlung, 1836.

Calderón de la Barca, Frances Erskine Inglis. *Life in Mexico: The Letters of Fanny Calderón de la Barca, with New Material from the Author's Private Journals*. Edited by Howard T. Fisher and Marion Hall Fisher. New York: Doubleday & Company, 1966.

Callcott, Wilfrid Hardy. *Church and State in Mexico, 1822–1857*. 1926. Reprint. New York: Octagon Books, 1971.

———. *Santa Anna: The Story of an Enigma Who Once Was Mexico*. Norman: University of Oklahoma Press, 1936.

Carreño, Alberto María, ed. *Jefes del ejército mexicano en 1847: Biografías de generales de division y de brigada y de coroneles del ejército mexicano por fines del año 1847*. Mexico City: Sociedad Mexicana de Geografía y Estadística, 1914.

Charno, Steven M., comp. *Latin American Newspapers in United States Libraries: A Union List*. Austin: University of Texas Press, 1968.

Cole, Garold. *American Travelers to Mexico, 1821–1982: A Descriptive Bibliography*. Troy, N.Y.: Whitston Publishing, 1978.

Diario exacto de Zacatecas, remitido por un curioso a un amigo de esta capital. Mexico City: Imprenta de la Testamentaria de Valdés, 1835.

Diccionario Porrúa de historia, biografía y geografía de México. 3rd ed. 2 vols. Mexico City: Editorial Porrúa, 1970–1971.

Douglas, Claude L. *Thunder on the Gulf: Story of the Texas Navy*. 1936. Reprint. Austin: Graphic Ideas, 1972.

Dyer, Joseph O. *The Early History of Galveston: Centenary Edition Part I*. Galveston: Joseph O. Dyer, 1916.

"Eduard Harkort—'der schwarze Prinz.'" *Westfalenland* 23 (1932): 109–10.

Ehrenberg, H[ermann]. *Der Freiheitskampf in Texas im Jahre 1836*. Leipzig: Otto Wigand, 1844.

Ehrenberg, Herman. *With Milam and Fannin: Adventures of a German Boy in Texas' Revolution*. Translated by Charlotte Churchill. Edited by Henry Smith. Dallas: Tardy Publishing Company, 1935.

Gammel, H. P. N., comp. *The Laws of Texas, 1822–1897* . . . 10 vols. Austin: Gammel Book Co., 1898.

García de Miranda, Enriqueta, and Zaida Falcón de Gyves. *Atlas: Nuevo atlas Porrúa de la república mexicana.* 2nd ed. Mexico City: Editorial Porrúa, 1974.

García Purón, Manuel. *México y sus gobernantes: Biografías.* 2nd ed. Revised by Heriberto García Rivas. Mexico City: Librería de Manuel Porrúa, 1970.

General Land Office. *Abstract of all Original Texas Land Titles, Comprising Grants and Locations to August 31, 1941.* Compiled by Bascom Giles. 8 vols. Austin: General Land Office, 1942.

Gilliam, Albert M. *Travels over the Table Lands and Cordilleras of Mexico during the Years 1843 and 44; including a Description of California, the Principal Cities and Mining Districts of that Republic and the Biographies of Iturbide and Santa Anna.* Philadelphia: John W. Moore, and London: Wiley & Putnam, 1846.

Gillispie, Charles Coulston, ed. *Dictionary of Scientific Biography.* 16 vols. New York: Charles Scribner's Sons, 1970–80.

Gilmore, Newton R. "British Mining Ventures in Early National Mexico." Ph.D. dissertation, University of California, Berkeley, 1956.

Grayson, Peter W. "The Release of Stephen F. Austin from Prison." *Quarterly of the Texas State Historical Association* 14 (October, 1910): 155–63.

Green, Thomas J. *Journal of the Texian Expedition against Mier, Subsequent Imprisonment of the Author, His Sufferings, and Final Escape from the Castle of Perote* . . . 1845. Reprint. Austin: Steck Company, 1935.

Gunn, Drewey Wayne. *Mexico in American and British Letters: A Bibliography of Fiction and Travel Books, Citing Original Editions.* Metuchen, N.J.: Scarecrow Press, 1974.

Hale, Charles A. *Mexican Liberalism in the Age of Mora, 1821–1853.* New Haven, Conn.: Yale University Press, 1968.

Hanighen, Frank C. *Santa Anna: The Napoleon of the West.* New York: Coward-McCann, 1934.

Harkort, Eduard. *Aus Mejicanischen Gefängnissen: Bruchstück aus Eduard Harkorts hinterlassenen Papieren.* Edited by F. Gustav Kühne. Leipzig: Carl B. Lorck, 1858.

———. *Noticias geográfico-políticas, del territorio de Colima, escritas por el coronel ingeniero d[on] Eduardo Harcort, en el año de 1834, y publicadas en 1842 por Ramón de la Vega.* Edited by Ramón de la Vega. Mexico City: S. Pérez, 1842.

———. *Die Probirkunst mit dem Löthrohre oder Versuch einer Anweisung, wie man Erze, Mineralien und Hüttenproducte mit Hülfe des Löthrohrs auf verschiedene Metallgehalte mit hinreichender Genauigkeit untersuchen kann. Erstes Heft: Die Silberproben.* Freiberg: Craz & Gerlach, 1827.

Humboldt, Alexander von. *Political Essay on the Kingdom of New Spain.* Edited by Mary Maples Dunn. New York: Alfred A. Knopf, 1972.

Jenkins, John H., ed. *The Papers of the Texas Revolution 1835–1836*. 10 vols. Austin: Presidial Press, 1973.

Jones, Oakah L., Jr. *Santa Anna*. New York: Twayne Publishers, 1968.

Klotzbach, Kurt. "Eduard Harkort: Pionier und Abenteurer in Mexiko und Texas." *Heimatbuch Hagen + Mark: Hagener Heimatkalender 1981* 22 (1980):63–66.

Koppe, Carl Wilhelm. *Mexicanische Zustände aus den Jahren 1830 bis 1832* . . . Edited by Eduard Wiedenmann and Hermann Hauff. 2 vols. Stuttgart: Verlag der J. G. Cotta'schen Buchhandlung, 1837.

Kruse, Hans, ed. *Deutsche Briefe aus Mexiko, mit einer Geschichte des Deutsch-Amerikanischen Bergwerkvereins 1824–1838*. Essen a. d. Ruhr: Verlagsbuchhandlung G. D. Baedeker, 1923.

Lockett, Marjorie, et al., eds. *Fodor's Mexico 1979*. New York: David McKay Co., 1978.

Lyon, George F. *Journal of a Residence and Tour in the Republic of Mexico in the Year 1826 with Some Account of the Mines of That Country*. 2 vols. 1828. Reprint. Port Washington, N.Y. Kennikat Press, 1971.

McCutchan, Joseph D. *Mier Expedition Diary: A Texan Prisoner's Account*. Edited by Joseph Milton Nance. Austin: University of Texas Press, 1978.

McGrath, J. J., and Walace Hawkins. "Perote Fort—Where Texans Were Imprisoned." *Southwestern Historical Quarterly* 48 (January, 1945): 340–45.

Magner, James A. *Men of Mexico*. 2nd ed. Milwaukee: Bruce Publishing, 1943.

Maissin, Eugene. *The French in Mexico and Texas (1838–1839)*. Translated . . . with introduction and notes by James L. Shepherd III. Salado, Tex.: Anson Jones Press, 1961.

Memorial and Genealogical Record of Southwest Texas, Containing Biographical Histories and Genealogical Records of Many Leading Men and Prominent Families. Chicago: Goodspeed Bros., 1894.

Mexican Company. *Extracts from the Report of Mr. Justus Ludwig von Uslar, (Chief Director of the Mines in the Service of the Mexican Company), Relative to the "Negociacion" of Yavesia, in the State of Oaxaca*. Dated San Antonio de Padua, (Oaxaca) 6th January, 1828. London: [J. Plummer], 1828.

———. *Report of the Directors of the Mexican Company, Presented at the Second Annual General Meeting of the Proprietors*, . . . London: J. Plummer, 1827.

———. *Report of the Directors of the Mexican Company Presented at the Third Annual General Meeting of the Proprietors*, . . . London: J. Plummer, 1828.

Meyer, Michael C., and William L. Sherman. *The Course of Mexican History*. New York: Oxford University Press, 1979.

Miller, Thomas Lloyd, comp. *Bounty and Donation Land Grants of Texas 1835–1888*. Austin: University of Texas Press, 1967.

Miquel i Vergés, José María. *Diccionario de Insurgentes*. Mexico City: Editorial Porrúa, 1969.

Mirafuentes Galván, José Luis, and Arturo Soberón Mora, comps. *Mapas y planos antiguos de Colima y del occidente de México (1521–1904)*. Mexico City: Consorcio Minero Benito Juárez peña colorada, [1978].

Mühlenpfordt, Eduard. *Versuch einer getreuen Schilderung der Republik Mexiko*. 1844. Reprint. Graz: Akademische Druck- und Verlagsanstalt, 1969.

Muñoz, Rafael F. *Santa Anna: El que todo lo ganó y todo lo perdió*. Madrid: Espasa-Calpe, 1936.

Nance, Joseph Milton. *After San Jacinto: The Texas-Mexican Frontier, 1836–1841*. Austin: University of Texas Press, 1963.

Newton, Lewis W., and Herbert P. Gambrell. *Texas Yesterday & Today*. Dallas: Turner Company, 1949.

Orozco y Berra, Manuel, comp. *Materiales para una cartografía mexicana*. Mexico City: Imprenta del Gobierno en Palacio, 1871.

Peral, Miguel Angel. *Diccionario biográfico mexicano*. Mexico City: Editorial P.A.C., [1944].

Pferdekamp, Wilhelm. *Auf Humboldts Spuren: Deutsche im jungen Mexiko*. Munich: Max Hueber Verlag, 1958.

Pierce, Gerald S. *Texas under Arms: The Camps, Posts, Forts, & Military Towns of the Republic of Texas 1836–1846*. Austin: Encino Press, 1969.

Poggendorf, Johann C., comp. *Biographisch-Literarisches Handwörterbuch zur Geschichte der exacten Wissenschaften*. 2 vols. Leipzig: J. A. Barth, 1863.

Poinsett, Joel Roberts. *Notes on Mexico, Made in the Autumn of 1822. Accompanied by an Historical Sketch of the Revolution, and Translations of Official Reports on the Present State of That Country*. 1824, 1825. Reprint. New York: Frederick A. Praeger, 1969.

Pool, William C. *A Historical Atlas of Texas*. Austin: Encino Press, 1975.

Poyet, C. F. *Monografía de Xalapa*. Mexico City: Editorial Citaltépetl, 1962.

Ramírez, Santiago, ed. *Datos para la historia del Colegio de Minería*. Mexico City: Imprenta del Gobierno Federal en el Ex-Arzobispado 1890.

Randall, Robert W. *Real del Monte: A British Mining Venture in Mexico*. Austin: University of Texas Press, 1972.

Richert, Gertrud. *Johann Moritz Rugendas: Ein deutscher Maler des XIX. Jahrhunderts*. Berlin: Rembrandt-Verlag, 1959.

Rivera Cambas, Manuel. *Historia antigua y moderna de Jalapa y de las revoluciones del estado de Veracruz*. 2nd ed. 17 vols. Mexico City: Editorial Citaltépetl, 1959–60.

Robinson, Fay[ette]. *Mexico and Her Military Chieftains, From the Revolution of Hidalgo to the Present Time, . . .* 1851. Reprint. Glorieta, N.Mex.: Rio Grande Press, 1970.

Roeder, Ralph. *Juárez and His Mexico: A Biographical History*. 2 vols. New York: Viking Press, 1947.

Sánchez Lamego, Miguel A. *La invasión española de 1829*. Mexico City: Editorial Jus, 1971.

Santa Anna, Antonio López de. *The Eagle: The Autobiography of Santa Anna.* Translated by Sam Guyler and Jaime Platon. Edited by Ann Fears Crawford. Austin: Pemberton Press, 1967.

Santa Anna, Antonio López de, et al. *The Mexican Side of the Texas Revolution [1836] by the Chief Mexican Participants.* Translated and with notes by Carlos E. Castañeda. 1928. Reprint. Austin: Graphic Ideas, 1970.

Santamaría, Francisco J. *Diccionario de mejicanismos.* 3rd ed. Mexico City: Editorial Porrúa, 1978.

Sartorius, Carl. *Mexico about 1850.* Illustrations by Moritz Rugendas. 1858. Reprint. Stuttgart: F. A. Brockhaus Kommissions-Geschäft, 1961.

Schiffner, C[arl]. *Aus dem Leben alter Freiberger Bergstudenten und der Lehrkörper der Bergakademie.* 3 vols. Freiberg/Sachsen: Verlagsanstalt Ernst Mauckisch, 1935–40.

Schumacher, Martin. *Auslandsreisen deutscher Unternehmer 1750–1851, Unter besonderer Berücksichtigung von Rheinland und Westfalen.* Edited by Hermann Kellenbenz. Cologne: Rheinisch-Westfälisches Wirtschaftsarchiv zu Köln, 1968.

Scott, Henry Lee. *Military Dictionary: Comprising Technical Definitions; Information on Raising and Keeping Troops; Actual Service, . . . and Administration Relating to Land Forces.* 1861. Reprint. New York: Greenwood Press, 1968.

Sosa, Francisco. *Biografías de mexicanos destinguidos.* Mexico City: Oficina Tipográfica de la Secretaría de Fomento, 1884.

Stapp, William Preston. *The Prisoners of Perote, Containing a Journal Kept by the Author, Who Was Captured by the Mexicans, at Mier, December 25, 1842, and Released from Perote, May 16, 1844.* 1845. Reprint. Austin: University of Texas Press, 1977.

Suárez y Navarro, Juan. *Historia de México y del General Antonio López de Santa Anna: Comprende los acontecimientos políticos que han tenido lugar en la Nación desde el año de 1821 hasta 1848.* 2 vols. Mexico City: Ignacio Cumplido, 1850–51.

Tamayo, Jorge L. *Geografía general de México.* 2 vols. Mexico City: Talleres Gráficos de la Nación, 1949.

Tayloe, Edward Thornton. *Mexico 1825–1828: The Journal and Correspondence of Edward Thornton Tayloe.* Edited by C. Harvey Gardiner. Chapel Hill: University of North Carolina Press, 1959.

Terry, T. Philip. *Terry's Guide to Mexico: The New Standard Guidebook to the Mexican Republic . . .* rev. ed. Hingham, Mass.: n.p., 1940.

Thompson, Waddy. *Recollections of Mexico.* New York: Wiley & Putnam, 1847.

Toor, Frances. *Frances Toor's New Guide to Mexico . . .* Mexico City: Frances Toor Studios, 1944.

———. *A Treasury of Mexican Folkways.* New York: Crown, 1947.

Torner, Florentino M., ed. *Resumen integral de México a través de los siglos: Historia general y completa . . . por los reputados escritores . . . bajo la dirección de Vicente Riva Palacio*. 2nd ed. 5 vols. Mexico City: Compañía General de Ediciones, 1952–53.

Trueheart, James L. *The Perote Prisoners: Being the Diary of James L. Trueheart Printed for the First Time Together with an Historical Introduction*. Edited by Frederick C. Chabot. San Antonio: Naylor, 1934.

Tudor, Henry. *Narrative of a Tour in North America; Comprising Mexico, the Mines of Real del Monte, the United States, and the British Colonies: With an Excursion to the Island of Cuba: In a Series of Letters Written in the Years 1831–2*. 2 vols. London: James Duncan, 1834.

Villaseñor y Villaseñor, Alejandro. *Biografías de los héroes y caudillos de la independencia*. 2 vols. Mexico City: Editorial Jus, 1962.

Waldeck, Jean Frédéric. *Voyage pittoresque et archéologique dans la province d'Yucatán (Amérique centrale) pendant les années 1834 et 1835*. Paris: Bellizard Dufour, 1838.

Ward, H[enry] G[eorge]. *Mexico in 1827, By H. G. Ward, Esq., His Majesty's Chargé d'Affaires in That Country during the Years 1825, 1826, and Part of 1827*. 2 vols. London: Henry Colburn, 1828.

Wauchope, Robert, ed. *Handbook of American Indians*. 16 vols. Austin: University of Texas Press, 1964–76.

Webb, Walter Prescott, H. Bailey Carroll, and Eldon Stephen Branda, eds. *The Handbook of Texas*. 3 vols. Austin: Texas State Historical Association, 1952, 1976.

Williams, Amelia W., and Eugene C. Barker, eds. *The Writings of Sam Houston 1813–1863*. 8 vols. Austin: University of Texas Press, 1938–43.

Winkhaus, Eberhard. *Wir stammen aus Bauern- und Schmiedegeschlecht: Genealogie eines süderländischen Sippenkreises und der ihm angehörenden Industriepioniere*. Görlitz: C. A. Starke, 1932.

Winkler, Ernest W., ed. "The Bexar and Dawson Prisoners." *Quarterly of the Texas State Historical Association* 13 (April, 1910): 292–324.

Yoakum, H[enderson K]. *History of Texas from Its First Settlement in 1685 to Its Annexation to the United States in 1846*. 2 vols. 1855. Reprint. Austin: Steck Company, 1935.

Zavala, Lorenzo de. *Ensayo crítico de las revoluciones de México desde 1808 hasta 1830*. Edited by Manuel González Ramírez. Mexico City: Editorial Porrúa, 1969.

Index